UNDERSTANDING CRIMINOLOGICAL RESEARCH

SAGE has been part of the global academic community since 1965, supporting high quality research and learning that transforms society and our understanding of individuals, groups and cultures. SAGE is the independent, innovative, natural home for authors, editors and societies who share our commitment and passion for the social sciences.

Find out more at: **www.sagepublications.com**

UNDERSTANDING CRIMINOLOGICAL RESEARCH

a guide to data analysis

JOHN MARTYN CHAMBERLAIN

Los Angeles | London | New Delhi
Singapore | Washington DC

Los Angeles | London | New Delhi
Singapore | Washington DC

SAGE Publications Ltd
1 Oliver's Yard
55 City Road
London EC1Y 1SP

SAGE Publications Inc.
2455 Teller Road
Thousand Oaks, California 91320

SAGE Publications India Pvt Ltd
B 1/I 1 Mohan Cooperative Industrial Area
Mathura Road
New Delhi 110 044

SAGE Publications Asia-Pacific Pte Ltd
3 Church Street
#10-04 Samsung Hub
Singapore 049483

Editor: Natalie Aguilera
Editorial assistant: James Piper
Production editor: Rachel Eley
Copyeditor: Jill Birch
Proofreader: Jonathan Hopkins
Marketing manager: Sally Ransom
Cover design: Wendy Scott
Typeset by: C&M Digitals (P) Ltd, Chennai, India
Printed by: MPG Books Group, Bodmin, Cornwall

Library of Congress Control Number: 2012933330

British Library Cataloguing in Publication data

A catalogue record for this book is available from
the British Library

MIX
Paper from
responsible sources
FSC® C018575

ISBN 978-1-4462-0857-1
ISBN 978-1-4462-0858-8 (pbk)

For my daughter Freyja,
because she understands why I still need her hand to hold,
particularly when crossing the street.

For my nana Freda,
as without her I wouldn't have taken this path.

Contents

About the Author

Dr Chamberlain is a Senior Lecturer in Criminology and Social Policy in the Department of Social Science at Loughborough University. His academic background and research interests cross over the fields of criminology and medical sociology. Drawing on both fields, over the last decade and a half he has conducted research in a range of topics, including the care and treatment of mentally disordered offenders within the prison system, the identification and punishment of health practitioners who deliberately harm patients, as well as the surveillance and control of civil disobedience and public protest by crime control agencies, such as the police. Currently he is conducting research into contemporary developments in the risk management and treatment of offenders classified by the criminal justice system as dangerous, including violent and sex offenders, mentally disordered offenders and terrorists.

1

An Autobiographical Introduction

CHAPTER OVERVIEW

Chapter 1 introduces the focus of this book on providing an introduction to how qualitative and quantitative data analysis is undertaken by criminologists. The chapter outlines the importance of numbers and words for exploring criminal life and discusses how, although criminology is a highly diverse and fragmented discipline, at its centre lies a common commitment to undertaking rigorous and systematic empirical research as a member of a broader academic community. The chapter ends with a brief summary of subsequent chapter content.

CHAPTER CONTENTS

The importance of words and numbers
The triangle of criminology
Purpose and structure of this book
Chapter reading list

The Importance of Words and Numbers

This book provides an introduction to different forms of data analysis used by criminologists to explore and examine the social world using words and numbers. A range of approaches to the analysis of narrative and numeric data are examined, including grounded theory analysis, narrative analysis, discourse analysis, univariate analysis and bivariate analysis. There are several research methods texts specific to criminology which provide students with help managing a research project (i.e. King and Wincup 2007; Crowe and Semmens 2008; Davies et al. 2011). Yet these texts don't focus in detail on the mechanics of doing different forms of data analysis. In addition to providing practical examples of how to do data analysis this book seeks to contextualise its content to help the reader understand the underlying key principles that serve to shape the analytic process. It does this by outlining the historical development of the different analytical strategies it discusses within the emergence of qualitative and quantitative research within criminology as an academic discipline. Self-study questions and further readings on a range of issues pertinent to the collection and analysis of criminological data, including research design and the presentation of empirical findings, are also provided. Although written with the budding criminologist in mind, students studying other social science subjects will also find it a useful text. After all, sociologists, psychologists, geographers, as well as communication and media analysts, all examine the world in which we live using words and numbers.

When I was an undergraduate student one of my favourite tutors used to like to end each lecture she gave with what she called 'question time', so each week we had to take it in turns to ask her a question. The question could be about anything we wanted. It didn't have to even be related to the topic we had just listened to. We were encouraged to speak our mind and constantly reminded that nothing was off limits and only a foolish person thinks there is such a thing as a stupid question. It was a small and friendly class entitled 'Humanity's place in Nature' which ran for the whole of the first year of my undergraduate degree on a Wednesday evening. It was as interesting as its title suggested. To this day I view it as one of the best classes I've attended and in no small part this was down to the lecturer who ran it. Each week we would explore our topic – the place of human beings within the universe – by examining an aspect of the history of western and eastern philosophy and religion. As we did so we learnt about the differences and similarities between, for example, Buddhism and Islam, Hellenistic and Continental philosophy, Psychotherapy and 'Hippie' Counter-Culture, as well as Cubism, Deep Ecology and Postmodernism.

As you can perhaps imagine, virtually all the questions we asked weren't that creative, or that memorable for that matter – although they certainly may have seemed so at the time. Nevertheless, our lecturer always used our questions as a starting place from which to develop a healthy exchange of ideas and opinions. Most importantly, she always reminded us what we were doing in her class: looking at the different ways human beings try to make sense of the world around them. She often talked about how humans liked to ask questions and seek answers by telling stories about the world and their place in it using a mixture of words and numbers. Indeed, one of the first things we do when we are children is learn the power of words and numbers for understanding and navigating the world around us. As we grow so does our appreciation of how they help us grasp its key features, reoccurring patterns and surprising events. She reminded us how each generation looks to both the past and the future as it attempts to explain why the world looks and behaves the way it does. In our long search for answers we have sometimes been lucky enough to uncover the hidden structures and patterns which seem to control our environment. What is more, she said, we have learnt to express these in the forms of numbers and words. We give them names and tell stories about how we came to find them. So we associate the discovery of gravity with the story of Newton and his apple tree. While in their more abstract forms they compress the complex world around us into an eloquent mathematical equation, such as $E = mc^2$, or some equally seductive narrative hypothesis that explains why things are the way they are.

Words and numbers not only provide us with access to the underlying structures present in the world around us, they also help us build a sense of self and allow us to communicate to others our own life story alongside that of the time and place in human history in which we live. But perhaps most importantly, they help us manipulate our environment and change it to get what we want. Harnessing the power of words and numbers, we have been able to change our surroundings, mass produce crops and livestock to sustain growing populations, eradicate certain diseases and contain still others, build extraordinary cities, as well as develop amazing information and communication technologies which make the global truly local. Important events from all over the world, which historically would have taken weeks or even months to reach us, now appear instantaneously on the screen in front of us. Coincidences, such as finding out that a new acquaintance also knows an old friend, are simply an expression of the underlying structures which drive the natural and social worlds we inhabit and the stories we in turn tell about them. After all, in a world built on probability and chance, but which nevertheless likes a good story, coincidences are bound to happen. What is more, they happen more often than we would care to admit.

My interest in how numbers and words can be used by the social sciences to examine the world around us has lasted throughout my undergraduate and post-graduate studies and into my subsequent academic career. During my Master's degree I conducted research in a prison in the United Kingdom, looking at the care and treatment of mentally disordered offenders. At this time (the mid-1990s) more formalised multi-agency working had been introduced nationally for the treatment of offenders who have mental health problems in prison as well as on their release into the community (James 2010). The numbers have consistently revealed that a disproportionately high level of mental illness and alcohol and drug abuse exists amongst the prison population. For example, a recent House of Commons report estimated that at least 70 per cent of prisoners in the United Kingdom suffer from two or more mental disorders, while noting that in the general population the comparative figures are 5 per cent for men and 2 per cent for women (Berman 2011). The situation was much the same when I was doing my research. Against this stark statistical background I sat and talked over cups of tea and biscuits to people whose life stories reinforced the complex nature of the problem of how best to care for individuals with mental health issues within an institutional environment primarily designed to punish wrongdoers. The narratives I collected to my mind revealed the presence of underlying socio-economic, cultural and ideological structures, which were at work shaping peoples lives and restricting the life opportunities and personal choices some individuals have available to them, particularly if they happen to be born in the wrong geographical area, look and act differently, come from a troubled family background, or just have had a run of bad luck. Each day I spent completing my research in the prison environment not only made me more grateful that I could go home to my family but also reminded me of the power of words for exploring the social world around me.

Yet it wasn't until I began my doctoral research looking at the reasons why health and social care professionals sometimes use their position to commit murder and other criminal acts – such as in the case of the general practitioner Harold Shipman, who killed some two hundred of his patients – that I really started to get to grips with a broader range of analytical approaches available in the social sciences to analyse words (or qualitative data analysis as it is more formally called). Up until this point I had primarily used what is called grounded theory to analyse the stories I collected. This approach is sometimes referred to as thematic analysis owing to its tendency to 'chunk' pieces of text (usually interview responses) into thematic categories. Grounded theory analysis is perhaps the most commonly used qualitative analysis method in the social sciences, and involves building up your story of what is happening and why from people's own accounts, instead of approaching them with some pre-existing theory in mind. We will look at this approach in more detail in Chapter 3 when we examine different strategies for collecting data, as well as in Chapter 4 where we discuss grounded theory analysis in detail. For the moment it is enough to say that it was at this point that I began to expand my analytical repertoire beyond grounded theory analysis through exploring how to incorporate narrative analysis and discourse analysis in my work. For me, these approaches opened up a range of new theoretical opportunities for critically exploring criminal life and the role played by language, power and social structure in shaping human agency. I hope after reading Chapters 5 and 6, which respectively discuss narrative analysis and discourse analysis, that the reader will agree with me that their emergence within the social sciences over the past three decades has done much to enhance the reach of the criminological imagination.

For all I valued having a range of different analytical approaches to help me look in different ways at qualitative data, I never forgot the emphasis placed by my undergraduate lecturer on using both words and numbers when exploring the world around us. But examining the world using numbers, or quantitative data analysis as it is more formally called, doesn't appeal to all students. Reviews of quantitative teaching in higher education in the United Kingdom by Williams et al. (2006, 2008) reveal the wariness social science students can feel towards quantitative methods teaching, with the research showing that two out of three would rather write an essay than analyse numeric data and do statistics. As my postgraduate studies progressed and I began my academic teaching career I increasingly recognised the importance of nurturing students' statistical skills and understanding of the role played by quantitative research in the ongoing intellectual development of the social sciences. My experience has shown that students may perhaps feel nervous when they find out they will be doing 'numbers analysis'. Nevertheless, if approached in the right way, quantitative methods teaching can significantly enhance their personal development and educational experience – partly through developing their awareness of the diverse range of statistically focused career and employment opportunities available to social science graduates, but mainly because, if managed carefully, quantitative teaching can enrich their understanding of the dynamic relationships which exist between criminological disciplinary discourse and practical real-world social problems and issues. Yet, to my mind, achieving this goal requires students be introduced to quantitative analysis in the first year of their studies, with this teaching being progressively deepened during subsequent years. This does not always happen in the United Kingdom – a state of affairs which deeply concerns the Economic and Social Research Council (ESRC) in its role as perhaps the key social science research funding body in the United Kingdom, which also grants PhD studentship bursaries (ESRC 2011).

In a recent report the ESRC strategic advisor on quantitative methods recommended after reviewing teaching provision nationally that cultural and institutional change was needed across the higher education sector 'to secure increased curriculum space for quantitative methods, including teaching in year 1 and more contact time for students' (MacInnes 2009: 27). In no small part this is why the introduction to quantitative data analysis covered in Chapters 7 and 8 of this book is specifically designed to introduce students to the main features of how the analysis of numbers is approached by criminologists. The goal is to provide a foundation to the analysis of numbers which students can apply in their own project work as well as subsequently build on as they move forward to examining more complex statistical procedures and techniques. Taken together Chapters 7 and 8 are an invitation for the reader to take the first step in what is a vitally important aspect of the study of the criminal life. More advanced students will find these chapters useful as an aide-memoire to the basics of doing quantitative data analysis.

This focus on outlining the key features of how quantitative research is undertaken by the criminological academic community brings us to an important point concerning the analysis of words and numbers. Our ability to ask questions, to listen, to observe and critically reflect on the world around us, is built on our ability to use words and numbers to negotiate everyday life – we use them to manage our personal finances, choose the right house to buy, make a case for a job promotion, or decide which political party to vote for. But as we will discuss in Chapters 2 and 3, criminological analysis may well be built on our everyday commonsense understandings concerning the world around us and how it works; however, as an academic discipline it also seeks to move beyond these. As such it has developed its own distinctive ways of examining the world which are often expressed in the form of key disciplinary concepts, theories and perspectives. A key theme of this book is that criminological research is a systematic and accumulative endeavour, undertaken by a community of scholars, all of whom contribute to a growing corpus of shared knowledge, even when they disagree with each other. Indeed, many academics, myself included, would say this is especially the case when they disagree with each other. Consequently Chapter 2 discusses, amongst other things, what is commonly referred to as the literature review and how this plays a key role in shaping criminological research even when we adopt a grounded theory approach. But for the moment I think it is important to focus on the fact that criminology is a highly diverse and fragmented discipline – no one viewpoint dominates, no one theory explains all. For this brings us to what I like to call the triangle of criminology.

The Triangle of Criminology

When asked about the undergraduate criminology degree course I teach I often find myself talking to prospective students (and sometimes their parents) about the triangle of criminology. I find this is a useful device for reinforcing the multidisciplinary nature of criminology. So I explain that, like a triangle, criminology can be said to be made up of three interconnected 'angles': administrative criminology, biological and psychological criminology, and finally, sociological criminology. I find the metaphor of a triangle works quite well as it reinforces how each discipline is connected to each other and all are concerned (but in different ways) by a shared concern with crime and deviance, which consequently can be said to lie at the centre of the triangle (see Figure 1.1). Typically I point out that saying the subject matter of criminology is crime is more than a little problematic. Although it may seem like common sense to say criminologists are concerned with crime, we need to ask ourselves if we really want to restrict our thinking to a topic whose content and boundaries are defined by the state and its institutionalised agencies of social control, i.e. the legal system, the police and so on. Shouldn't criminology as an independent academic discipline be concerned with critically analysing the lawmakers and lawkeepers just as much as the lawbreakers? Although we may feel we have a strong innate sense of right and wrong the fact of the matter is that crime is a social construct and indeed definitions surrounding what constitutes a criminal act change over time. For example, homosexuality was once considered a crime in the United Kingdom. What is more, definitions of what is a crime also vary by geographical location. For example, the age of consent for sexual intercourse varies worldwide, indeed within Europe alone it is 13 in Spain and 16 in the United Kingdom. It is for these reasons that criminologists usually add the concept of deviance when discussing the focus of their disciplinary subject.

Deviance is usually defined as behaviour which may not necessarily be illegal but nevertheless deviates from what is perceived as normal group behaviour. Hence including it in the focus of criminology allows us to examine both the social construction of 'the other' and so the processes by which certain behaviours come to be labelled as 'criminal' while others do not.

Figure 1.1 The triangle of criminology

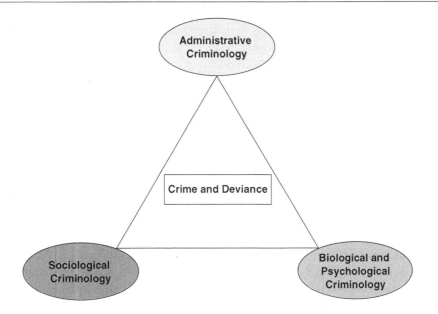

Being the subject matter of criminology, crime and deviance lie at the centre of our criminological triangle. Our next step is to consider the angles of our triangle. Let us begin with administrative criminology. Within criminology, administrative criminology is often taken to refer to a distinctive policy-oriented disciplinary development that emerged in the United Kingdom in the 1980s; it is concerned with situational crime prevention, that is, the measures taken at a local level to close down the opportunity for crime through preventive strategies such as the use of CCTV, the employment of shop security, the design of urban or city centre space, and so on. However, what I am referring to here under the banner of administrative criminology is the structure and processes of the criminal justice system and its associated agencies of social control, i.e. the police, legal system and so on. Students studying undergraduate criminology programmes tend to expect that they will be taught about how the criminal justice system in the United Kingdom is organised and operates in practice, what its underlying principles and key procedures and who its key social actors are, as well as how certain key historical and contemporary legislative developments have impacted on the policing of crime and punishment of offenders. As part of this, students may well also explore the origins of criminology as an academic discipline and so be introduced to the next angle in our triangle: biological and psychological criminology.

A concern with crime and punishment may have existed for as long as recorded history yet it is only in the last 150 years or so that a distinctively scientific form of criminology has emerged. As we will discuss in Chapter 3, from the nineteenth century onwards we see an increasing emphasis on incorporating within criminology the methodological techniques of modern science with the result that a growing emphasis was placed by criminologists on collecting empirical evidence and engaging in practical experiment. While the focus of administrative criminology could be said to be on how society manages and deals practically with the problem of crime and deviance via a criminal justice system, with biological and psychological criminology the emphasis is very much about looking at the causes of crime and using the tools of modern science to do so. Most importantly, it is about looking at the causes of crime within the context of evolutionary, genetic or psychological predispositions to commit crime. Forerunners of this approach in the nineteenth century were Lombroso, Ferri and Garofalo, who sought to identify 'the criminal type' – which they felt was a throwback to an earlier stage in human evolution and so inferior to the normal population – through collecting and scrutinising the physical features of offenders. Their research led them to conclude that common indicators of 'the criminal type' included large cheekbones, flat noses and large eyebrows. Following Darwin's evolutionary theory such 'abnormalities' were perceived to be inherited from one generation to the next, creating a predisposition to crime within certain sections of society (who just also happened to be the poor, dispossessed and socially excluded).

More recently a range of biochemical factors have been discussed as possible biological triggers for crime: hormone imbalances, serotonin levels, testosterone, vitamin B deficiency and hyperactivity have all been suggested as risk factors for a propensity for aggression and violence, which in turn may lead to criminality (Rowe 2002). It is also worth noting that the growth of psychiatry as a medical discipline was tied up with the development of early research surrounding the criminal type, for its focus on organic and so biological explanations for mental illness fitted well with a growing political and cultural emphasis on value-neutral science and natural (as opposed to religious) explanations for human behaviour and social problems. Over the last several decades psychological explanations have joined the debate through locating possible causes of criminal behaviour within responses to traumatic life experiences, such as childhood abandonment or instances of physical and sexual abuse (Howitt 2006).

The viewpoint that certain sections of society are inherently 'bad' or 'criminal' may not carry the immediate sense of legitimacy it perhaps once did amongst political elites and professional groups, including criminologists. Yet the idea that criminality is immutably connected to some underlying element of human nature, which may lie dormant within certain individuals unless certain biological or psychological trigger events occur, nevertheless to some degree still influences commonly held notions concerning why some people commit crime. The popularity of this viewpoint for political elites which advocate a more punitive approach towards crime to some extent lies in the fact that the analytical focus stays on individuals rather than the social environments in which they live. This leads us to our next angle in our criminological triangle: sociological criminology. Here the emphasis remains on looking at the causes of crime, but the focus shifts from looking for this inside individuals towards searching for it within the broader social conditions in which people live.

It would be oversimplistic to say that biological and psychological perspectives concerning crime do not recognise the importance of 'the social' when examining human behaviour. But their focus typically remains on an individual's familial background and social relationships, particularly during childhood and key transitional life stages from puberty to adulthood, rather than the key sociological themes of power, inequality and social structure. Within sociological criminology, emphasis is placed on exploring crime in relation to the unequal gender, class, race and ethnicity relations present in society. These social constructs are held to shape human behaviour as well as the opportunities and choices an individual has available to them. A concern with exploitive social relationships, social exclusion, as well as the unequal distribution of social opportunity, lies at the centre of sociological criminology. Hence, sometimes the terms critical criminology, radical criminology and sociological criminology are used interchangeably to describe this approach – while the more recent development of cultural criminology serves to further complicate matters. Key analytical concepts for this approach to criminology include patriarchy, institutional racism, social disorganisation, differential association and differential opportunity, strain, status frustration, labelling and social control. This brings to the foreground the point that criminology is a broad church incorporating a variety of perspectives or movements, including the sociology of deviance, left and right realism, feminism, subculture analysis, victimology, cultural criminology, postmodernism and peacemaking criminology (Tierney 2006).

This broad brushstroke outline of the criminological triangle reinforces three key issues relating to the study of crime and deviance. First, when exploring a topic we need to consider the relevance of each angle of our triangle even if we wish to focus our attention on one aspect of it. For example, with the issue of domestic violence we may be primarily concerned with exploring the impact of culture and ideology in the form of patriarchy on the experience of victim reporting (sociological criminology). But we must also consider how the criminal justice system responds to this offence, both punitively and in terms of offender rehabilitation, particularly if we are interested in critically evaluating whether how victims are treated by the legal system has changed over time (which is a concern for administrative criminology, but in some respects sociological forms of criminology too). It would also be useful to identify what is known about the profile of the offender, the effectiveness of offender treatment and victim support programmes, as well as what the personal, emotional and psychological impact for victims may be of reporting this offence and subsequently giving evidence in court (psychological criminology).

Recognising the need to view 'all the angles' surrounding a topic leads us to the second key issue highlighted by our discussion of the triangle of criminology. Namely, criminology may have its own disciplinary academic corpus in the form of published research, journal articles, books and so on, but it nevertheless does borrow empirical findings, viewpoints and conclusions from a range of other academic disciplines, including social policy, law, biology, philosophy, medicine, sociology, genetics, education, history, economics, psychology (social and forensic) and geography, to name but a few. Criminology is inherently a fragmented discipline and is arguably better off for being so. For one of the key consequences of the fact that no one theoretical perspective holds sway over criminology's intellectual foundations is that it always welcomes alternative opinions and viewpoints, which in turn means it remains ever open to new theoretical insights and empirical research possibilities.

This point brings us to our third and final issue, which also is one of the key themes running through the subsequent chapters of this book. Criminology may well be a fragmented discipline but as a social science what distinguishes it from everyday commonsense discourse is a commitment shared by its members to rigorously exploring and testing disciplinary assumptions and theories through engaging in systematic empirical inquiry. This does not mean armchair theorising is not valued as highly as empirical inquiry. Both are needed in equal measure for any academic discipline to flourish and grow. But it does mean that criminological research is often designed and undertaken by individuals with academic and policy-making communities in mind, a fact we perhaps can see most clearly in the role of the published literature surrounding the topic in helping a researcher formulate their initial research question, design a project to answer it, analyse their findings, as well as subsequently consider what the implications of their results may be.

Purpose and Structure of this Book

The act of doing criminological research requires that we undertake a commitment to incorporating the work of others within our own thinking about a topic, and open up our research findings to critical peer appraisal. Ensuring that we can justify how we went about analysing our research data is a central feature of this process: when we present our findings it is necessary to outline not only why we asked the research question we did and collected our data in a certain way; we must also critically discuss how we went about analysing our data. This book seeks to make this process a little easier for the first-time researcher through outlining the main features of different approaches to qualitative and quantitative data analysis against the background of their emergence within the development of criminology as an academic discipline. Hence it has two key aims:

1   To provide an introduction to different forms of qualitative and quantitative data analysis, as well as to place this discussion within the context of the development of criminology as an academic discipline.
2   To outline key features of the research process and provide guidance and further readings to help students plan a research project.

The following chapters are structured in such a way as to fulfil these aims. Chapter 2 discusses the importance of deskwork and the need to carefully organise and plan a research project before conducting fieldwork. The chapter also focuses on the process of moving from initially identifying a broad research area to subsequently focusing this down into a researchable topic with a clear question to answer. The role played in this process by study skills, project management, assessment criteria and the existing academic literature are also outlined. Following on from this discussion Chapter 3 acts as a bridge between Chapter 2 and subsequent chapters, which are concerned with different data analysis techniques; hence it discusses project planning and research design and management issues, including making contacts, gaining access and obtaining ethical approval to conduct research. In doing so the chapter examines important aspects of the history and conduct of criminological research, including the role of criminological theory in initial research design.

Chapters 4, 5 and 6 are concerned with qualitative data analysis, and discuss, respectively, grounded theory analysis, narrative analysis and discourse analysis. Each chapter follows a similar format, first outlining the history of each approach to the analysis of words, before detailing their main analytical principles using illustrative examples from published research to help the reader apply what they have learned in their own research. Chapters 7 and 8 follow a similar format although they discuss, respectively, univariate and bivariate quantitative data analysis. The focus here is on exploring how to summarise statistical data and identify possible relationships between two variables, such as gender and the fear of crime. Finally Chapter 9 returns to the theme of deskwork and discusses the purpose of doing criminological research alongside the writing-up and dissemination of research findings.

Box 1.1

Self-study tasks, case studies, recommended readings and chapter review activities

Each chapter has study boxes which contain self-study tasks, illustrative case study examples of key points, recommended readings, as well as chapter review activities.

Self-study tasks are provided to help the reader: first, develop their own research project and identify an appropriate topic and question given their practical circumstances; second, design an empirical study using a qualitative, quantitative or mixed-methods approach; and third, write up and present research findings after completing the data analysis process.

Illustrative case studies are provided throughout the book to help the reader understand key issues and points as well as how the forms of data analysis outlined are conducted so they can apply them in their own research. The examples used are drawn from internationally published academic sources to help the reader contextualise their learning within criminology as a critical discipline concerned with examining criminological life using a variety of sources and materials.

Recommended further readings are provided at key points during chapters to act as resources and help the reader examine a topic or issue in greater detail. Not all the further readings are book-based; some useful website references are also provided.

Chapter review self-study activities can be found at the end of each chapter. These take the form of tasks which can be completed using the content of a chapter as well as the further readings provided therein. Completing these task activities will help the reader to further consolidate their learning.

Taken together the contents of this book are an invitation to the reader to enter the world of numbers and words as a means to capture and explore criminological life in all its colourful hues. It is up to the reader to decide how they respond. Although in my experience I have found that most students relish the challenge of doing their own research project, nevertheless often a little nervousness and self-doubt creeps in. Furthermore, just as there are no easy and straightforward answers to the problem of crime, similarly there are no easy options when it comes to entering the world of *doing* criminological research and data analysis. However, the first-time researcher should not underestimate their ability to successfully manage a research project. After all, they already use words and numbers to explore and understand the world around them. Indeed, this ability is essential to completing a whole host of everyday tasks. Nor should the first-time researcher underestimate the value of a 'can do' attitude, dogged persistence, as well as a good dollop of sheer luck and serendipity, particularly if they are going to successfully negotiate all the potential and actual problems which lie before them when they begin a practical research project. This said, each person must learn for themselves the truth of the axiom that no research project ever goes completely to plan no matter how well planned it may be. The resources, guidelines and rules of thumb scattered throughout this book should, however, make this journey of self-discovery a little easier.

CHAPTER READING LIST

Berman, G. (2011) *Prison Population Statistics.* London: House of Commons Library.

Crowe, I. and Semmens, N. (2008) *Researching Criminology.* London: McGraw-Hill.

Davies, P., Francis, P. and Jupp, V. (2011) *Doing Criminological Research.* London: Sage Publications.

ESRC (2011) *Undergraduate Quantitative Methods Initiative Curriculum Innovation and Researcher Development Initiative Call Specification.* Available at: http://www.esrc.ac.uk/funding-and-guidance/funding-opportunities/15407/latest-opportunity-13.aspx

James, D.V. (2010) Diversion of mentally disordered people from the criminal justice system in England and Wales: an overview, *International Journal of Law and Psychiatry,* 33(4): 241–8.

Howitt, D. (2006) *Introduction to Forensic and Criminal Psychology.* London: Prentice Hall.

King, R. and Wincup, E. (2007) *Doing Research on Crime and Justice* (2nd edn). Oxford: Oxford University Press.

MacInnes, J. (2009) *Proposals to Support and Improve the Teaching of Quantitative Research Methods at Undergraduate Level in the UK.* ESRC Strategic Advisor Report. Available at http://www.esrc.ac.uk/_images/Undergraduate_quantitative_research_methods_tcm8-2722.pdf

Rowe, D. (2002) *Biology and Crime.* Los Angeles: Roxbury.

Tierney, J. (2006) *Criminology: Theory and Context* (2nd edn). Harlow, Essex: Pearson Education.

Williams, M., Payne, G., Hodgkinson, L. and Poade, D. (2006) *Student Perceptions and Experiences of Quantitative Methods.* University of Plymouth.

Williams, M., Payne, G. and Hodgkinson, L. (2008) Does sociology count? Student attitudes to the teaching of quantitative methods, *Sociology,* 42(5): 1003–22.

2

Getting Started: Focusing on Deskwork

CHAPTER OVERVIEW

This chapter discusses the importance of deskwork and the need to carefully organise and plan a research project before conducting fieldwork. The main features of deskwork are introduced. The process of moving from initially identifying a broad research area to subsequently focusing this down into researchable topic with a clear question to answer is discussed. The role played in this process by study skills, project management, assessment criteria and the existing academic literature is outlined. The goal of criminological research in answering inductive, qualitative, 'what is happening?' questions as well as deductive, quantitative, 'why is it happening?' questions is explored. Exercises, further readings and review activities are provided to aid initial project development.

CHAPTER CONTENTS

The importance of deskwork

Formulating an initial research area

- *Review your study skills*
- *Get organised and develop a filing system*
- *Know your assessment criteria*

Developing a research topic with a clear question to answer

- *Focusing on what is doable: the square of crime*
- *The literature review and research question development*

The Importance of Deskwork

This chapter gives a general introduction to initial research project development. It provides a necessary background to the main focus of subsequent chapters: the collection and analysis of criminological research data. The chapter is written with the first-time researcher in mind and contains review activities and recommended further readings. It introduces some important elements of doing criminological research that will be explored further in subsequent chapters, including the need to question commonsense knowledge and shared assumptions surrounding crime and deviance, alongside the role within this of inductive, qualitative, 'what is happening?' questions and deductive, quantitative, 'why is it happening?' questions.

The previous chapter discussed how criminology is a fragmented discipline which draws on a range of differing theoretical perspectives and expert discourses when dealing with its subject matter. Some criminologists focus on the complex interplay between social inequality and injustice and commonly shared notions of deviance and criminality, highlighting as they do how social categories such as race, class and gender play key roles in the production and consumption of crime in advanced post-industrial societies. Others are not so concerned with wider social circumstance and power relations. Instead they busy themselves with exploring offender profiling and biological and psychological explanations of crime. But regardless of their differences criminologists share in common a questioning attitude towards the world around them. They are interested in why things are the way they are and happen the way they do. So they may ask questions like 'Why in the US are African-American men more likely to be given the death penalty than white men?', or 'Why do graffiti artists "tag" social spaces and objects when they know it is illegal to do so?', or 'Why do women feel reluctant to report domestic violence?' What is more, to answer their questions criminologists comparatively analyse death penalty statistics over time and collect the life stories of individuals on death row, spend time with people who graffiti public places such as shopping centres, as well as work with women who have been a victim of domestic violence to explore how their voices have been silenced.

Criminological research is not just done for the sake of academic disciplinary progress but to influence government and lobby for changes in social policy and the criminal justice system (although conducting criminological research for its own sake is certainly not a bad thing). This brings to the foreground issues relating to research ethics and the complex social-political role played by criminology as a knowledge-producing and -consuming discipline: is a value-neutral model of criminology possible or even desirable? These questions have been touched on in Chapter 1 and are looked at in more detail as the politics and ethics of doing criminological research are explored in later chapters. For now it is enough to recognise that it is its potential to engender social change which makes criminology so rewarding: it can make a real practical difference to people's everyday lives. Yet it is only through conducting high-quality research that this goal can be realised. It is the task of this chapter to lay the foundations on which this can be accomplished by offering the reader guidance on how to initially develop their research project.

It is presumed the reader is an undergraduate or postgraduate student who has to complete a piece of empirical fieldwork on their own, but under the supervision of an experienced tutor, for an assessed piece of coursework. In this book the term fieldwork is used quite broadly to mean the collection of the information (or data if you prefer) to answer your research question. This definition covers what are referred to as primary forms of data (when you collect your own data) and secondary forms of data (when you use data which has been collected by others for your own purposes). Designing and carrying out a project to answer a research question can seem like a daunting task to the first-time criminological researcher. It is therefore perhaps unsurprising that fieldwork is often approached with an equal mixture of excitement and anxiety by students who haven't done it before (as well as those who have!). Following the guidance offered in this chapter should bring to the foreground the enjoyable and rewarding elements of conducting criminological research. It is written to help alleviate your fears by taking you through how to manage your research project and avoid common mistakes and pitfalls.

It is a key theme of this book that fieldwork begins and ends with deskwork. Of course in today's information-rich age of mobile interconnectivity it is no longer appropriate to imagine a researcher sitting alone at a large wooden desk, surrounded by their data, books and other papers, furiously 'doing research', while a well-inked calendar full of plans, appointments and deadlines hangs on a nearby wall as a constant reminder of just how far behind with their work they are. Without doubt the computer, the internet and mobile technology have together transformed the nature and location of deskwork. A researcher may well still work at a desk but the possession of a laptop and mobile phone makes at least some elements of their workspace portable and even virtual. Indeed it is now possible for a criminologist sitting at their desk in London to interview somebody sitting in their living room in New York, or indeed anywhere else in the world, using the internet and associated online communication technologies such as Skype. The rapid growth of information technology over the last three decades has undoubtedly transformed the practice of doing criminological research and will continue to do so for the foreseeable future. Nevertheless it is important for the beginning researcher to recognise that regardless of the extent to which they are plugged into the world of mobile internet technology, deskwork remains *the* place where their plans come together. It therefore needs to be approached as carefully and methodically as possible.

We will now begin to look at some of the key features of deskwork (see Box 2.1). The rest of this chapter will focus on important initial aspects of deskwork: formulating initial ideas, reviewing the literature and developing a research question. Chapter 3 focuses on qualitative and quantitative research strategies and data collection, discussing as it does so project planning and research design, making contacts, gaining access, alongside the management of fieldwork. Chapters 4, 5 and 6, which focus on qualitative data, alongside Chapters 7 and 8 which focus on quantitative data, discuss different forms of data analysis used by criminologists. Finally Chapter 9 discusses the writing-up of research findings.

Box 2.1

Seven key elements of deskwork

It is useful to divide criminological research into two parts: fieldwork and deskwork. Deskwork happens before, during and after fieldwork. Key elements of deskwork include:

1 **Formulating an initial research area, focusing on study skills and dealing with assessment criteria.**
2 **Reviewing the literature and developing a research topic with a clear question to answer.**
3 Project planning and research design.
4 Making contacts, gaining access and obtaining ethical approval to conduct your research.
5 Managing your fieldwork: timetabling.
6 Conducting data analysis.
7 Writing up your findings and research dissemination.

Organisation of book chapters

This book outlines key features of qualitative and quantitative criminological research and data analysis. Each element of deskwork is looked at:

- Chapter 2 discusses deskwork elements 1 and 2.
- Chapter 3 discusses deskwork elements 3, 4 and 5.
- Chapters 4, 5, 6, 7 and 8 discuss deskwork elements 3 and 6.
- Chapter 9 discusses deskwork element 7.

Formulating an Initial Research Area _____

Having project work to do can be the only time during their studies that a student gets to set the question they must answer. In my experience I have found the majority welcome this opportunity and can quite easily identify an area of criminology which personally interests them and they would like to look into in greater detail. The hints and tips on formulating a research project found in the rest of this chapter should help those students who are perhaps struggling with this task, in addition to supporting those who have a clearer idea of what they want to do, but as first-time researchers feel they would perhaps benefit from some additional guidance. To begin with I always ask students to identify at least one broad area of criminology that interests them. Perhaps a series of lectures or even an entire teaching module has inspired your criminological imagination? Books, academic journals, magazines, newspaper articles, films, documentaries and TV programmes can all inspire you to look at a particular area of criminal life for a research project. Never choose a research area because you think your tutor likes it and that alone will help you get a good grade (in fact often the reverse is true). The first rule of choosing your research area is the same as with any other task: when you have the choice of what to do always choose something that stimulates your interest and creativity. But if nothing immediately catches your imagination it is useful to remember we can initially define a research area as a generalised thematic grouping which comes under the broad disciplinary remit of criminology, such as 'victimology', 'white collar and corporate crime', 'prisons and imprisonment', 'youth and crime', or 'mental illness and crime'. These groupings are often used as chapter headings in introductory criminology textbooks to help familiarise the reader with the main features of substantive disciplinary topics and their associated key themes, issues and questions, such as Tim Newburn's *Criminology* (2007), James Treadwell's *Criminology (Sage Course Companions)* (2006) or Larry Siegel's *Criminology: The Core* (2010). For this reason they can be useful for helping students to initially identify a research area they would like to look into in greater depth. But this is only the first step involved in developing a project: a research area must be focused down into a topic with a clear and answerable research question. We will discuss that process shortly. First we need to pay attention to three important aspects of deskwork which together shape the initial development of a project: 'study skills', 'getting organised' and 'assessment criteria'.

Review your study skills _____

> It is a goal of higher education to enable students to become critical thinkers and independent learners.
>
> (Matthews and Jessel 1998: 242)

We began the chapter by recognising the importance of deskwork when doing criminological research. What we now need to do before we start to develop our initial ideas further is to reflect on where, when and how we do our best deskwork. Recognising how you prefer to approach your studies and manage your learning is an important aspect of your higher education learning experience. There has been a rapid growth in the provision of specialist guidance and support for students in recent years as universities increasingly recognise they need to help students take greater control of their learning by supporting them to develop their study skills. Students are now able to access workshops on a range of study skill topics, such as time management, critical thinking, exam preparation and essay writing. There is also a range of study skill guides and books available (i.e. Cottrell 2003; Holtom 2007).

The increasing focus on developing students' study skills is in part related to widening participation and promoting equality of opportunity within higher education. The widening participation agenda is guided by the admirable principle that factors such as having a disability should not bar an individual from studying in higher education. It has been estimated that at least 10 per cent of students attending higher education are registered with a disability, with learning difficulties such as dyslexia most common (Barrington 2004). It has been suggested that a key strategy by which teachers can pay attention to students' diverse needs is to bear in mind they may well possess different learning styles (Thomas et al. 2002). The concept of learning style comes from the belief that individuals favour some particular method of interacting with, taking in and processing information (Sprenger 2003). The literature on the topic is extensive, with several different questionnaire inventories available, all of which claim to identify students' preferred style of learning. The inventories share in common the assumption that identifying students' learning style preferences helps improve academic achievement. But however grounded in common sense this position may seem, there is in fact little hard, reliable quantifiable research evidence to support it (Stahl 2002). Some educationalists, such as Brookfield (2006), have advised tutors and students to be wary of learning styles inventories as they tend to pigeon-hole learners and ignore the fact that people often adopt different styles of learning depending on the context they find themselves in and the nature of the learning task they are faced with.

Although it is important to acknowledge the limitations of the concept of learning style it can nevertheless be a useful educational tool. Hargreaves (2005: 11) has noted that 'many teachers are successfully using learning styles as a means of getting students to reflect deeply on their learning and thus develop their meta-cognitive capacities.' By meta-cognitive capacities Hargreaves means our ability to develop our self-awareness of how we approach learning tasks. Doing a research project is a complex and demanding task that can help develop your meta-cognitive capacities through calling on you to develop a range of study and interpersonal skills, including your critical thinking, time management, communication, negotiating and multi-tasking skills (Harrison et al. 2005). So it is fine to be nervous about the fact that you may have to test your communication and negotiation skills by standing outside of the local shopping centre on a wet and windy Saturday morning persuading busy people to spare some time out of their hectic day to complete your questionnaire. The sense of personal achievement that happens when you get your questionnaires completed and hand in your resulting research report is very much part of the intended learning process. So why not view your project as a deliberate opportunity to develop as a learner and expand your meta-cognitive capacities? I have found students can benefit immensely from reflecting on their study skill needs at the beginning on their project to help target areas for development as they complete their research. This task must be approached in an open and honest fashion. For example, if you tend to leave writing your essays until a few days before they are due, perhaps sometimes even finishing an essay the morning of the hand-in deadline, it is important to ask yourself if this approach really does help you to produce high-quality work and achieve the grades you are capable of. Your focus should always remain on successfully completing your research project but you certainly will not lose anything by reading a study skills book for helpful tips on how to better manage your learning, or by signing up for that critical thinking workshop you have been putting off, as well as – perhaps most importantly – by taking some time to reflect on feedback you have received from your tutors on your marked coursework as you start to plan your research project.

Box 2.2

Preparing for deskwork: review your study skills

Managing a research project can be a complex and demanding task. The initial planning stage is an ideal place to take some time to reflect on your study skills to identify your academic strengths and areas for personal development. Critically reflecting on how you manage learning tasks, as well as signing up for study skill support workshops and seminars (often provided free of charge by university departments), can help you to plan your study workload and better manage competing demands on your time as you complete your project.

Recommended reading

Greasley, P. (2011) *Doing Essays and Assignments: Essential Tips for Students*. London: Sage Publications.

Harrison, J., Simpson, M., Harrison, O. and Martin, E. (2005) *Study Skills for Criminology (Sage Study Skills Series)*. London: Sage Publications.

Northedge, A. (2005) *The Good Study Guide* (2nd edn). Milton Keynes: Open University Press.

Get organised and develop a filing system

Regardless of whether you intend to use your research project as an opportunity to brush up on your study skills the fact of the matter is that being organised is key to the successful management of deskwork. The beginning of a project, when you are trying to turn your initial thoughts into a doable piece of research, is an ideal time to focus on how you will manage your project at a day-to-day level. Even with a relatively small-scale research project it can be quite easy to quickly lose track of things, particularly when you start reviewing books, journal articles and other information sources. If you are not careful a brief conversation with your supervisor, a quick trip to the library, alongside a trawl through an online journal database, can within a short space of time lead to your desk being lost under a jumbled pile of notes, books, journal articles and other research-related paraphernalia. Personally I like to keep a written diary of my research to help keep on top of things. Each project I do has its own diary. This is my own personal record of the research process as it unfolds over time, and I use it at each and every stage of the life cycle of a project: from the initial development of a topic through to the collection of data and eventual dissemination of findings. These days I like to keep an electronic diary. But in the past I have used the more traditional notepad and pen method. In my diary I keep a personal record of events, information, ideas and critical reflections, each of which I put under one of five subheadings:

1 Project ideas and literature
2 Project planning and research design
3 Appointments and deadlines
4 Fieldwork notes
5 Miscellaneous

Any insights I may have into answering my research question as a result of doing an interview or reading a journal article go under 'project ideas and literature' while a brief record of arrangements I made to set up an interview along with its date and time go under 'appointments and deadlines'. Each entry heading has a corresponding paper file that I keep in a large filing cabinet next to my desk. For example, paper copies of journal articles go into the cabinet folder marked 'project ideas and literature', ethical application forms go into a folder marked 'project planning and research design', while a list of names and contact details goes into 'appointments and deadlines'. I find this cross-linked filing system helps me to stay on top of my research. Of course it is down to each individual to develop by a process of trial and error their own way of organising and managing their workload. You certainly don't need to keep a research diary if you don't want to. But I would strongly advise you to put in place a personal filing system to make the storage and retrieval of information simple and efficient. It will save you a lot of time in the long run.

Box 2.3

Get organised: develop a filing system

It is important when you begin your project to develop a filing system that enables you to manage your research as well as store and retrieve any information you need as efficiently and quickly as possible. It is up to you how to plan this. An academic calendar, some colour file folders and a box of Post-it notes can be just as efficient as a large filing cabinet.

Recommended reading

Burgess, R.G. (1981) Keeping a research diary, *Cambridge Journal of Education*, 11(1): 75–83.

Cottrell, S. (2012) *The Palgrave Student Planner (Palgrave Study Skills)*. London: Palgrave Macmillan.

Know your assessment criteria

It is important to reflect on your study skills and how you plan and manage learning tasks as you begin your project. But perhaps the most important factor you need to bear in mind at the early stages of your project is your expected research outcomes. All criminological research operates within practical constraints that to a certain degree pre-define what the purpose and outcomes of a project will be. One such constraint is the need to obtain funding to pay research costs. Government-sourced funding bodies, such as the Economic and Social Research Council (ESRC) in the United Kingdom, alongside the various criminal justice agencies and voluntary and charitable organisations that fund research, such as the Joseph Rowntree Foundation, have their own priorities and agendas when it comes to deciding which of the numerous applications they receive will get funded. Competition for funding can be fierce as a limited amount of money is available. Often less than 10 per cent of applications are successful (and even then there is no guarantee you will get all the money you ask for). So no matter how good their project ideas are, to maximise their chances of getting funding, criminologists often find that their carefully thought-through research plans need to be altered to fit in with a grant provider's aspirations, priorities and requirements. Leaving some types of funded PhD studentships to one side, the relatively small-scale research project that criminology students typically do as part of their studies does not tend to lead them to becoming involved with funding bodies. But one thing students do need to accommodate into their initial plans is the criteria of assessment used to judge the quality of their resulting project report.

Educationalists often hold that assessment drives learning (Brookfield 2006). Brown (2008: 40) argues that 'assessment requirements shape student behaviour. Students follow the cues we give them about what we regard as important. They regard marks as if they were money, asking "how much is this assignment worth?".' Research does seem to show that much like other students in higher education those who study criminology often pay particular attention to assessment demands when planning their learning (e.g. Case 2007). But completing a written essay or passing an exam is a little different from doing a practical research project. I have found that a mixture of excitement and anxiety about developing their own project, alongside a sense of uncertainty about just how to go about doing it, can lead some students to quite quickly lose track of the fact they are completing an assessed piece of coursework (a PhD is no different from an undergraduate dissertation in this regard). This can lead them to think they must do something complex, original and new to get a good grade, instead of remembering to keep their work objectives clear, simple and firmly focused on the assessment task at hand.

As you develop your initial research ideas it is important to remember that being asked to do a 3000-word interview-based study on a topic of your choice for the practical element of a second-year-undergraduate taught research-methods module is very different from doing a 12,000-word final year undergraduate research dissertation project, which in turn is very different from doing a 90,000-word postgraduate PhD thesis. The level of complexity and critical analysis required proportionally increases as you move from completing a final year undergraduate research dissertation to pursuing postgraduate research. Keep this in mind and talk to your tutor about just what is expected of you if you start to feel you are getting lost. But always remember, regardless of whether you are doing undergraduate or postgraduate research, your immediate goal is to identify a doable topic with a focused question to answer, not to revolutionise the world of criminological thought. Even a higher postgraduate degree like a PhD is meant to make a contribution to *existing* knowledge on a topic and must be presented in a certain approved format. Only after a productive post-PhD research career lasting many years will you find yourself in a position where you can change how the academic community thinks about your field of study.

It is not possible to state exactly the form in which you will be expected to write up and present your research as this can vary depending on the nature of the academic qualification you are pursuing. But you should expect to present your research in something along the lines of the following generic format and it would therefore be useful as you begin your project to spend some time familiarising yourself with it. Please remember that many undergraduate dissertations are literature reviews in their own right and these will follow a different format to the one proposed here. The associated further readings in Box 2.4 provide guidance on this type of dissertation project, if you should wish to find out more. As this book is concerned with empirical research projects it will stick to the following format. Indeed, we will return to it in Chapter 9 when we discuss the writing-up of research findings:

1 *Title page* (research title and author name).
2 *Abstract* (brief summary of research aims and key findings).
3 *Introduction* (overview of topic; statement of research aims and objectives; justification of why it is important; summary of subsequent chapter content).
4 *Literature review* (discussion of literature leading to the identification of key themes, issues, concepts and theories relevant to topic; identification of gaps in reviewed literature; statement of research aims and objectives in relation to these omissions).
5 *Methodology* (discussion of strengths and weaknesses of research strategy designed to meet stated research aims and objectives; consideration of access and research ethics alongside the process of data collection and analysis, i.e. questionnaire development and proposed statistical analysis procedures give the type of data collected).
6 *Findings* (clear thematically organised discussion of findings obtained using a mixture of text and graphs to illustrate key findings as appropriate).
7 *Discussion* (analysis of findings obtained and their contribution to existing literature based on a critical appraisal of whether and how they fill previously identified 'literature gaps'; consideration of possible next steps for future research on topic).
8 *Conclusion* (evaluation of implications and consequences of research findings).

Box 2.4

Focus on expected outcomes: format and assessment criteria

Managing a research project can be a complex task. A common pitfall to avoid early on is overestimating what is needed and not paying enough attention to expected outcomes: a 12,000-word undergraduate research dissertation has a different academic aim and expected submission format to a 90,000-word PhD thesis. So remain aware of exactly what is expected of you by knowing your assessment criteria. Thoroughly check available guidance on the format you are expected to submit your work in and use it to help organise your initial planning. If you are unclear about anything don't be afraid to ask your tutor questions concerning what is expected of you. Reviewing final year dissertations or PhD theses successfully submitted by previous students will also help you. You will usually find Master's and PhD theses in your campus library, while individual academic departments typically make their own arrangements to store previous undergraduate dissertations so current students can access them.

Developing a Research Topic with a Clear Question to Answer

The next stage of project development requires you to identify a more focused research topic. Because that is the thing about research areas: they are exactly that – a broad area of criminology which contains within it a whole range of thematic topics. What I generally advise students to do is look again at their introductory criminology textbooks, for example Tim Newburn's *Criminology* (2007), James Treadwell's *Criminology* (*Sage Course Companions*) (2006) or Larry Siegel's *Criminology: The Core* (2010). Chapters in such books tend to break down the content of a disciplinary area into a series of thematic subtopics with related key issues, questions and readings. So when you say you want to look at 'youth and crime' it could mean you want to look at one of any number of possible thematic topics within this broad disciplinary area. For instance, just a few of the topics which come under the broad disciplinary area 'youth and crime' include inner-city gang membership and knife crime, anti-social behaviour orders, teenage girls as the victims of sex crime, the use of internet chat rooms by paedophiles to groom children, as well as youth court sentencing patterns for violent offences in relation to race and social class background.

An invaluable feature of textbooks is that they tend to take the reader through topics by looking at quite broad questions that criminologists actively doing research in the field sometimes use to help orientate their own work as well as compare and contrast it to that of peers; e.g. Is the level of crime going up or down? Why do the media tend to focus more on street crime rather than white collar and corporate crime? Who are the real victims of environmental crime? Given their broad and open-ended nature such questions are not really appropriate for use in an undergraduate or postgraduate research project, as their primary purpose is to act as a spur for ongoing critical reflection and debate within the broader academic community, e.g. How can we ever know if crime is rising or falling when we aren't even sure if the recorded government statistics we have are accurate? But these types of question are nevertheless very helpful in orientating students towards the key features of a topic as they begin the process of thinking about what their research question may be.

Box 2.5

Find out what the broad issues, themes and questions surrounding your topic are

Criminological research areas typically contain several thematic topics, each of which will have their own key issues and pertinent questions that act as useful orientating devices for introducing a topic to the reader when they have no prior knowledge. You can use an introductory criminology course textbook to help you identify topics. Use the themes, issues, questions and further readings discussed by the author to help orientate your own project and guide your initial thoughts and broader reading. But your priority as you begin is to identify a doable project, so first complete the square of crime exercise in Box 2.6 *before* you thoroughly review the literature surrounding your topic.

Recommended reading

White, P. (2009) *Developing Research Questions*. London: Palgrave Macmillan.

Focusing on what is doable: the square of crime

The important thing to identify at this stage is a doable research project bearing in mind what we have already discussed in this chapter: what can you do given the time and resources you have to meet your assessment remit? Here I like to advise students to take a step back and return to basics to identify what is a doable research project for them given their personal interests and practical constraints. In fact I like to begin with what is on the surface a very simple but nevertheless core disciplinary question: what is the subject matter of criminology? The all-too-obvious answer to this question is of course 'crime'. Yet crime is a highly contested, historically situated and socially constructed concept that changes its character over time. Nevertheless focusing on it brings to the foreground that criminological research is by and large concerned with investigating one or more aspects of what has been termed 'the square of crime' (Matthews and Young 1992). That is, if we can broadly agree for the sake of argument that criminology is concerned with crime then we can equally hold that criminological research is concerned with one or more of the four key social actors involved: 1) the offender; 2) the victim; 3) the state and its agencies, i.e. police, courts, welfare services and so on; and 4) the general public.

I have found the square of crime can be a useful analytical tool for students to use as they begin to look for a doable research topic. Remember you are meant to be doing your own research project, which means collecting your own primary data or utilising secondary data sources for your own purposes. The idea here is that you use the square of crime as a tool to help you when you are initially trying to clarify your topic, that is, before you get too involved in intensively searching 'the literature'. You do this by first asking yourself which aspect of the square of crime you can feasibly look at and collect your own primary data on, given your research interests, available resources and assessment requirements (see the exercise detailed in Box 2.6). So if you think you want to look at the topic of knife crime and youth gang membership then the first question you might want to ask yourself is whether you have the time, resources and access to be able to collect data from the offender on this topic. Answering this question will help clarify your thinking by focusing on what is a doable project for you. An undergraduate student completing a final year dissertation project, which usually begins in late September when the semester starts and must be handed in several months later the following April or May, may not have the time and resources available to get the sustained access they need to obtain data from youth gang members on why they carry and use knives (there are also of course personal safety issues here which mean that even if a student could get access their tutor may well veto the project). But even though students may not be able to collect primary data from the offender they can nevertheless still look at the experiences and perceptions of the public on the topic (who may or may not have been the victim of knife crime), as well as look at the response of the state and its crime control agencies by analysing contemporary shifts in criminal justice policy and practice. So students may conclude that they would like to collect primary data from members of the public concerning their attitudes and beliefs about youth gang involvement with knife crime, as well as the response of the government and criminal justice agencies to this issue. Of course this is just a starting point. The next step is to look at relevant literature in the form of journal articles, books, reports and policy documents to flesh out these initial thoughts into a more focused research project with a clear and answerable research question. The usefulness of doing the square of crime exercise lies in that it keeps you focused on what is doable given your practical situation.

Box 2.6

The square of crime exercise

A key issue you must reflect on as you begin to focus down on a research topic is the collection of relevant primary and secondary forms of data bearing in mind the time, resource, assessment and access constraints you are operating within. The concept of the square of crime can be a useful analytical tool to develop your project by helping to clarify your initial ideas and target your empirical focus *before* you undertake an in-depth literature review to finalise your project topic and research question. The square of crime focuses on four key social actors typically involved in a criminological topic:

1 The offender
2 The victim
3 The state and its agencies (including the main political parties, the police, the courts, welfare services and so on)
4 The general public (including the media, special interest public groups such as charities and voluntary groups)

(Matthews and Young 1992)

Once you have identified a potential research area – e.g. gender and crime – and perhaps begun to tentatively identify a research topic within it – e.g. sex trafficking into the United Kingdom from Eastern Europe – the next thing you should do is reflect on the square of crime. First you need to identify whether you have the time, resources and access to collect your own primary data from:

1 *The victim* – i.e. are you able and willing to collect primary data from individuals who have been the victims of sex trafficking?
2 *The offender* – i.e. are you able and willing to collect primary data from individuals who have been convicted of sex trafficking?
3 *The state and its agencies* – i.e. are you able and willing to collect primary data from people who work within the criminal justice system and deal in some way with sex trafficking, such as the police, doctors, counsellors, judges, welfare services and so on?
4 *The general public* – i.e. are you able and willing to collect primary data from members of the public concerning sex trafficking or charitable and voluntary organisations who in some way work with victims and state agencies?

Whatever your answers are, think about how it will impact on your project and its aims and potential research question. It is also important to reflect on ethical and personal safety issues when considering if it is feasible to collect primary data from the different elements of the square of crime; i.e. aside from any practical difficulties, what ethical and personal safety issues do you think will be involved in getting access to convicted sex traffickers currently in prison, or women who have been the victim of sex trafficking? Remember, your supervisor will be able to advise you on such matters so ask them for help if you are finding this difficult.

Once you have some initial ideas about whom you can and cannot collect primary data from, repeat this process to identify if you think it will be possible to obtain secondary data for each part of the square of crime. Primary and secondary forms of data are discussed in more detail in Chapter 3. For now it is important to think about what qualitative 'narratives' and quantitative 'facts and figures' types of secondary data could be available relating to your topic and how you could get your hands on it; e.g. do you think the state and its agencies will have collected statistical data over time on the number of known sex trafficking victims and conviction rates for offenders and made this available to members of the public via online websites? Also, what about voluntary organisations, such as *Stop the Traffik*, who campaign to raise public awareness of the issue and provide support to the victims of sex trafficking? Do you think they will have published reports containing victims' narratives of how they came to be trafficked into sex work? Think about how the potential availability or unavailability of different types of secondary data for each part of the square of crime will impact on your project. This will help you get started with your literature review and prioritise the information you collect as you develop your project, collect your data, as well as write up your resulting research report.

Typically I find that completing this exercise helps student focus down on what is a doable project for them in terms of their likely empirical focus. It also reinforces that they will need to use secondary forms of data at various points in their project report: to provide background information, set the scene and justify the importance of their project; to help guide the collection of their own primary data; and perhaps most importantly, to help them interpret their research findings and discuss their relevance, importance and consequences.

Tip: I frequently ask students to bring one or two potential research topics to a tutorial session and work together in small groups of three or more on the square of crime exercise to help clarify and develop initial ideas. Working in groups can help alleviate worries and anxieties as well as provide insights and alternative points of view. Perhaps you could do something similar and complete the square of crime exercise with a friend who also has to complete a research project?

The literature review and research question development

Completing the square of crime exercise helps clarify possible lines of empirical inquiry in relation to a potential topic and in doing so prepares the ground for your review of relevant literature. It is presumed in this chapter that your research study needs to be completed within a relatively short timeframe, will be carried out by you alone, and that you possess limited personal resources (that is, you don't have research grant money to pay for a research assistant, cover travel costs and so on). Knowing who you can and cannot feasibly collect your own data from, alongside initially reflecting on the possible availability of secondary data sources, should help you initially decide if a topic is feasible for your purposes. But before we look at the process of using your literature review to help finalise your research question it is necessary to consider some key points about the nature and focus of criminological research.

Commonsense knowledge and criminological research

One of the tasks of criminology should be to question taken-for-granted assumptions regarding what crime and deviance are, what criminals are like, and so on. It should, in other words, question common-sense knowledge.

(Tierney 2006: 7)

An important thing to remember as you begin your research is that you are a fully paid-up member of the social world you are part of. I am often surprised by how students tend to underplay what they already know about a topic. In part this is why I ask them to use introductory criminology course textbooks to identify possible research topics as well as get them to complete the square of crime exercise. These are invaluable exercises for clarifying initial thoughts on a topic precisely because they remind us what we already know about an area of criminology which interests us. But we don't know things about an aspect of criminological life simply because we have attended a few lectures, read some books and journal articles, or completed some exercises designed to help us get started. Rather the processes of primary socialisation have provided us with a wealth of interpersonal shared knowledge about the world around us, including those parts of it we have not had direct personal contact with, which we can draw on to help us develop our ideas. Sociologists often argue that core cultural values and social mores are transmitted and internalised from one generation to the next by key primary socialisation mechanisms, such as the family and educational institutions (Carrabine et al. 2009). Whether or not we choose to accept this we certainly do spend a considerable amount of time learning how to act in social situations as we move through shared rites of passage from childhood to adulthood and into old age. In a very real sense our idea of who we are is a socially shared experience obtained through looking at ourselves through the eyes of others and responding to their changing expectations of us as sons or daughters, friends or family, husbands or wives, teachers or pupils, work colleagues or customers, and so on. A key consequence of this is that we possess a range of typified stocks of taken-for-granted knowledge and commonsensical assumptions concerning the nature of self, others and our social environments (Marshall 1998). These provide us with cognitive maps concerning what is going on in the terrain around us as we go about our daily lives.

Of course, we can't always fully articulate what we know or why we behave the way we do in social situations. Much of our knowledge is tacit and tentative, firmly grounded in the experiential realm of hunches and gut feelings. But it is vitally important to use our existing knowledge as both topic and resource, as we begin to formulate our research plans, by articulating what we already know and using our creative imagination to fuel our research. We may not possess direct personal experience of the area of criminological life we wish to pursue as a possible research topic. But we do have the next best thing: our creative ability to navigate the world around us by drawing on our commonsense knowledge and putting ourselves in another person's shoes. So we may never have been arrested by the police for being drunk and disorderly but can still creatively imagine what it would be like to end an evening of drinking alcohol in a police cell, as well as – perhaps most importantly, given we are researchers – construct in our heads differing possible scenarios to explain why we might find ourselves in this situation (Do we have a mental health problem? Have we unwittingly drunk something laced with a hallucinogenic drug? Are we experiencing a painful marital breakdown?). Furthermore, in today's world of mass communications and mobile interconnectivity, our mental maps of the world around us are increasingly plugged into the world of 24-hour news media, multi-channel TV, reality shows and electronic social networking sites. We are living in a time in human history where it is possible to participate in a whole range of shared human experiences, live as they happen, from the comfort of our own sitting room: from the day-to-day happenings in the lives of reality TV stars, wannabe music icons and soap opera actors, to the drama of mass civil protest against corrupt state government, or the collective outpouring of grief when a popular public figure unexpectedly dies. Modern information and communication technologies continue to transform the immediacy and range of our contact with the world around us. They open up previously closed off areas of social life to routine everyday inspection. In doing so, they feed our criminological imagination and enable us to explore criminology in previously unthought-of ways.

As a critical social science criminology seeks to both capture and go beyond everyday commonsense knowledge and our shared understandings of the world around us, not least of all because experience shows that people can be misled and subject to manipulative ideas and false ideologies. Recognising this is particularly important as we move from researching lawbreakers to investigating lawmakers and the crimes of the powerful, e.g. state-sponsored acts of genocide or human rights violations by the police during legitimate civil protest. Although criminological analysis must arguably always be rooted in commonsense knowledge and understandings in a very real sense, its bespoken task as a critical discipline lies in systematically collecting, explicating and elaborating on people's conceptions of their social world while also paying close attention to whose interests are being served and whose voices are being silenced when we research and think about crime and deviance in particular ways. This reinforces the need to look at the ethical and political contingencies which permeate through criminological research. We will return to this, and the important role played by the abstract conceptualisation of commonsense knowledge to the development of criminology as an academic discipline, in the next chapter. For now it is necessary to focus on how the drive to both capture and move beyond everyday understandings of crime and deviance means it is possible to argue that two generic research questions underpin criminological research: 'what is happening here?' and 'why is it happening?'

From 'what is happening here?' to 'why is it happening?'

As criminological research arguably builds on and seeks to question commonsense knowledge it can be conceptualised as a process of moving from initially exploring and describing an area of criminal life to subsequently explaining it (albeit with varying degrees of predictive success given the fundamentally unpredictable nature of human behaviour). Often our primary purpose, when we first approach a new topic we are perhaps unfamiliar with, is exploratory and descriptive: the goal is to answer the deceptively simple question, 'what is happening here?' This type of research is what Pugh (2010: 46) calls 'intelligence gathering'. Here a researcher often does not have a specific theory guiding their research (although they may well have a good hunch or two about what is going on), but rather their broad focus is to answer the question, 'what is happening here?' So they adopt a deliberative, investigative stance and concern themselves with systematically collecting information about an area of criminal life so they can paint as accurate a picture as possible of it. The researcher seeks to rigorously build up a picture of what is happening from accounts provided by the social actors involved, often in their own words, using a range of research methods and tools, i.e. interviews, observation, questionnaires and so on. This approach is frequently (but by no means exclusively) associated with *inductive* and *qualitative research*, both of which are discussed in Chapter 3. For some criminologists the production of rich narrative accounts of 'what is happening here?' in an area of criminal life is the primary goal of criminological research (Brookman et al. 1999). Certainly, exploring and describing criminal life, which often leads to the identification of new insights into the nature of crime and deviance, to some extent justifies the legitimacy of criminology as an academic discipline with a strong policy orientation. One only has to think of the role played by criminology in the United Kingdom over the last three decades in raising the profile of domestic violence to recognise the value of a criminological research agenda that actively seeks to make sure the narrative life stories of previously silenced voices are heard (Walklate 2004).

But once we have an account of what is happening we often begin to develop working hypotheses about why things happen the way they do. Here we are beginning to move beyond social actors' own commonsense knowledge and shared understandings and towards a more abstract and empirically informed theory of why things happen the way they do. Gradually our focus is shifting towards prediction in the form of testing a hypothesis based upon what we already know. This approach is often associated with *deductive* and *quantitative research*, both of which are discussed in Chapter 3. Of course, not all quantitative research is concerned with *why* questions and hypothesis testing, just as not all qualitative research is concerned with *what* questions and inductive hypothesis generation. But it is useful to bear in mind at this stage in our discussion that in the classic experiment a review of previous research leads the researcher to identify an independent and dependent variable, and a hypothesis is formed that variation in the independent variable is associated with variation in the dependent variable. For instance, we may review prior research concerning age and fear of being attacked and from this form the conclusion that the older a person gets (the independent variable) the more afraid they are of being attacked (the dependent variable). We could then proceed to test this hypothesis using the results of a large-scale survey data-set. For some, being able to answer 'why is it happening?' questions is the goal of good criminological research (Noaks and Wincup 2004), not least of all because the answers gained often seem to have a practical application, and so can be used as an evidential base to guide professional practice within the criminal justice system as well as lobby government and influence policy formation. But qualitative research outcomes are equally often used to inform policy formation and guide professional practice within the criminal justice system (Brookman et al. 1999). We will discuss in Chapter 3 how we must utilise a mix of both 'what is happening?', qualitative approaches and 'why is it happening?', quantitative approaches if we are to obtain a rounded snapshot of criminal life in all its colourful hues.

Getting on with your literature review

The differences between inductive, qualitative, 'what is happening?' questions and deductive, quantitative, 'why is it happening?' questions in part reflect the dichotomy between 'theory-after' and 'theory-first' research. Punch (1998: 16) says that:

> in theory-first research, we start with a theory, deduce hypotheses from it, and design a study to test these hypotheses. This is theory verification. In theory-after research, we do not start with theory. Instead, the aim is to end up with a theory, developed systematically from the data we have collected. This is theory generation.

We will discuss the role of theory-before and theory-after research models in criminological research in Chapter 3. The important thing to remember at this point is that no one research approach is inherently better than the other; rather your choice is based on the research question you are asking. Having completed the square of crime exercise in Box 2.6 you should have a clearer idea about who you can feasibly collect your own primary data from and this will help clarify what is a researchable question for you given your practical situation. But now you need to reflect further on whether you think you are going to be able to answer a 'what is happening?' or 'why is it happening?' research question. To do this you need to complete a literature review. Of course, the fact that you can draw on your own commonsense knowledge and are studying criminology does mean you are able to put together some basic ideas about what a researchable question may look like.

Following up the example of 'sex trafficking' first discussed in Box 2.6, after reviewing your options you may have decided the most feasible project you can do for your final year research dissertation is to look at the attitudes and beliefs of members of the public concerning the nature and extent of the sex trafficking trade in the United Kingdom in order to identify how their views compare to the case studies and facts and figures published in government, police and charitable organisational reports. Of course, this is presuming that the case studies and facts and figures available via various office-published reports and documents are accurate and consistent with one another (this is an issue you would have to address in your dissertation). But nevertheless your initial 'what is happening?' research question may well be something like 'An analysis of the attitudes and beliefs of members of the public towards sex trafficking'. This does seem like a doable project which quite possibly involves devising and distributing some questionnaires as well as maybe even conducting some interviews. But it could perhaps be a little more focused, i.e. is it concerned with child or adult sex trafficking? A key purpose of the literature review is to help focus down our initial question further (see Jenson and Matheson 2011).

Box 2.7 summarises the three aims of doing a literature review: to summarise the current scholarly corpus, to place your research within this body of work, and to help refine your research question. This is why your decision to use a theory-after or theory-first research model comes after you complete your review. At its core an academic literature review is concerned with identifying relevant information in the form of published academic articles and books, policy documents, narrative case studies and statistical data. Online web content, newspaper articles and other forms of narrative and visual media can also be of use. The range of possible sources reinforces the necessity of putting a good filing system in place early on in a project. Together these sources will build a clearer (but still partial and incomplete) picture of your topic. The reason why the picture painted by a review is always partial and incomplete is because in a very real sense all criminology topics are ongoing disciplinary projects open to flux and change as a result of shifts in criminal justice policy and practice alongside broader socio-economic, cultural and political change. It is important to focus on 'blind spots' or 'gaps' in our current understanding of a topic to justify the importance and relevance of our research before we embark on it, as well as (just as importantly), to help place our findings in a broader context and discuss their implications. In short, researchers utilise 'the literature' when identifying a topic and doable question, when designing their research instruments, when collecting and interpreting data, as well as when writing up and presenting their findings (Jenson and Matheson 2011). One thing I have found is that students often get quite concerned about what is expected of them. Of course doing a literature review is meant to be a challenge but it is certainly a doable one. I have found that it can be useful to break a review into three overlapping phases. First is the 'information collection phase' where you are mainly concerned with identifying relevant sources of information. Talking to your supervisor, fellow students or even a friendly librarian can all help identify possible information sources. A good place to begin is the university library catalogue. This usually includes electronic access to a broad range of journals, periodicals, newspapers and e-resources in addition to the books and other paper documents physically located on the library shelves. Online internet search engines such as Google Scholar can also be useful in identifying relevant material. But not everything you identify will be relevant. This is where the craft skill of doing a literature review comes in (Hart 1998). Only by getting your hands dirty and learning to search and find relevant information through a process of trial and error will you eventually become adept at crafting a literature review (Hart 2001). Some helpful further readings on getting started with your review can be found in Box 2.7.

The second phase of your review is where you begin the process of bringing some logical order to the information you have collected together. This is what I like to call the 'listing phase' as it involves your reading and summarising a range of relevant texts. In short, being able to produce a good literature review is 'part of your academic development – of becoming an expert in the field' (Hart 1998: 1). This implies that you must study the literature surrounding your topic with insight and so adopt an informed evaluative stance towards it, not simply summarise it as if it were a shopping list, or what Haywood and Wragg (1982: 2) call the 'furniture sale catalogue, in which everything merits a one-paragraph entry no matter how skilfully it has been conducted: Bloggs (1975) found this,

Smith (1976) found that, Jones (1977) found the other, Bloggs, Smith and Jones (1978) found happiness in heaven'. I strongly agree with this sentiment. But I would also argue that at the beginning of a project you are primarily concerned with organising the growing number of papers on your desk into some sort of patterned whole. So it can be useful to produce a descriptive list of key author names, policy documents, relevant theoretical frameworks, research findings and so on. This can bring a sense of order to the diverse range of materials you are reading and so help you to tell a good story about the current state of knowledge surrounding your topic.

I would argue the 'listing phase' is a necessary stepping stone to the final 'evaluative phase'. The key difference between these two phases is that in the listing phase you tend to organise your literature thematically and chronologically into key issues, debates and ideas, but in the evaluative phase you seek to build on this analytically through comparing and contrasting different research findings and theoretical explanations surrounding your topic, with the aim of drawing informed conclusions regarding the current state of knowledge. It is in the evaluative phase that you bring your critical analysis skills to your reading to produce a synthesised critique of your topic. Of course, the level of detail and analysis required for a literature review written for a PhD thesis will be different to that for a final year research dissertation project. This is why it is important to keep your assessment criteria in mind when you begin planning your research. But regardless of such matters your aim is to show the reader you know what other people have written about your topic, as well as to clarify and make explicit the relationship between your research and prior scholarship. Identifying what has been said previously about your topic helps highlight 'gaps' your research can fill and in doing so focuses your topic into a clear and doable research question. Take again our topic of 'sex trafficking'. Before you began your review you decided after doing the square of crime exercise that your working 'what is happening?' question would be: 'An analysis of the attitudes and beliefs of members of the public towards sex trafficking'. Now imagine that as you completed your review you identified that although there seems to have been a growing awareness on behalf of the state and criminal justice agencies of the need to tackle 'import sex trafficking' into the United Kingdom from overseas, very little attention seems to have been given to 'export sex trafficking' of children and adults from the United Kingdom into European countries and even worldwide. So you may decide for your dissertation research project to critically review current government efforts to raise the public profile of this particular aspect of your topic through looking at the awareness of the general public of the nature and extent of 'export sex trafficking' from the United Kingdom to European countries and beyond. So your more focused 'what is happening here?' question might now be: 'An examination of the awareness of members of the public of export sex trafficking of adults and children from the United Kingdom to mainland Europe and other countries worldwide'.

Box 2.7

The three aims and phases of the literature review

Doing a literature review is an organic process and often you will end up at a completely different point from where you started. Research questions change as a researcher reviews relevant information sources on their topic and identifies new ideas and possible avenues of inquiry. It is important to bear in mind as you begin that the core aims of reviewing the literature are threefold:

1   To build up a picture of the terrain surrounding a topic to highlight its key themes, pertinent issues and ongoing debates, which you will subsequently communicate to whoever will read your research project report in order to demonstrate your grasp of your field of study.
2   To identify current gaps in knowledge in the scholarly corpus that your research can seek to fill, in part. An important evaluative element of your review is its focus on the limitations of current research and thinking surrounding your topic. Remember not to be over-ambitious: your aim is to make a small but nevertheless important contribution to some aspect of your topic.
3   To focus down your initial ideas into a doable research question. As you conduct your literature review you will encounter existing research and ideas surrounding your topic which will open up a range of new possibilities in terms of helping you refine your existing question.

The literature review process can be divided into three overlapping phases:

1   *Information collection phase*: identify and collect published material relevant to your topic from journal articles, books, policy documents and other resources (e.g. online websites and blogs). This stage will involve you using your campus library catalogue and electronic/online search engines and resources.
2   *Listing phase*: thematically and chronologically list the key debates, authors, ideas, concepts and theories surrounding your topic. The aim here is to be able to give a detailed account of relevant literature surrounding your topic.
3   *Evaluative phase*: comparatively evaluate your key themes, issues, ideas, concepts and theories to identify the limitations of current research and thinking surrounding your topic. The aim here is to select what is important, and analytically synthesise your material to highlight current gaps in the scholarly corpus in order to demonstrate where your research fits against this background.

Recommended reading

Hart, C. (1998) *Doing a Literature Review: Releasing the Social Science Research Imagination*. London: Sage Publications.

Hart, C. (2001) *Doing a Literature Search: A Comprehensive Guide for the Social Sciences*. London: Sage Publications.

Jenson, J. and Matheson, L. (2011) *Doing Your Literature Review: Traditional and Systematic Approaches*. London: Sage Publications.

Conclusion

The chapter has focused on the importance of deskwork, the process of developing a doable research question, alongside the role of commonsense knowledge and the literature review in developing a research project. It has provided a general introduction to initial project development to give a necessary background to subsequent chapters which focus on the analysis of criminological research data. I find the fact that criminology research topics are generally (but not exclusively) shaped by an underlying focus on some aspect of crime and deviance (including quite possibly criminal justice policy and practice in relation to these social constructs) does make the identification and selection of student research projects perhaps a little easier when compared to other social science disciplines. Of course, this is not always the case and the exercises and further readings provided in this chapter are designed to help the reader begin their project regardless of whether they have a clearly focused topic or not. In the next chapter we will look at the next stages of project development: research design, access and ethics.

CHAPTER REVIEW ACTIVITIES

1 Identify the study-skills development workshops (i.e. time management, critical thinking and so on) provided by your university. Often these are advertised by library services but your tutor should also be able to help you identify relevant courses. Once you have done this write a short essay of no more than 1000 words on why you think you do or do not need to attend each workshop on offer. Use the feedback you have already received from your tutors on assessed coursework to justify your arguments.

2 Write a short essay of no more than 1000 words exploring what is meant by commonsense knowledge and how modern information and communication technologies such as the internet and mobile phone have transformed our understanding of the world around us while also expanding the gaze of our criminological imagination. When providing your answer remember to discuss the role you think commonsense knowledge and information resources such as the internet will play in your project.

3 Identify three possible research topics and complete the square of crime exercise in Box 2.6. Write a short essay of no more than 1000 words explaining the difference between 'what is happening?' and 'why is it happening?' research questions, and critically reflect on which type of question you think would be most appropriate for each of your topics.

CHAPTER READING LIST

Barrington, E. (2004) Teaching to student diversity in higher education: how multiple intelligence theory can help, *Teaching in Higher Education*, 9(4): 421–34.

Brookfield, S.D. (2006) *The Skillful Teacher: On Technique, Trust, and Responsiveness in the Classroom* (2nd edn). New York: Jossey Bass.

Brookman, F., Noaks, L. and Wincup, E. (1999) *Qualitative Research in Criminology*. Aldershot: Ashgate Publishing.

Brown, S. (2008) A respect for marks, *Times Higher Education Supplement*. 16 October 2008: 39–41.

Burgess, R.G. (1981) Keeping a research diary, *Cambridge Journal of Education*, 11(1): 75–83.

Carrabine, E., Cox, P., Lee, M., Plummer, K. and South, N. (2009) *Criminology: A Sociological Introduction* (2nd edn). London: Routledge.

Case, S. (2007) Reconfiguring and realigning the assessment feedback processes for an undergraduate criminology degree, *Assessment and Evaluation in Higher Education*, 3: 285–99. Available at: http://www.informaworld.com/smpp/title~db=all~content=t713402663~tab=issueslist~branches=32 - v3232

Cottrell, S. (2003) *The Study Skills Handbook*. London: Palgrave Macmillan.

Cottrell, S. (2010) *The Palgrave Student Planner (Palgrave Study Skills)*. London: Palgrave Macmillan.

Greasley, P. (2011) *Doing Essays and Assignments: Essential Tips for Students*. London: Sage Publications.

Hargreaves, D. (2005) *About Learning: Report of the Learning Working Group*. London: Demos (download from http://www.demos.co.uk/publications/aboutlearning).

Harrison, J., Simpson, M., Harrison, O. and Martin, E. (2005) *Study Skills for Criminology (Sage Study Skills Series)*. London: Sage Publications.

Hart, C. (1998) *Doing a Literature Review: Releasing the Social Science Research Imagination*. London: Sage Publications.

Hart, C. (2001) *Doing a Literature Search: A Comprehensive Guide for the Social Sciences*. London: Sage Publications.

Haywood, P. and Wragg E.D. (1982) *Evaluating the Literature*. Rediguide 2, University of Nottingham School of Education.

Holtom, E. (2007) *Study Skills (Guide to Smart Learning)*. London: Galore Park Publishing.

Jenson, J. and Matheson, L. (2011) *Doing Your Literature Review: Traditional and Systematic Approaches*. London: Sage Publications.

(Continued)

(Continued)

Levin, P. (2007) *Excellent Dissertations.* Maidenhead: Open University Press.

Marshall, G. (1998) *Dictionary of Sociology.* Oxford: Oxford University Press.

Matthews, B. and Jessel, J. (1998) Reflective and reflexive practice in initial teacher education: a critical case study, *Teaching in Higher Education,* 3(2): 231–43.

Matthews, R. and Young, J. (eds) (1992) *Rethinking Criminology: The Realist Debate.* London: Sage Publications.

Newburn, T. (2007) *Criminology.* Oxford: Willan Publishing.

Noaks, L. and Wincup, E. (2004) *Criminological Research: Understanding Qualitative Methods.* London: Sage Publications.

Northedge, A. (2005) *The Good Study Guide* (2nd edn). Milton Keynes: Open University Press.

Pugh, E. (2010) *How to Get a PhD: A Handbook for Students and their Supervisors* (5th edn). Maidenhead: Open University Press.

Punch, K.E. (1998) *Introduction to Social Research: Quantitative and Qualitative Approaches.* London: Sage Publications.

Race, P. (2005) *Making Learning Happen.* London: Sage Publications.

Siegel, L. (2010) *Criminology: The core* (4th edn). Independence, KY: Wadsworth Publishing.

Sprenger, M. (2003) *Differentiation through Learning Styles and Memory.* Thousand Oaks: Corwin Press.

Stahl, S.A. (2002) Different strokes for different folks? In L. Abbeduto (ed.) *Taking Sides: Clashing on Controversial Issues in Educational Psychology.* New York: McGraw-Hill.

Thomas, L., Slack K. and Casey, L. (2002) *Student Services: Effective Approaches to Retaining Students in Higher Education.* Institute for Access Students, Staffordshire University.

Tierney, J. (2006) *Criminology: Theory and Context* (2nd edn). Harlow, Essex: Pearson Education.

Treadwell, J. (2006) *Criminology* (*Sage Course Companions Series*). London: Sage Publications.

Walklate, S. (2004) *Gender, Crime and Criminal Justice* (2nd edn). Cullompton, Devon: Willan Publishing.

Walliman, N. (2004) *Your Undergraduate Dissertation: The Essential Guide for Success.* London: Sage Publications.

White, P. (2009) *Developing Research Questions.* London: Palgrave Macmillan.

3

Qualitative and Quantitative Fieldwork Strategies

CHAPTER OVERVIEW

This chapter acts as a bridge between Chapter 2 and subsequent chapters concerned with different data analysis strategies. It discusses three elements of deskwork: project planning and research design; making contacts, gaining access and obtaining ethical approval to conduct research; and finally, managing your fieldwork (see Box 3.1). In doing so it examines important aspects of the history and conduct of criminological research, including the role of theory in initial research design. Exercises, further readings and review activities are provided to help the reader get to grips with the issues discussed.

CHAPTER CONTENTS

Project planning and research design

- *From early classical and positivist criminology to modern experimental criminology*
  - *Experimental criminology and randomised control trials*
  - *Survey-based criminology*
- *The emergence of sociological criminology*
  - *Qualitative research methods*
  - *Mixing methods*
- *Designing your research project*

Project Planning and Research Design

Box 3.1

Seven key elements of deskwork

1. Formulating an initial research area, focusing on study skills and dealing with assessment criteria.
2. Reviewing the literature and developing a research topic with a clear question to answer.
3. **Project planning and research design.**
4. **Making contacts, gaining access and obtaining ethical approval to conduct your research.**
5. **Managing your fieldwork: timetabling.**
6. Conducting data analysis.
7. Writing up your findings and research dissemination.

Having completed your literature review and formulated your research question you are now ready to design your empirical study. This is an important point. Everything you do next is dictated by your research question. So your immediate goal once your question is finalised is to develop an appropriate strategy to collect the data you need to answer it. To help you begin this process we will first explore the development of four key approaches to criminological research: experimental, survey, qualitative and mixed methods.

From early classical and positivist criminology to modern experimental criminology

Often the adoption of a scientific approach to a topic of study is assumed to mean you are going to be objective and value-neutral. Emphasis is placed on identifying and systematically collecting 'the facts' through careful observation and experiment. This approach to inquiry emerged in the seventeenth century as a direct result of the Enlightenment. This was an intellectual movement which argued for the value of focusing on natural instead of religious explanations for events. It argued that by applying their innate reason and engaging in active experimentalism human beings could discover laws of nature and even perhaps change things to their liking. Early technological advances such as the development of the modern steam engine occurred as a direct result of this approach and led, as the eighteenth century progressed, to what is now commonly referred to as the industrial revolution. This signalled the early beginnings of the modern era of mass production and consumption. As the industrial revolution took hold across western nation-states during the nineteenth century there was a gradual shift in population distribution from rural to urban areas. City-based factory work in particular was attractive to the poor and working classes living in rural areas because it seemed to offer more opportunities for economic prosperity and social ladder climbing than toiling day after day in a field had done for their forebears. The resulting relatively rapid shift towards city living caused considerable organisational and structural strain on existing urbanised areas at the same time that a growing governmental concern with maintaining social order emerged as democratic and liberal ideas began to challenge existing elitist social hierarchies and monarchical governing structures. Like other human sciences emerging at this time – such as public health, psychiatry, psychology and sociology – criminology was born out of the governmental need to provide workable solutions to a raft of social problems, most notably criminal justice administration, penology and the planning and policing of growing urban cityscapes.

Criminology emerged at a point in history where rapid socio-economic and political change was occurring at the same time that natural explanation for human behaviour began to replace more traditional religious explanation. To begin with, what is now called classical criminology concerned itself with the governmental project of mapping crime patterns and monitoring the criminal justice system to establish a fair, efficient and regulated method of justice to support in turn a better-regulated social order. Classical criminology's emphasis on rational action and free-will was inspired by utilitarian political philosophy. This holds that people try to maximise pleasure and minimise pain so they rationally calculate the costs and benefits before acting to achieve desired goals. Classical criminology signalled the beginning of a shift away from religious explanations for crime and criminality as social elites sought to maintain social order through establishing a more rationalistic system of punishment to deter would-be offenders (Radzinowicz 1999).

Yet classicism did not thoroughly engage in observation and experiment, preferring instead to 'armchair theorise'. In contrast – spurred on by achievements of natural and social scientists, including Charles Darwin and Auguste Comte – positivist criminology emerged in the form of 'the Lombrosian project', which built on the modern scientific principle of careful observation and experiment

(Garland 2002). Drawing on Darwinian evolutionary theory, Lombrosian criminology popularised the idea that it was possible to 'spot the criminal type'. It argued that criminals were a distinctive type of biologically determined human being who were physically and psychologically different from law-abiding citizens. The Lombrosian project signalled the beginning of widespread penal expansionism and experimentalism across European countries, with prisons becoming vast experimental laboratories where a raft of newly emerging professionals (notably psychiatrists, penal reformers and criminologists) sought to identify and contain criminality under the guise of developing scientifically informed, efficient punishment systems and effective rehabilitative regimes.

The central idea of the Lombrosian project that criminals represented a different type of human being was subsequently widely discredited, but it is nevertheless recognised today as marking the early beginnings of the 'scientific study of the criminal and the conditions under which he commits crime' (Wolfgang 1973: 286). For Garland (2002), amongst others, the historical heritage of criminology as an empirically grounded scientific enterprise is what makes it an academic discipline with a strong policy orientation. Although it oversimplifies matters somewhat it is conceptually useful to hold that policy-oriented criminology is concerned with the governmental management of crime while its theoretical counterpart searches for its causes (Noaks and Wincup 2004). Positivism's roundly scientific contribution to criminology lives on today in a particular type of policy-oriented criminology: experimental criminology. Positivism assumes there is an objective reality that exists independently of human beings, and emphasises the need for a researcher to engage in systematic observation and experiment in a value-neutral and dispassionate manner in order to discover underlying causal laws of behaviour. Experimental criminologists working in the criminal justice system by and large utilise this approach to inform policy-making through focusing on obtaining statistical evidence of 'what works' in relation to a range of criminal justice policy initiatives, interventions and crime reduction strategies. These include prison administration, community-based crime prevention, rehabilitative diversion schemes for youth and adult offenders with mental health problems, domestic violence programmes, as well as interventions to tackle alcohol and substance-abuse-related crime (Sherman 2012).

Experimental criminology and randomised control trials

Experimental criminology grew to dominance in the twentieth century, particularly in the post-Second World War years. This saw from the 1950s onwards the establishment of experimental criminology research centres in the United Kingdom at Cambridge University, in the USA at the University of California, in Australia at Melbourne University, in Norway at the University of Oslo, and in

Israel at the Hebrew University of Jerusalem (Knepper 2007). These all shared the aim of providing governments with independent crime-based facts to inform policy development in as scientific and value-neutral a manner as possible. At its purist, experimental criminology advocates a clear division of labour between policy-makers and criminologists:

> *Criminologists supply facts, policymakers make choices about values and priorities. From this point of view, researchers ought to remain indifferent in the content of policies. It is not the criminologist's job to advocate for particular policies but only to advise policymakers about which of their programmes work.*

> (Knepper 2007: 9)

Experimental criminology utilises the research model of the randomised control trial (see Box 3.2). As the era of risk-averse evidence-based criminal justice policy and practice has emerged internationally over the last three decades, the role of experimental criminology has arguably become more important than ever before. However from an international perspective the majority of criminological research remains non-experimental, and furthermore, experimental criminology is perhaps more dominant in American criminology than other countries (Sherman 2012). Yet a general bias within criminology towards quantitative criminology, in the form of both experimental and survey-based research, can be deduced from examining the methodology adopted by empirical research studies published in leading criminology and criminal justice journals (Kleck et al. 2006). For example Tewksbury, Dabney and Copes (2010) undertook a detailed content analysis of leading academic journals. They found that only 5.7 per cent of published articles in American criminology and criminal justice journals (*Criminology, Criminology and Public Policy*) relied on qualitative data and analysis compared to 27.2 per cent in leading international journals (*British Journal of Criminology, Australian and New Zealand Journal of Criminology* and *Canadian Journal of Criminology*).

Survey-based criminology

Although the findings of Tewksbury, Dabney and Copes (2010) reinforce the preference for quantitative criminology in America (that is, at least in terms of published research in leading academic journals) they also demonstrate more generally the relatively heavy emphasis placed internationally on quantitative methods within criminology (again, at least in terms of published research in leading academic journals). This is perhaps to be expected. The use of large-scale survey methods to capture snapshots of criminal activity and the victim experience of crime, alongside the dynamics of criminal justice processes and outcomes, is tightly

Box 3.2

The randomised control trial

Experimental criminology uses the randomised control trial (RCT) and is generally concerned with 'why is it happening?' research questions as it often seeks to test a pre-existing hypothesis. There are seven elements to experimental research:

1 Independent variable
2 Dependent variable
3 Pre-test
4 Post-test
5 Experimental group
6 Control group
7 Random assignment

(Source: Sherman 2012)

An *independent variable*, as we briefly discussed in Chapter 2, is presumed to be associated with a *dependent variable*, i.e. if age is the *independent variable* then fear of being attacked is the *dependent variable* when we hypothesise that the older you are the more afraid you are of being attacked. An RCT is a controlled field experiment where the researcher deliberately seeks to manipulate a dependent variable by introducing change to an independent variable. The *pre-test* is the measurement of the dependent variable undertaken by the researcher prior to the introduction of modification to the independent variable to deliberately induce change in the dependent variable. The *post-test* is the measurement of the dependent variable by the researcher after the manipulation of the independent variable to see if there has indeed been any change. In an RCT the sample is divided into two groups: the *experimental group* (where the independent variable is changed) and the *control group* (where the independent variable is left as it is). *Random assignment* involves the allocation of a sample of individuals into either the experimental group or the control group without their knowing which group they are in, in a deliberate attempt to reduce bias and induce rigour into the research process.

The RCT originated in the laboratory of medical research (Sherman 2012). An example of RCT in experimental criminology is Pager (2007). Pager wanted to identify the impact of race and the possession of a criminal record on a male offender's chances of finding paid employment on their release from prison. He designed an experiment whereby he tested the impact of his two independent variables (race and having a criminal record) on his dependent variable (being offered paid employment). His sample was made up of student volunteers who did not have any prior criminal convictions. He carefully selected his sample to control for key factors, such as age differences, and gave everybody some training in interview presentation skills. He then divided his sample into two, with each part being made up of the same number of white and black participants. One half were given a fake curriculum vitae which indicated that they had a minor criminal conviction (the experimental group) and the other half had an equally fake curriculum vitae indicating that they didn't have a criminal conviction (the control group). He found that individuals with a criminal record *and* black sample members, regardless of whether they had a conviction or not, were less likely to be offered a job. White individuals with a criminal record were more likely to be given a job than black individuals who did not have a criminal record – a finding that directly contravenes anti-discriminatory legislation.

Advocates of experimental criminology and RCT argue that they provide the strongest evidence it is possible to obtain for the existence of relationships between variables. It is certainly the case that governments and policy-makers are attracted to experimental methods in evaluating interventions for offenders (Knepper 2007). However, RCT arguably possesses an overly simplistic view of causality. Causality does not exist in the empirical data itself but rather in the eyes of the researcher conducting the experiment who brings their own ideas and interpretations to their data. Furthermore it is difficult to obtain unbiased samples free from participant bias, as well as control for all possible variables in the complex social laboratory in which the experimental criminologist operates, e.g. prisons, courts or high-crime city centre areas. For example Pager's (2007) study could be criticised for not being able to fully control for subtle individual differences between sample members in terms of their interview presentation of self (i.e. their dress, demeanour, verbal and non-verbal response to interview questions and so on) alongside other key factors outside of the direct control of the researcher, such as the training of the person conducting the job interview.

Recommended reading

Sherman, L.W. (2012) *Experimental Criminology*. Cambridge: Cambridge University Press.

bound up with the emergence of criminology as a discipline, as well as the contemporary development of policy-oriented criminology as it has sought to generate a statistical evidence base from which to influence governmental practice. Statistical information on crime patterns was first gathered in Europe in the nineteenth century by early classical and experimental criminologists as well as in the early part of the twentieth century in American criminology by researchers and academics working in Chicago (Knepper 2007). As the twentieth century progressed governments internationally recognised the value of systematically collecting statistical information to inform decision-making and policy development.

Box 3.3

The survey

According to Simmons (2001) survey-based criminology can be used to collect information concerning respondent attributes (e.g. are you male or female?), behaviour (e.g. how many days a week do you smoke cannabis?), attitudes (e.g. I think cannabis should be legalised) and beliefs (e.g. people who smoke cannabis do not do regular physical exercise). Researchers use surveys to collect large-scale descriptive statistical information on a topic of interest and/or for analytical purposes to test for a correlation between two or more variables. Surveys can be concerned with 'what is happening?' and 'why is it happening?' research questions. The key elements of the survey include:

1 Variable identification (independent variables and dependent variables)
2 Question formulation and research instrument design
3 Sampling
4 Piloting
5 Distribution and return
6 Data analysis

Variable identification involves the conceptualisation and categorisation of the key information needed to answer your research question. When collecting descriptive statistical information on a topic this involves a mixture of attributes, behaviour, attitudes and beliefs. When a researcher possesses a hypothesis they wish to test, the descriptive statistical information will consist of a mixture of *independent variables* and *dependent variables*, i.e. respondent attributes such as age, gender and socio-economic status in relation to their self-reported behaviours, attitudes and beliefs, such as if they walk home alone at night after visiting a nightclub, or believe that sexual assault crime is on the rise. *Question formulation* requires the researcher to transform variable information into a series of answerable questions for collection, e.g. what is your age? Have you been a victim of burglary in the last 12 months? Surveys use a mixture of open questions (when respondents can answer how they wish) and closed questions (when respondents have to select an answer). It is important to make sure a survey avoids asking leading questions (which supply respondents with an idea of how they are expected to reply) and double-barrelled questions (which ask respondents about two things at the same time). During *research instrument design* the ordering of the questions is decided and the method by which respondents will be required to answer them finalised. Are you going to do a postal or online questionnaire that respondents will complete themselves, or are you going to ask the questions yourself, either face to face or via the telephone? *Sampling* requires you to consider how you will select respondents to complete your survey. This is a complicated issue but, generally speaking, surveys seek to obtain a sample from a larger study population; for example, students studying at one university could be used as a sample of the national student population. Sampling can be either longitudinal, when a survey is repeated to gather data over time, or cross-sectional, when a survey is administered once to a targeted sample of a study population. During *piloting* the survey is administered to a small number of individuals to check that the questions asked are clear and understandable and are presented in a naturally flowing order. *Distribution and return* involves making the necessary arrangements for sending out a survey to respondents and ensuring they can return it once completed. Are you going to ask respondents to return their questionnaire via a self-addressed envelope? The *data analysis* stage is where you engage in the analysis of your resulting empirical data. We look at statistical data analysis in Chapters 7 and 8.

When you design your own survey you are doing *primary data analysis*. But surveys are also used by governments internationally to gather information for a mixture of policy development and evaluation reasons on a range of topics, including assault, burglary, motor vehicle theft, rape and robbery. In the United States the National Crime Victimization Survey (NCVS) is administered annually by the Bureau of Justice Statistics while the Uniform Crime Report (UCR) is compiled by the FBI. In the United Kingdom the Crime Survey for England and Wales (CSEW) is administered annually by the Home Office while the United Nations publishes international Crime Trends and Operations of Criminal Justice (CTOCJ). When the results of these surveys are used by criminologists for their own purposes this is called *secondary data analysis*. Although victimisation surveys such as the CSEW do include invaluable information concerning activity not always formally reported elsewhere, they have been criticised by some criminologists for not including some types of crime (i.e. white collar crime) and respondents (i.e. communal residents such as people living in hostels, hotels or nursing homes) as well as in some cases inadvertently capping the number of times a respondent can report they have been a victim of crime (see Coleman and Moynihan (1996) and Farrell and Pease (2007) for further discussion of such issues).

Recommended reading

Bushway, S. and Westburd, D. (2005) *Quantitative Methods in Criminology*. Aldershot: Ashgate Publishing.

Coleman, C. and Moynihan, J. (1996) *Understanding Crime Data: Haunted by the Dark Figure*. Milton Keynes: Open University Press.

Farrell, G. and Pease, K. (2007) The sting in the British Crime Survey tail: Multiple victimisations. In M. Maxfield and M. Hough (eds) *Surveying Crime in the 21st Century*. Cullompton, Devon: Willan Publishing.

Some useful website sources for official crime statistics

The UK Home Office: http://www.homeoffice.gov.uk

Federal Bureau of Investigation: http://www.fbi.gov

Bureau of Justice Statistics: http://bjs.ojp.usdoj.gov

United Nations Office on Drugs and Crime: http://www.unodc.org

Australian Bureau of Statistics: http://www.abs.gov.au

Canada Statistics Source: http://www.statcan.gc.ca

The practical utility of the information provided by victim surveys, police operational statistics, court sentencing outcome data, crime reporting patterns in urban and rural areas, alongside a wealth of other criminal justice outcome data, has been held by some to reinforce the validity of the viewpoint that the methods of the natural sciences are appropriate for understanding crime and criminality, and furthermore, for making both these social constructs amenable to governmental manipulation and control (Sherman 2012). Survey-based criminology enables the large-scale collection of descriptive statistical information (i.e. the prevalence of burglary) as well as the use of analytical statistics where correlation tests are applied to two or more variables (e.g. if a person has been a victim of burglary in relation to whether they live in an urban or rural area) in order to test a hypothesis (i.e. that people in rural areas are less likely to be victims of burglary than their city-dwelling counterparts) (see Box 3.3). Survey-based criminology typically distributes questionnaires and/or conducts survey interviews with a target sample from a larger study population. More recently the internet and modern mobile technologies have made electronic and online surveys possible. I have found online surveys to be popular with students (particularly those who are computer savvy) as they can be relatively time efficient and a cheap way of reaching a target audience. I have found Survey Monkey (surveymonkey.com) to be a useful resource to help students construct online questionnaires.

The emergence of sociological criminology

Experimental and survey-based criminology have been associated with positivism and the viewpoint that social sciences such as criminology should adopt the methods of the natural sciences to identify underlying causal patterns at work when crime occurs. As already discussed, positivism argues for a distinction between facts and values. This perhaps can be most clearly seen in the experimentalist viewpoint that it is the role of criminology to produce facts to advise policy-makers without considering the values at play in the governmental decision-making process. Yet it is arguable that criminology must not be limited to the research questions suggested by the social control priorities of the governmental project. To argue otherwise denies it the ability to operate independently and if need be focus its attention on the state and its crime control agencies when their actions engender harm. Furthermore, policy-oriented quantitative criminology encounters problems when it tries to promote evidence-based decision making under the guise of a social-scientific cloak of objectivity and neutrality, not least of all because there is no such thing as an 'ideology-free zone' (Knepper 2007: 9).

Given its subject matter criminological research is often concerned with the poor, vulnerable, socially excluded and politically disenfranchised, all of whom do not necessarily have a recognised public platform to independently air their experiences and viewpoints. If criminological research outputs can be used to legitimise governmental interventions as best-evidenced exercises then it is important to ask 'whose side are we on?' when we conduct our research (a point we will return to later when we discuss research ethics). Answering this question was particularly important to the development of sociologically-informed criminology in the latter part of the twentieth century.

The post-war period may have seen the rise of experimental and survey-based criminology as distinctive quantitative forms of policy-oriented criminology, but it also saw the emergence of the sociological study of crime and deviance on both sides of the Atlantic. This focused variously on the role played by negative societal labelling in the creation of deviance and delinquency; how the socio-cultural characteristics of neighbourhoods and economic urban zones were involved in the production and consumption of criminal activity; as well as how crime could be generated as a result of strain caused by the tension between cultural expectations surrounding social opportunity and prosperity and the socio-economic material reality faced by individuals (Tierney 2006). When injected into an emerging, broader sociological critique of social inequality, as caused by a toxic mix of class-based politics, racial prejudice and gender-based violence against women, the result was a veritable explosion from the 1960s onward of academic research concerned with exploring deviance and crime from anything but the perspective of the governmental crime control project. The response to the question of 'whose side are we on?' was, by and large, 'the underdog' as opposed to the authorities and power elites (Young 2011), a position diametrically opposed to the value-neutral ideals of quantitative criminology. The emergence of the sociology of crime and deviance provided the conceptual, empirical and ethical foundation stones on which critical criminology would develop as an analytical and policy-oriented discipline over the next four decades.

Qualitative research methods

Focusing on the processes by which deviance, delinquency, crime and criminal careers are socially constructed by forces external to individual biology and psychology led to an increasing recognition amongst criminologists that they needed to look at commonsense conceptions and understandings of social action. This signalled the beginning of an 'interpretive turn' within criminology and a concurrent growth in the use of qualitative research methods to explore the lived experiences and personal understandings of individuals labelled by society as deviant and delinquent, the victims of crime, those categorised as convicted criminals, alongside members of the agencies of crime control. Although the value and role of quantitative statistical data in the development of criminology during this period should not be ignored or underplayed, qualitative methods undoubtedly played a foundational role in the development of sociological criminology. Qualitative criminological research uses a range of methods – including face-to-face interviews, participant observation and documentary analysis – to capture and examine lived experience as well as the meanings people attribute to their actions and the differing socio-cultural worlds they live their lives in (see Box 3.4). Ethical issues run through qualitative research owing to its emphasis on the researcher interacting directly with research informants (a point we will touch upon again later).

Key to this approach is the concept of *verstehen*. First associated with the writing of the German sociologist Max Weber (1864–1920) verstehen translates from the German as meaningful understanding and involves putting yourself in the shoes of others to see things from their perspective. Our commonsense knowledge provides us with everyday understandings from which we can organise and explain events in the world around us. A researcher can draw on and use their commonsense knowledge to aid their research and help develop emphatic understanding of another person's world view as they seek to construct a thick descriptive narrative account of it. But at the same time it must be acknowledged that this can be a difficult and somewhat time-consuming task. Prolonged exposure to 'in house' cultural understandings and associated ways of seeing and acting in the world is necessary if one wishes to move beyond surface understandings and explanations for human behaviour.

Yet the question of whether it is truly possible to understand the experience of others without some sort of shared common point of reference has hung over qualitative research for the last four decades. Feminist authors in particular have argued for the need to account for the fragmented and pluralistic nature of social reality as they have sought to emphasise the patriarchal ideological constraints which surround the shared female experience of contemporary social life. A central criticism levelled at qualitative accounts of criminal life is that they are the researcher's own interpretation of events. In qualitative research no account of social reality and its criminal life can ever be held to be the final, objective version of events. But to most qualitative researchers the recognition that it is possible for several contradictory accounts of social life to co-exist with one another is not a weakness of this approach to studying criminal life, rather it is one of its key strengths. Meanwhile, the concept of *reflexivity* has emerged as qualitative researchers have sought to partially address the constitutive role of the researcher in the production of rich, qualitative accounts of social life. Broadly speaking reflexivity involves exploring 'the ways in which a researcher's involvement with a particular study influences, acts upon and informs such research' (Nightingale and Cromby 1999: 228). Reflexivity requires the researcher to make explicit their presence within the research process and offer a detailed account of how this has affected their research. Just how have their methodological choices and personal beliefs and values impacted on the production of their account of an aspect of contemporary criminal life? But it is important here to avoid overly obsessive self-referential 'navel gazing'. The aim in acknowledging the researcher's role in the production of qualitative data is to enhance the rigour of the research process, not to focus on highlighting its limitations so as to undermine its inherent value and contribution to existing knowledge (see further readings provided in Box 3.4).

Box 3.4

Qualitative research methods

Qualitative research methods seek to capture the social actor's lived experience, behaviour and points of view on a topic. Individuals are assumed to create their social worlds by organising their own understandings of it and giving it meaning. Because of this, qualitative research is not as concerned with statistical sampling and generalisation as is survey-based research. Additionally, instead of attempting to pre-define independent and dependent variables beforehand, qualitative researchers tend to highlight the importance of social context and seek to inductively build an understanding of causality in terms of the meanings people assign to their own and other people's actions. As such, qualitative research can be concerned with 'what is happening?' as well as 'why is it happening?' research questions. The key methods used by qualitative research are:

1 Interviews
2 Observation
3 Documents (e.g. criminal records)
4 Media and visual content

Interviews can come in many formats, including one to one, group, telephone and online forms via internet chatrooms and media technologies such as Skype. Whereas interviews are usually separated from the social action they are concerned with, exploring *observations* in contrast can be placed on a continuum in relation to the amount of researcher participation involved. On one side of the continuum the researcher directly participates in the social activity and cultural ways of life belonging to the people they are studying (known as the *participant observer role*) while on the other side of the continuum they act as a complete observer not taking part in what is going on (known as the *complete observer role*). Formal *documents* such as police reports or medical records are often used in research to analyse organisational administrative procedures and processes. *Media and visual content* includes video and audio recordings, newspaper articles, TV broadcasts, photos, emails, voicemail recordings and webpage content. Such items can be invaluable when looking at the media representation of crime. The most common form of qualitative data used in analysis is text, e.g. transcripts of interviews or audio recordings, observational notes concerning behaviour and talk, as well as webpage or chatroom content. In this book, Chapter 4 looks at grounded theory analysis, Chapter 5 narrative analysis and Chapter 6 discourse analysis.

A key issue that needs to be addressed by the qualitative researcher in their account of their findings is how they sought to address the central issue of whether or not what they report is a 'true' interpretation of criminal life, or simply their

(Continued)

(Continued)

own subjective offering of what respondents say and do based on their personal selection of what is important; hence the need to adopt a *reflexive* stance when conducting qualitative research. When you begin your project, one tried and tested method of learning to master the skill of reflexivity is to read previously published research accounts: just how did the author try to make sure they let their informants' own voices and experiences dominate the account offered and how far did they succeed in this task? Qualitative research methods have a long and rich history in criminological research and all researchers can and should draw on these invaluable resources when planning their projects. An early example is *The Professional Thief* by Sutherland (1937) which gives a detailed account of various strategies employed by professional thieves, including pickpockets, shoplifters and conmen, as reported by Sutherland's chief informant, Chic Conwell (the professional thief of the title). *Outsiders: Studies in the Sociology of Deviance* by Becker (1963) offers a seminal account of the study of deviance, focusing on marijuana users and jazz musicians. More recently, qualitative methods have been used to explore a range of criminological topics, including steroid abuse amongst body builders, cop culture, court processes and sentencing procedures, subcultures and youth gang memberships, victim accounts of sexual abuse and rape, violence against the police, domestic violence and organised crime (see Bartels and Richards 2011; Brookman et al. 1999; Noaks and Wincup 2004).

Recommended reading

Bartels, L. and Richards, K. (2011) *Qualitative Criminology*. Sydney: Federation Press.

Brookman, F., Noaks, L. and Wincup, E. (1999) *Qualitative Research in Criminology*. Aldershot: Ashgate Publishing.

May, T. and Perry, B. (2010) *Social Research and Reflexivity: Content, Consequences and Context*. London: Sage Publications.

Noaks, L. and Wincup, E. (2004) *Criminological Research: Understanding Qualitative Methods*. London: Sage Publications.

Some useful websites

SAGE Methodspace: http://www.methodspace.com/

National Centre for Research Methods: http://www.ncrm.ac.uk

Some criminologists stick rigidly and exclusively to one research approach – often on the basis that their preferred approach is better than the alternative. This position is usually (but not exclusively) adopted by criminologists with a preference for using a quantitative approach. But the last three decades have seen an increasing shift towards a risk-averse, evidenced-based governmental crime control project (Young 2011). Evidence-based governance judges the utility of information on the basis of its practical usefulness in the day-to-day management of a social problem. There has been a growing recognition amongst policy-oriented criminologists that it is now necessary to justify their choice of research strategy on the instrumental grounds of its utility in answering their research question rather than on an ideological preference for quantitative over qualitative approaches (or vice versa). But this is not the only driver for change. Nor for some is it the most important. There is certainly some use in highlighting distinctions between qualitative and quantitative approaches in criminological research, particularly when first introducing them to students in the classroom.

At a basic level, quantitative and qualitative research do seem to deal with different types of research questions, the former being more concerned with numbers and the value-neutral identification of social facts and the latter with words and the interpretive understanding of the social construction of meaning. Yet both strategies are arguably needed if we are to obtain a holistic picture of criminological life, and in practice most criminologists do use both numbers and words in their research. For example, we don't just want to know how much domestic violence there is at a national level; we also want to develop a deeper understanding of the underlying reasons why it happens and what stops individuals reporting it when it does. We can only achieve that by talking to people. The need to utilise both words and numbers to explore issues if we are to more fully understand them beyond a surface level has led to an increasing focus on 'mixing methods' in contemporary criminological research. Here a researcher may use one-to-one interviews with a small number of people (qualitative research) to initially explore an issue and help develop a questionnaire for large-scale distribution (quantitative research). Similarly, quantitative data analysis outputs, in terms of the rejection of a hypothesis central to a researcher's current understanding of their topic, could lead to them conducting a series of follow-up focus groups to explore in detail why there is an apparent mismatch between their expectations of what their data will show and what respondents actually reported (see Box 3.5 for an example of mixing methods, and the readings provided in Box 3.4 for further discussion).

Box 3.5

Mixing methods

Criminologists are increasingly recognising the value of mixing qualitative and quantitative methods when exploring a topic. One example of the value of mixing methods is provided by Tulloch (2000) and her study of age, gender and fear of crime in Australia. Reviewing the literature on her topic Tulloch noted that research in western nation-states seems to show links between a person's fear of crime and their gender and age. But she also noted the limitations of large-scale data-sets in terms of capturing shifting perceptions of social threats, which she argued could not be fully captured via answers to survey questions such as 'I feel safe walking home at night'. Tulloch decided to use a series of follow-up interviews and focus groups to supplement her questionnaire survey and statistical analysis. She noted that her questionnaire findings did indeed show that in the Australian context, much like in other western nations, age and gender appear to be important factors at play in shaping respondents' perceptions of risk. But her qualitative data allowed her to also build up a richer understanding of her topic through showing how research participants' self-reported perceptions of risk were shaped by noc-turnal movement through neighbourhoods using different modes of transport, as well as by constructing different types of individuals as 'others' and potential threats to personal safety, e.g. older respondents tended to view teenagers as potential threats while young women tended to view unknown men as potential threats. Tulloch concluded that by mixing methods she has been able to capture a richer and more dynamic picture of fear of crime and how social categorisation based on stereotypical 'othering' informs perceptions of risk over different social spaces within urbanised areas.

Designing your research project

So far the chapter has introduced some major approaches to doing criminological research. At the early stage of your project your first real task is to decide which of these you think will be most appropriate for answering your research question: experimental, survey, qualitative or mixed methods? In an ideal world this decision will be based solely on the ability of an approach to provide a framework within which you can get an answer to your research question. But in my experience of supervising undergraduate project work I have found it necessary to advise students to pay close attention to the proposed research context and available resources. For example, you may like to do an experiment similar to Pager's (2007) on the influence of race and criminal convictions on subsequent employment chances as part of a broader concern with the impact of anti-discriminatory legislation on employment practices (see Box 3.2 for details of Pager's study). Your interest may even lie in expanding on this work by seeing what happens if the sample is replaced with female instead of male offenders. But do you really have the practical resources available in terms of the time, money and skills needed to advertise for participants and train them in interview techniques before waiting for appropriate job opportunities to arise, as Pager did? For most undergraduate students completing dissertation project work within a relatively short time period, the answer here would be a resounding no. Similarly you might be able to get access to conduct research with offenders convicted of domestic violence in two rural and urban areas to explore the relationships that exist between geographical area, treatment programme provision and reoffending patterns. But you may not have the time and resources to interview all your respondents as you would like to, particularly if you haven't got access to regular reliable transport. Of course, consideration of resource and contextual factors should have played a key role in the initial identification of a particular topic as doable or not when you completed the square of crime exercise in Chapter 2 (see Box 2.6). Nevertheless a certain amount of reflection on such matters should also occur as you decide which research approach and associated method to adopt. So instead of conducting interviews, maybe owing to your practical situation could you perhaps obtain your domestic violence data using a questionnaire and possibly even a single follow-up focus group?

Triangulation, validity, reliability and generalisation

The initial decision-making stage is also the time where you must consider issues to do with validity, reliability and generalisation. It is important to think about triangulation in relation to these concepts. At its most basic, triangulation involves using different sources of information to answer your research question. Triangulation comes in different forms: 'data triangulation', which involves using different types of data concerning the same topic; 'investigator triangulation', which involves using different researchers in the same project to collect and analyse data; 'theoretical triangulation', which involves using different theories in the same study; and finally 'methodological triangulation', which involves using different methods to study a topic (Silverman 2000). Typically as assessed pieces of coursework, undergraduate and postgraduate research projects must be sole-authored. This makes the option of investigator triangulation inherently problematic. However, it is certainly the case that students can and should if possible utilise multiple theories, methods and types of data in their projects, particularly as they seek to deal with design issues relating to validity and reliability.

Reliability refers to whether a test, procedure or question will give the same results if repeated. A study is said to be reliable if similar results would be obtained by others using the same questions. When designing your project it is important to make sure that different researchers asking the same question or doing the same experimental test would elicit the same response. But it is equally important here not to confuse such considerations with the fact that different people will reply to your questions differently. As Punch (1998: 100) notes, 'when a measure has low reliability, some of the differences in scores between people which it produces are spurious differences, not real differences.' Some qualitative researchers argue that reliability is impossible to achieve because different researchers will always produce different versions of the world. There may well be some truth in this but regardless of such matters it is important to consider the reliability of your questionnaire and interview questions as you formulate them, because this enables you to embed your project within the broader conversation surrounding your topic within the academic community. Triangulating different methods and data can demonstrate to others how a researcher has sought to address reliability issues in a clear and transparent manner by looking at their topic from different angles in a way others can replicate to see whether they obtain a similar result (and so further demonstrate the reliability of the original data). The recommended readings in Box 3.8 provide detailed guidance which you may like to refer to as you consider reliability when you begin to design your research project.

Validity is concerned with making sure your study measures what it sets out to measure. A study is said to be valid if it accurately reflects the reality of the beliefs or behaviours of those from whom the data was collected. It is important to remember that a question can be reliable but not valid: it could be reliably obtaining the same response on all occasions but not actually measuring what it is meant to measure. Like reliability, validity is seen as inherently problematic by some qualitative researchers, since they feel it can ignore the fact that people can and do interpret the world around them differently. But validity is nevertheless important, as considering it requires that we engage in concept measurement and this can help clarify exactly how we will go about collecting the information needed. For example, suppose you wanted to measure people's fear of crime. You may choose to measure your concept 'fear of crime' in a questionnaire using a scaled response to the question 'I feel safe walking home alone from work at night in the dark'. This usually involves using the possible responses *Strongly Agree, Agree, Neither Agree nor Disagree, Disagree* and *Strongly Disagree*. On the surface this does seem to be a reasonable measure of a person's fear of crime because it allows us to ascertain their self-reported perception of the level of threat to their personal safety they feel when they find themselves in a potentially vulnerable situation. So it does seem at first glance that asking people this question will enable us to identify if their self-reported fear of crime is associated with their age, gender or geographical location (that is, as long as we also include a series of questions in our questionnaire to elicit this information!). But it is highly debatable if the question 'I feel safe walking home alone from work at night in the dark' actually enables us to obtain a valid measure of the concept we are interested in. Fear of crime is a multi-dimensional concept involving a range of perceived possible risks to personal safety, including violent assault, sexual assault or mugging and theft to name but a few. Furthermore, why limit oneself to night-time when threats to personal safety occur during the daytime as well? What we actually need to do is develop a battery of questions relating to a range of possible perceived threats to personal safety in different circumstances and locations which when taken together will enable us to holistically measure the concept 'fear of crime' and how this changes for respondents in different situations over a period of time. After all it would be highly useful to find out if people believe that they are more likely to have their purse or wallet stolen as they walk home on a warm summer evening than a cold winter night. At the very least, knowing this would enable us to help develop targeted crime prevention strategies. As this discussion shows, validity can then be quite an involved concept. The further readings in Box 3.8 provide guidance which you may like to refer to as you consider validity when you begin to design your research project.

Statistical and analytical generalisation

Generalisation is concerned with the impact of research findings. As social scientists we would naturally like our findings from our sample to hold true in wider circumstances. In other words generalisation is concerned with the applicability of our findings for similar groups and settings beyond our research site(s). It is with the concept of generalisation that key differences between qualitative and quantitative approaches come to the foreground. For example, in a hypothetical large-scale quantitative survey project where 5000 male and 5000 female university students were randomly selected we might find that 47 per cent of women compared to 13 per cent of men were afraid of being sexually assaulted as they walked home alone at night when living off-campus, compared to 38 per cent of women to 9 per cent of men who lived on-campus. We discuss statistical generalisation in Chapters 7 and 8, which deal with quantitative data analysis. For the moment it is enough to consider that given this finding we could conclude by generalising that female students fear being sexually assaulted more than male students regardless of whether they live on-campus or not, but that they feel safer living on-campus than off-campus, as do male students. Findings such as these by and large possess a clear practical purpose through providing generalisable statistical evidence for the conclusions made. For this reason it is sometimes argued that survey and experimental research are superior research tools to qualitative approaches. It is argued that no matter how interesting or insightful the findings of qualitative research projects are, they cannot provide the same large-scale evidential base for policy-making that quantitative research can. It is certainly the case that qualitative research often deals with smaller samples and therefore does not seem to have the statistical generalising power that quantitative research seems to possess. But qualitative research samples are not random in the sense that typically people are included in the research on the grounds that they are the right people to speak to given the topic, i.e. male and female students if we are investigating fear of sexual assault on and off university campus. This is because qualitative research is concerned with analytical, not statistical, generalisation.

We discuss analytical generalisation when we look at grounded theory analysis and narrative forms of qualitative data analysis in Chapters 4 and 5. For the moment it is enough to say that, if approached systematically and rigorously, qualitative research can generate concepts that are useful for thinking outside of the immediate research setting in which they were conceived and at the very least can be used as 'sensitising devices' by other researchers in different contexts to help frame their own research. For example, instead of conducting a large-scale quantitative survey of 5000 male and 5000 female students' fear of sexual assault we might conduct a series of one-to-one qualitative interviews with a relatively small sample of 30 respondents, 15 male and 15 female. During these interviews we might note that more female than male interviewees expressed concerns about walking home at night after going out for the evening with their friends. However, regardless of whether they report they are afraid of being attacked or not, all our interviewees might talk about different types of what we can call 'defensive strategies' they and their friends use when they find themselves in potentially threatening situations. We also may be able to identify that some of these defensive strategies are gendered, with girls on occasion adopting different strategies from boys. So both boys and girls may report that they or their friends sometimes use 'phone chatting' to make it appear they are not alone by talking to an imaginary person on the phone as they walk home down a badly lit footpath. But more girls than boys may report using 'book reading' where they pretend to read while sitting on a train station platform waiting for their train home, as they want to avoid making eye contact with strangers. In contrast, boys may report using 'phone gaming' in a similar situation where they pretend to play a game on their mobile phone but in fact are keeping a watchful eye on a bunch of unknown people acting boisterously on the train platform in case their actions escalate and possibly become personally threatening to them. We might therefore conclude that although more girls than boys voiced concerns about being attacked as they made their way home at night, both male and female respondents reported that they and their fellow students engaged in a number of defensive strategies in an attempt to counter perceived threats to personal safety and negotiate safe passage through different social contexts, e.g. train stations, poorly-lit footpaths and so on, some of which appear to be gendered in the sense of being more used by girls than boys (or vice versa). Under such circumstances we could justifiably argue that we have identified a useful analytical concept – namely defensive strategy – that other researchers could apply in their own research when exploring this topic

and could also inform policy-making in regard to the formation of crime prevention strategies. As this example demonstrates, analytical generalisation reinforces
the shared nature of criminological research. It reminds us that criminological
research is a collective undertaking which involves individual members of the
academic community sharing their research findings with their peers in order to
advance knowledge.

Theory and research: deduction and induction

Consideration of statistical and analytical generalisation brings to the foreground
the need to consider the place of theory in your research project. When we talk
about theory we are concerning ourselves with abstract conceptualisation. In a
very real sense we do this every day of our lives. Conceptualisation is necessary
because the real world of jobs, mortgages, relationships, social events and so on is
highly complex, so we need to simplify it into stocks of commonsense knowledge
of how to behave in particular social situations to guide our own actions.
Criminological theory is arguably a more abstract form of everyday forms of conceptualisation. In Chapter 2 we talked about how social science criminology tries
to both capture and move beyond commonsense understandings of the world
around us as it seeks to build up an explanatory picture of the causes and consequences of crime. Of course this is not always the case. Much high-quality qualitative and quantitative criminological research is descriptive and exploratory, solely
concerned with building up a rigorous empirical account of 'what is happening
here?' in regards to a topic, using commonsense knowledge and the statistical patterns of collective human behaviour. Such research is often justified on the grounds
of intrinsic value (maybe because it is exploring a new area of criminal life about
which we know little) or its practical utility in aiding policy-development. It is
certainly the case that large-scale descriptive statistical surveys such as the CSEW
provide us with a wealth of information from which we can build up a picture of
the nature and distribution of crime in the United Kingdom. Surveys like the CSEW
are undoubtedly highly useful tools for influencing policy formation *and* aiding
the critical analysis of the governmental crime control project without necessarily
moving into the more abstract realm of criminological theory. Some qualitative
criminological researchers also argue that their research goal is not the production
or confirmation of criminological theory as such, but rather increasing our understanding of crime through bringing to the foreground the life stories of previously
silenced victims who for various reasons have been unable to make their voices
heard. Researchers working with victims of domestic violence, childhood sexual
abuse and human trafficking sometimes adopt this position, arguing somewhat
understandably as they do so that they do not want to undervalue the often highly

distressing narratives of their research participants by overlaying them with their own conceptual abstractions and formal theories. In some situations a criminologist needs to take a step back and solely act as a facilitator through which a previously silenced voice can be heard.

Yet as an academic discipline criminology does possess its own way of looking at the world. Abstract concepts, such as 'relative deprivation', 'differential reinforcement', 'moral panic' and 'underclass' help criminologists explore and explain deviance and crime. Arguably it is therefore important to think about what role (if any) they might play in your project at the initial design stage. Chapter 2 touched upon the difference between 'theory-first' and 'theory-after' research (Punch 1998). Theory-first research is frequently called hypothetico-deductive research. This approach involves, first, collecting current information on a topic; second, the generation of a hypothesis or theory based on deduction which might explain the information; and third, the testing of said hypothesis or theory with the aim of confirming or refuting it (Layder 2005). It should be noted that the hypothesis tested in such circumstances are restricted to a relatively narrow field of study – usually particular types of social institution or social action – and so have difficulty dealing with what is nominally referred to as 'grand theory'. Grand theories are highly abstract, concerned with 'whole societies and the processes involved in their development, or with very general aspects of social reality such as the relationship between agency and structure or micro and macro levels of analysis' (Layder 1998: 14). Grand theories are generally not testable in the sense of being operationalisable into discrete variables for analysis. Merton (1967) argued that much theorising in social sciences is highly abstract and speculative, without firm anchorage in empirical data. He was particularly concerned with dominant grand theories of the time in Anglo-American sociology, notably Marxism and Parson's theory of social systems. Although he recognised the need for the social sciences to have such theories, Merton argued that sociology and criminology needed to concern themselves with linking empirical data to theory by focusing in a very practical way on developing theories concerned with particular social circumstances. He called these 'theories of the middle range' (Merton 1967). Such theories are abstract so they can be applied to different social phenomena, but they are nevertheless restricted to a specific set of social circumstance: 'middle-range theory involves abstraction of course, but they are close enough to the observed data to be incorporated in propositions that permit empirical testing' (Merton 1967: 39). For Merton a theory has two basic components: concepts and presumed relations between them. A concept such as 'race', for example, must be operationally definable as an empirical variable, which in terms of 'race' means 'white', 'Asian' and so on. Under this model of the research process it must be possible to empirically test for assumptions between conceptual variables, such as for example 'gender' in relation to 'fear of crime' as stated in the form of the hypothesis 'women more than men are afraid of being a victim of crime'.

Box 3.6

Hypothetico-deductive research: social control theory

An example of a hypothetico-deductive middle-range theory in criminology is found in Hirschi's (1969) Social Control Theory (SCT). This asks the question 'why do people not break the law?' to which it replies 'because of social bonds'. In other words SCT assumes that people are free to break the law in any number of ways but certain controls stop them. Hirschi argues that these controls are located in the social bonds which tie individuals together and engender law-abiding behaviour. He defines four types of bond, stating that 'elements of social bonding include attachment to families, commitment to social norms and institutions (school, employment), involvement in activities, and the belief that these things are important' (Hirschi 1969: 16). Importantly SCT hypothesises that the presence of these four social bonds helps to prevent criminal behaviour and encourage lawful behaviour. Each of the four bonds can be operationalised into variables against which it is possible to obtain empirical data. Hirschi (1969) provides empirical data from over 4000 informants aged between 12 and 17 years old. He operationalised and tested his four concepts – 'attachment', 'commitment', 'involvement' and 'beliefs' – and doing so showed that rule-breaking behaviour and delinquency did seem to occur: in children from families with poor emotional ties between children and parents ('attachment'); when children felt they did not have much to lose from not meeting expectations surrounding participation in educational study ('commitment'), as well as perhaps not investing much personal time and energy in organised social activities such as sports or other leisure pursuits ('involvement'); and finally, when children did not seem to recognise the value of rules to regulate behaviour amongst people ('beliefs'). Since Hirschi's original formulation, SCT has been subject to further empirical study and although by no means conclusive the evidence does seem to tentatively support the theory, although it has been criticised for its tendency to focus on young male offenders and its inability to account for some forms of offending behaviour, e.g. white collar crime (Tierney 2006).

In the hypothetico-deductive model of the research process, criminologists tend to be concerned with the 'theory-first' testing of middle-range theory. Its key strength is that it emphasises the role played by theory in the conduct of research, and encourages careful and precise formulations of theory in the form of hypotheses for rigorous empirical testing. We will look at theory-testing approaches in Chapters 7 and 8 when we look at quantitative data analysis. For the moment it is important to note that given the emphasis placed on testing a hypothesis this model of the research process has been criticised for its inability to deal with 'grand theory', its tendency to favour quantitative over qualitative methods, as well as (perhaps most importantly) – because it can unduly restrict the researchers' focus on testing and refining their hypothesis – it may lead to them unintentionally omitting important pieces of information that may emerge during the research process. This latter point in particular has been taken up by researchers who advocate a theory-after model of the research process in the form of grounded theory research. Grounded theory argues that concepts and their relationships (in other words, theory) should be grounded in research participants' own everyday understandings of reality, as it appears in specific social and cultural contexts. Within this approach a researcher should approach their topic in an open and unbiased manner and avoid pre-defining concepts before they collect data. Grounded theory was first developed by Glaser and Strauss (1967). Like Merton (1967) they sought to promote more specific middle-range theories which deal with situated social behaviour across a range of similar contexts. As they carefully studied the social world of dying hospital patients Glaser and Strauss became increasingly concerned about the inability of grand theory to provide concepts to help them understand the processes by which such dying patients moved through the hospital environment and the roles played by relatives and medical staff within this. However, unlike Merton they did not feel they should be deductively testing pre-formulated theory in the form of a hypothesis. Instead they wanted to adopt an inductive approach, building theoretical concepts up from the research participants' own accounts of the trajectory a dying patient followed once they entered hospital (see Box 3.7).

Box 3.7

Grounded theory: 'awareness contexts'

Grounded theory is concerned with the inductive development of middle-range theory. An example of a grounded theory is provided by Glaser and Strauss (1967) in their study of dying hospital patients. Using the accounts provided by their research participants they generated the concept of 'awareness contexts' which encapsulated the different degrees of knowledge and mutual understanding which existed between patients, relatives and hospital staff as the dying trajectory unfolded. Glaser and Strauss identified four different types of awareness contexts, each related to the level of understanding possessed by a patient about their imminent death: 'closed awareness' patients were not aware they were about to die even though members of hospital staff and sometimes their immediate relatives where; 'suspicion awareness' occurred when patients suspected they were dying but did not know for certain; 'mutual-pretence awareness' occurred when patients knew they were dying but acted like they were recovering, and hospital staff played along with the pretence; finally, with 'open awareness', patients knew they were going to die and openly discussed the matter with staff and relatives. Glaser and Strauss found that most research participants possessed 'closed awareness' of their imminent death, reflecting the patronising approach towards patients on behalf of health care professionals who tended to dominate health care provision at the time. The concept of 'awareness contexts' is grounded in respondents' own accounts so as to be recognisable to them, but abstract enough to be generalisable to other contexts and so utilisable by researchers across a range of different situations. For example Hooper (1992) was concerned with types of contextual awareness present in the relationships of victims of childhood sexual abuse with other people and how these changed over time as they themselves became parents.

Grounded theory is then inductive, with the researcher building up a conceptual framework from informants' accounts. Glaser and Strauss (1967: 3) say that:

> *We suggest as the best approach an initial, systematic discovery of the theory from the data of social research. Then one can be relatively sure that the theory will fit and work. And since the categories are discovered by examination of the data, laymen involved in the area to which the theory applies will usually be able to understand it, while sociologists who work on other areas will recognise an understandable theory linked with the data of a given area.*

A key strength of this approach is that the researcher is not testing for a hypothesis and so to some extent predetermining what is important; rather they allow the data to speak for itself, which often results in unexpected informant-led insights and understandings of events. This focus on avoiding analysis derived from already defined concepts, which researchers typically identify when they conduct their literature review, has led some critics to argue that grounded theory studies can be idiosyncratic, overly context specific, and so somehow 'weaker' than quantitative methods.

Typically, grounded theory studies will be qualitative in nature and they therefore often will not possess the statistical predictive power of large-scale quantitative studies, but as we have already discussed when we touched upon analytical generalisation, this does not mean it is somehow less rigorous or generalisable than survey or experimental research. Indeed grounded theory 'uses a systematic set of procedures to develop an inductively derived theory about a phenomenon' (see Strauss and Corbin 1990: 24). Two key procedures here are use of the 'constant comparative method' and 'theoretical sampling'. In the former, codes are applied to data and refined through a comparative process that essentially involves cross-checking emergent concepts using different research informant accounts and possibly even different types of data. In the latter, research participants are selected on the basis that they will help to extend, confirm or refute emerging concepts so the researcher's analysis can be broadened through accounting for what are called deviant cases: instances which do not confirm the researcher's interpretation of what is happening. We will discuss these procedures in Chapter 4 when we look at grounded theory analysis.

Grounded theory has been a very popular approach to data collection and analysis amongst researchers, and remains so today. However, it has been criticised as outdated by some qualitative researchers influenced by postmodernism who seek alternative approaches to exploring social life, as we will discuss in Chapter 5 when we look at narrative analysis. One perhaps justifiable criticism of grounded theory is that unlike statistical analysis no firm prescriptive procedures exist, rather just guidelines and rules of thumb, so it is very much a craft skill that is learnt by doing. This does leave it open to the charge that it is difficult to quality control the resulting analyses undertaken in its name. Silverman (2000) discusses several grounded theory studies that clearly would have benefited from a more rigorous application of available guidance, and you may wish to look at these if you intend to adopt a grounded theory approach in your own research (see further readings provided in Box 3.8). But perhaps the most important criticism of grounded theory is that, as members of an academic discipline that possesses a history of ideas – in the form of relevant theories, concepts and empirical research findings – it is impossible for a researcher to approach their topic without bringing some preconceptions with them. As you conducted your literature review to help refine your topic and research question you will have identified relevant empirical findings and conceptual frameworks that will inevitably shape how you both plan and conduct your research. Layder (1998, 2005) has suggested that it would be more appropriate to utilise what he calls 'adaptive theory'. This values both deductive and inductive approaches to the production of knowledge but argues that there are no theory-neutral facts so a researcher must be reflexive and discuss their role in the production of an account of some aspect of social life. Here the concepts and theories that a researcher brings with them to their study are used as 'orientating devices' to help begin the process of data collection and analysis. So a research project may still be inductive in the sense that primary focus is being given to new concepts and theories emerging from data, but by explicitly acknowledging the role of prior ideas in this process the researcher possesses a powerful tool to reflexively justify their resulting account of their topic and place their findings within the broader academic conversation surrounding it. Given that you have already completed a literature review of your topic which has revealed relevant empirical findings and conceptual frameworks, you may wish to adopt this approach in your research. But you are strongly advised to use the further readings provided in Box 3.8 to help you design your project as well as to discuss such matters in detail with your research supervisor, before you come to any final decisions.

Box 3.8

Research design

When undertaking undergraduate or postgraduate project work it is important to seek the guidance of your supervisor when designing your research. Your choice of research design is determined by your research question. There are four basic approaches available: experimental, survey, qualitative and mixed methods. It is important to begin by asking yourself if your question is concerned with numbers or words (or a mixture of the two) as well as to consider your practical circumstances and the assessment criteria you must meet. Key design issues you will need to consider are validity, reliability, generalisation (analytical and statistical), reflexivity and the role that existing criminological theory and published empirical research will all play in your research: are you undertaking an inductive or deductive study? The recommended readings below will help you to consider such matters.

Recommended reading

Bachman, R. and Schutt, R.K. (2011) *The Practice of Research in Criminology and Criminal Justice.* London: Sage Publications.

Creswell, J.D. (2008) *Research Design: Qualitative, Quantitative and Mixed Method Approaches* (3rd edn). London: Sage Publications.

Flick, U. (2011) *Introducing Research Methodology: A Beginner's Guide to Doing a Research Project.* London: Sage Publications.

Hammersley, M. (2010) *Methodology: Who Needs It?* London: Sage Publications.

Silverman, D. (2000) *Doing Qualitative Research: A Practical Handbook.* Thousand Oaks, CA: Sage Publications.

Making Contacts, Gaining Access and Obtaining Ethical Approval to Conduct Your Research

When you were asked to complete the square of crime exercise in Chapter 2 (see Box 2.6) you were advised to consider how you would gain access to potential research participants, given the practical constraints you are operating under as a student of criminology. Gaining access can seem on the face of it to be a straightforward matter but what are known as 'gatekeepers', who sponsor your access, are often needed. You may want to solicit the opinions of members of the public on the topic of wallet and handbag theft in public spaces by standing in a shopping centre and asking passers-by to complete a short questionnaire. Although it may seem that you don't need approval from anybody to gain access to possible respondents in such circumstances you may actually have to seek permission from local retail outlets and shopping centre owners before you can conduct your research. This is not something you want to find out the hard way when you are approached by shopping centre security staff.

Gaining access to speak to the people you are interested in talking to is rarely straightforward. This is particularly the case when you are dealing with certain types of individuals and institutional contexts where admission is restricted; for instance police stations and prisons would fall within this category. In such cases access to research informants must be carefully negotiated and maintained throughout the data collection phase. This can be a difficult task and it will undoubtedly stretch your presentational, communication and negotiation skills. Under such circumstances adhering to an appropriate dress code, and thinking carefully about what you will say and how you will act, are always a must. Possession of a thick skin, unwillingness to give up in the face of adversity, alongside the ability to smile and be very polite even when dealing with rejection and outright rudeness, are all distinct advantages when doing project work. Access issues can also have a direct impact on your research as sometimes the people who sponsor your entry into a research site may set certain conditions that you must adhere to. They may ask to see a report of your findings before you publish it or even require a member of staff to sit in on your interviews. As criminology students your research supervisor will advise and help you with access issues. One particular gatekeeper you will need to successfully negotiate early on in your project at the design stage is your university research ethics committee.

Research ethics

The default position adopted by most criminologists is that you must obtain informed consent to conduct your research. It is certainly the case that university ethics committees, which review research proposals to ensure probity, will require you to detail not just your research question and how you plan to collect your data, but also the steps you intend to take to ensure you protect research participants from undue coercion, duress and harm. This means your research informants must know what your study is about and freely agree to participate. A careful record of consent obtained must be kept. You will need to construct a project information sheet and consent form for your project and consider how these will be securely stored once completed (see Box 3.9). There is an argument, however, that sometimes it is necessary to engage in covert research where the researcher deliberately hides the fact they are conducting research from participants. In such circumstances it is often argued that it is necessary to hide one's intentions for the greater good. One example of such research from the United Kingdom is *The Secret Policeman* (2003). Here an investigative journalist called Mark Daly spent six months working undercover to identify if police officers discriminated against minority groups. Daly joined the police as a trainee to achieve his research aims. Using hidden cameras and microphones he recorded incidents where fellow recruits and serving police officers voiced racist opinions, and the resulting TV programme led to several police officers tendering their resignations. Daly argued his research was necessary given that police officers who possess racist attitudes are typically unlikely to freely voice their opinions under normal interview conditions. He argued that he needed to create an identity which would allow him to access his informants' social world in such a way that they would act around him as they would in everyday situations. In other words Daly was attempting to eliminate researcher bias from his investigation. However justifiable such research may seem, it can be dangerous and it is unlikely that undergraduate and postgraduate students will be granted permission to undertake covert research. So if you are considering such a project you must discuss the matter thoroughly with your supervisor before proceeding, as you will need to approach obtaining ethical approval to conduct your study very carefully.

A final ethical issue that criminologists must consider in their research, which we have already touched on in this chapter, is 'whose side are we on?' (Becker 1967). In his now famous 1966 presidential address to the Society for the Study of Social

Problems in America, Becker discussed how it was impossible to conduct research free from personal and political bias. Becker pointed out that much research in the social sciences is conducted by the powerful on the powerless, that is, groups of individuals who are unable to get their voices heard. This is particularly the case in criminology where research is often conducted with groups of individuals who are labelled as deviant or criminal. Becker argued that social scientists need to act to make sure the experiences and opinions of research participants are heard and that a researcher's own attitudes and beliefs are acknowledged in their research accounts. For Becker, amongst many others, the social sciences possess an ethical duty to ensure that those with the power to label, control and punish, do hear and respond to the voices of those they seek to govern. It is important to consider such matters in your own research as well as to acknowledge your own place in your research. We touch on such matters again in Chapter 9 when we look at the final aspect of deskwork: the writing-up and dissemination of research findings.

Box 3.9

Access and research ethics

Gaining access to the people you need to speak to needs careful thought and it is important to discuss such matters with your research supervisor as you begin to formulate your design strategy to answer your research question. You will have to gain approval to conduct your research from your university research ethics committee. This will be concerned with ensuring you obtain informed consent from research participants, and you will be expected to design a consent form and a project information sheet which describes your project aims and expected outcomes alongside why a person is being asked to participate. You will also have to discuss how you intend to ensure research participants' confidentiality and anonymity as well as how you will securely store and subsequently dispose of key project information. The further readings and websites listed below should assist you as you consider such matters.

Recommended reading

Hope, T. and Waters, R. (2008) *Critically Thinking About the Uses of Research*. Centre for Crime and Justice, Studies, King's College London.

Israel, M. and Hay, I. (2006) *Research Ethics for Social Scientists*. London: Sage Publications.

Some useful websites

American Society of Criminology: http://www.asc41.com

British Criminology Society: http://www.britsoccrim.org

European Society of Criminology: http://esc-eurocrim.org

Managing your Fieldwork: Timetabling

We have already touched on how gaining and maintaining access to research respondents is an ongoing task which requires careful handling throughout the fieldwork stage of your study. As you consider the design of your research and how you are going to collect the information you need to answer your research question you also need to carefully consider time management. Final year undergraduate dissertation project work and single year postgraduate Master's degree research typically occur over a period of several months. Doctorate research may take longer, but it equally needs careful time management. Time flies. Once your initial literature review has been completed, which can take anywhere between a couple of months for undergraduate degrees and as much as a year or more for PhD research, a study has to be designed, ethics committees have to be successfully negotiated and access to research informants obtained, before you even begin to collect your data.

In my experience first-time researchers tend to grossly underestimate the time it will take to both initially develop and design their project as well as subsequently collect and analyse their data, let alone disseminate their findings. For example, a one-hour interview can take at least several hours to fully transcribe, so if you have conducted twenty interviews this means virtually a month of your time will be taken up with transcription. Furthermore no matter how engaging a research project may be you also need to manage your other academic studies and keep up your social and personal life, as well as perhaps even work part-time to help fund your studies. This is why I always advise my students to carefully plan four overlapping project milestones at the design stage: 1) research ethics, 2) fieldwork, 3) data analysis and 4) write-up and dissemination. So if you have several months to complete your project and at the end of month two have completed your initial literature review and formulated a research question that you and your supervisor are both happy with, then you may wish to set aside a month to gain ethical approval to conduct your research, a month to complete your fieldwork and gather your data, a month to format and analyse your data, as well as a month to write up your findings. Of course, in practice, fieldwork and data analysis can and do often overlap, but it is nevertheless important to have a firm series of deadlines in mind when completing project management tasks (see Box 3.10 for further readings).

Box 3.10

Project timetable

As you begin designing your study it is important to consider how you will effectively manage your time. As early as possible you should create a timeline covering key project milestones: from initially gaining ethical approval, to collecting your data, undertaking data analysis, and subsequently producing a report of your findings in a required format.

Conclusion

This chapter has provided a link between the previous chapter which discussed initial project development and subsequent chapters which deal with the analysis of criminological data. In doing so it has introduced you to the basics of research design in criminology and provided further resources and key readings from which you can begin the process of designing your own study to answer your research question. As you design your research you will need to consider several important design issues (reliability, validity, generalisation, triangulation), alongside the role played by theory in the conduct of criminological research. Use the further readings provided and complete the chapter review activities to help you with this task.

CHAPTER REVIEW ACTIVITIES

1   Write a 1000-word essay outlining the strengths and weaknesses of the four key research design strategies used in criminology: experimental, survey, qualitative and mixed methods. Discuss which strategy you will use in your own research and justify your choice on the basis of its ability to help you answer your research question(s) given your practical circumstances when compared to the alternative approaches available.

2   Write a 1000-word essay outlining the key differences between inductive 'theory-after' and deductive 'theory-first' research, bearing in mind the role that will be played by existing criminological research findings and conceptual frameworks in your own proposed research project.

3   Write a 1500-word essay which defines analytical and statistical generalisation and discusses their relative strengths and weaknesses. As part of this discussion, outline which approach to generalisation you will use in your own research, bearing in mind key design issues such as validity, reliability and reflexivity.

4   Design a project information sheet and consent form for your research project. Pilot it with at least five individuals and ask them to provide you with written feedback on the accuracy and clarity of your proposed project documentation.

CHAPTER READING LIST

Bachman, R. and Schutt, R.K. (2011) *The Practice of Research in Criminology and Criminal Justice*. London: Sage Publications.

Bartels, L. and Richards, K. (2011) *Qualitative Criminology*. Sydney: Federation Press.

Becker, H. (1963) *Outsiders: Studies in the Sociology of Deviance*. New York: The Free Press.

Becker, H. (1967) Whose side are we on? *Social Problems*, 14: 239–47.

Brookman, F., Noaks, L. and Wincup, E. (1999) *Qualitative Research in Criminology*. Aldershot: Ashgate Publishing.

Bushway, S. and Westburd, D. (2005) *Quantitative Methods in Criminology*. Aldershot: Ashgate Publishing.

Coleman, C. and Moynihan, J. (1996) *Understanding Crime Data: Haunted by the Dark Figure*. Milton Keynes: Open University Press.

Creswell, J.D. (2008) *Research Design: Qualitative, Quantitative and Mixed Method Approaches* (3rd edn). London: Sage Publications.

Evans, C. (2008) *Time Management for Dummies*. London: John Wiley and Sons.

Farrell, G. and Pease, K. (2007) The sting in the British Crime Survey tail: Multiple victimisations. In M. Maxfield and M. Hough (eds) *Surveying Crime in the 21st Century*. Cullompton: Willan Publishing.

Flick, U. (2011) *Introducing Research Methodology: A Beginners Guide to Doing a Research Project*. London: Sage Publications.

Garland, D. (2002) The development of British criminology. In M. Maguire, R. Morgan and R. Reiner (eds) *The Oxford Handbook of Criminology* (4th edn). Oxford: Clarendon Press.

Glaser, B. and Strauss, A. (1967) *The Discovery of Grounded Theory*. New York: Aldine.

Hammersley, M. (2010) *Methodology: Who Needs It?* London: Sage Publications.

Hirschi, T. (1969) *Causes of Delinquency*. Berkeley: University of California Press.

Hooper, C.A. (1992) *Mothers Surviving Child Sex Abuse*. Tavistock: Routledge.

Hope, T. and Waters, R. (2008) *Critically Thinking About the Uses of Research*. Centre for Crime and Justice Studies, King's College London.

Israel, M. and Hay, I. (2006) *Research Ethics for Social Scientists*. London: Sage Publications.

Kleck, G., Tank, J. and Bellows, J.J. (2006) What methods are most frequently used in research in criminology and criminal justice? *Criminal Justice Education*, 21: 503–25.

Knepper, P. (2007) *Criminology and Social Policy*. London: Sage Publications.

Layder, D. (1998) *Sociological Practice: Linking Theory and Social Practice*. London: Sage Publications.

Layder, D. (2005) *Understanding Social Theory* (2nd edn). London: Sage Publications.

Levan, P. (2007) *Skilful Time Management* (*Student-Friendly Guides*). Milton Keynes: Open University Press.

May, T. and Perry, B. (2010) *Social Research and Reflexivity: Content, Consequences and Context*. London: Sage Publications.

Merton, R. (1967) *On Theoretical Sociology*. New York: Free Press.

Nightingale, D.J. and Cromby, J. (eds) (1999) *Social Constructionist Psychology: A Critical Analysis of Theory and Practice*. Buckingham: Open University Press.

Noaks, L. and Wincup, E. (2004) *Criminological Research: Understanding Qualitative Methods*. London: Sage Publications.

Pager, D. (2007) *Marked Race: Crime and Finding Work in an Era of Mass Incarceration*. Chicago: Chicago University Press.

Punch, K.E. (1998) *Introduction to Social Research: Quantitative and Qualitative Approaches*. London: Sage Publications.

Radzinowicz, L. (1999) *Adventures in Criminology*. London: Routledge.

Sherman, L.W. (2012) *Experimental Criminology*. Cambridge: University of Cambridge.

Silverman, D. (2000) *Doing Qualitative Research: A Practical Handbook*. Thousand Oaks, CA: Sage Publications.

Simmons, J. (2001) *Review of Crime Statistics: A Discussion Document*. London: Home Office.

Strauss, A.L. and Corbin, J. (1990) *Basics of Qualitative Research*. London: Sage Publications.

Sutherland, E. H. (1937) *The Professional Thief: By a Professional Thief. Annotated and Interpreted by Edwin H. Sutherland*. Chicago: University of Chicago Press.

Tewksbury, R., Dabney, D. and Copes, H. (2010) The prominence of qualitative research in criminology and criminal justice scholarship, *Criminal Justice Education*, 17: 297–322.

Tierney, J. (2006) *Criminology: Theory and Context* (2nd edn). Harlow, Essex: Pearson Education.

Tulloch, M. (2000) The meaning of age differences in the fear of crime, *British Journal of Criminology*, 40: 451–67.

Walliman, N. (2011) *Your Research Project: Designing and Planning Your Work* (3rd edn). London: Sage Publications.

Wolfgang, M.E. (1973) Cesare Lombroso. In H. Mannheim (ed.) *Pioneers in Criminology* (2nd edn). Montclair, NJ: Patterson Smith.

Young, J. (2011) *The Criminological Imagination*. Cambridge: Polity Press.

4

Grounded Theory Analysis

CHAPTER OVERVIEW

In this chapter we will look at grounded theory analysis. This involves the creation and application of conceptual codes to chunks of textual research data which encapsulate the common themes or categories therein in a more abstract form, to enable tentative analytical generalisation beyond the research setting under study. The chapter outlines the main principles of grounded theory analysis so you can apply these as you initially design your project, as well as, perhaps most importantly, collect and analyse your own empirical data (see Box 4.1). Examples, further readings and exercises are provided to develop your understanding of grounded theory analysis and help you to apply this approach in your own research.

CHAPTER CONTENTS

Introduction

> **Box 4.1**
>
> ## Seven key elements of deskwork
>
> 1 Formulating an initial research area, focusing on study skills and dealing with assessment criteria.
> 2 Reviewing the literature and developing a research topic with a clear question to answer.
> 3 **Project planning and research design.**
> 4 Making contacts, gaining access and obtaining ethical approval to conduct your research.
> 5 Managing your fieldwork: timetabling.
> 6 **Conducting data analysis.**
> 7 Writing up your findings and research dissemination.

Consideration of which data analysis technique to use occurs at the initial research design stage of a project. This chapter looks at a particular type of qualitative data analysis technique called grounded theory analysis. As such it is primarily concerned with the analysis of textual data. This is typically obtained via formal research methods such as interviews and observation, but it can also include a range of different types of data sources, such as diaries, advertisements, government policy legislation as well as institutional reports. Grounded theory analysis involves the creation and application of conceptual codes to chunks of textual research data which encapsulate the common themes or categories therein in a more abstract form to enable tentative analytical generalisation beyond the research setting under study. Arguably this process lies at the centre of all forms of qualitative data analyses which seek to move beyond being solely a description of how research participants understand and respond to social phenomena. At first glance grounded theory may seem to be the most popular form of qualitative data analysis in the social sciences. A cursory perusal of published qualitative research in leading social science academic journals will reveal that authors often state they have adopted a grounded theory approach to the analysis of research data. It is important to recognise here that some researchers use the term grounded theory to indicate that they did not seek to apply pre-existing theory to their data. Rather they have sought to allow theory to inductively emerge from their data. In such cases a researcher may well have engaged in a thematic form of analysis to generate an analytical framework to tell a story about what they have found, which they hope could be of use beyond the particular research setting they have studied. However, they may not have followed key grounded theory principles and procedures, particularly theoretical sampling (which is discussed later in this chapter). Yet this should not be taken as a criticism of such research. Far from it. For unlike with quantitative data analysis, no clear-cut definitive rules for doing qualitative data analysis exist. Rather, it is very much a craft skill which each researcher must personally develop through gaining practical experience of doing empirical research and analysing qualitative data. Of course, general principles and rules of thumb have developed over the last several decades as qualitative research methods have become increasingly used in the social sciences.

In this chapter we will outline the main features of grounded theory under the purview of looking at it as a general research strategy which broadly adopts a thematic stance towards data analysis, in addition to providing useful guidelines on the conduct of fieldwork and collection of research data. In doing so the chapter explores key issues already touched on in Chapter 3 relating to the development of grounded theory. Examples and further readings are provided to help the reader reflect on how much of the grounded theory approach to data collection and analysis they would like to use in their own research, while at the same time developing their understanding of how to undertake this form of analysis.

Grounded Theory Analysis and Research Design

It is necessary to begin by briefly outlining the historical development of grounded theory in the social sciences as this highlights some important epistemological issues regarding the nature of the social world and how we as social scientists gain knowledge of it, which we will also touch on in Chapter 5 when we discuss narrative analysis. Chapter 3 focused on highlighting differences between grounded theory and positivism. It was discussed how grounded theory was originally developed by Glaser and Strauss (1967), first, to highlight the importance of producing and testing 'middle range theory' instead of focusing on the often conceptually unhelpful grand narratives of abstract social scientific theory; and second, to advocate the value of conducting inductive data analysis using qualitative data to generate theory. Yet grounded theory and positivism share in common a realist epistemological position whereby a single objective social reality is held to exist independently of a social actor's knowledge of it, which acts on them and constrains their behaviour.

Both also argue that the purpose of research is to capture this underlying shared reality. The realist position appears commonsensical: as we go about our everyday lives we typically assume the world around us existed before we were born and indeed will continue to exist after we die. What is more, human beings who live, work and play together tend to possess shared values and beliefs about the nature of the world in which they live, which guide how they interact with each other, in part because these shared values and beliefs are internalised by individuals from a young age through the processes of socialisation. Furthermore, these objectively and materially confront us on a day-to-day basis as external 'social facts' in the form of social organisations and institutions which embody communally shared values and ideals that act to channel individual human behaviour in socially acceptable ways.

Realism has been increasingly challenged over the last few decades by the rise of anti-realist postmodern positions. For example post-structuralism highlights the contingent nature of human knowledge, holding that accounts of the world are social constructions which do not exist independently of the social actor and the language they use to describe the world around them (Searle 1999). The intellectual heritage of postmodernism lies in the traditions of idealist and relativist western philosophy. This suggests that we cannot know anything about the so-called 'real world' – rather everything we experience is mediated through mental and linguistic constructs. Owing to its relativistic take on the nature of human knowledge the postmodernist anti-realist viewpoint accords equal validity to all perspectives and voices. In doing so it often also denies that any one ethical position can be privileged over another. This is a state of affairs some individuals find difficult to accept, as although they may recognise the historically situated and socially constructed nature of human beliefs and values, it is also possible to argue that moral absolutes do exist in the social world – particularly in regard to what constitutes appropriate behaviour towards other individuals, given the embodied nature of the shared human condition. Hence varying points of extreme exist in the anti-realist postmodern position. Some stress the socially constructed nature of social reality. They acknowledge the active role played by individuals within this process without doing away with the idea that social reality exists externally to the individual and constrains their behaviour. Others insist that the social world does not exist independently of the social actor and the language used to describe it. For example, Potter (1996: 98) argues, '[the world] … is constituted in one way or another as people talk about it, write about it and argue it.' Whether one agrees with their arguments or not, anti-realist positions bring to the foreground the idea that researchers present their own interpretation of the social world rather than a definitive account of it, a point we will look at again when we examine narrative analysis in Chapter 5. We must now turn to look at the consequences of such arguments for the development of grounded theory.

From objectivist to constructivist grounded theory

The emergence of constructivism as part of the growth of postmodernism has led to grounded theorists (e.g. Glaser and Strauss 1967; Corbin and Strauss 2008) being criticised for suggesting that the qualitative data collected by researchers reflects an underlying social reality which exists objectively to individual social actors and can be directly and accurately analysed by researchers. In an influential series of writings Charmaz (1995, 2000, 2002, 2006) argued that most grounded theory is what she calls 'objectivist' in that it aims to uncover a reality that exists external to the individual and in doing so implies that 'concepts inhere within the data, awaiting the researcher's discovery' (Charmaz 2000: 522). She advocates what she calls a 'constructivist' grounded theory approach which 'assumes that people create and maintain meaningful worlds through dialectical processes of conferring meaning on their realities and acting within them … [so] social reality does not exist independent of human action' (Charmaz 2000: 521). This constructivist approach consequently '[recognises] that the categories, concepts and theoretical level of analysis emerge from the researcher's interaction with the field and questions about the data' (Charmaz 2000: 522). Hence for constructivist grounded theorists, researchers and respondents in a very real sense co-create meaningful data together although the resulting account of social life offered remains the researcher's own interpretation.

Charmaz's arguments for a constructivist view of grounded theory are important for two interrelated reasons. First, her critique of objectivist grounded theory is in line with the argument made in Chapter 3 that qualitative research does not rely upon a purely inductive data analysis process, but rather an iterative–inductive one. Qualitative research is without a doubt primarily (though not exclusively) inductive in the sense that it typically (but not always) begins without a theoretically grounded formal hypothesis directly influencing the process of data analysis. This is due to the emphasis that is placed on gaining access to informants' own understandings of the research topic under investigation. But at the same time the process of data collection, data analysis and theory building is iterative in that it involves the researcher moving forward and backward between their developing theory and research data as their fieldwork progresses (although this is not always the case as we will discuss when we examine theoretical sampling). They actively seek to simultaneously expand upon and disprove their emerging ideas about what their data means. Consequently the research process must not be conceptualised in purely linear terms with theory inductively emerging from data in a relatively straightforward fashion. Rather it must be seen as a two-steps forward one-step back spiralling process of induction and deduction, involving theory building, testing and rebuilding, as the researcher completes their fieldwork by undertaking the interrelated tasks of data collection and analysis. A key consequence of the iterative–inductive nature of qualitative research is that it is designed to be open, fluid and flexible. This is important to remember at the research design stage.

The second reason why Charmaz's critique is important is that she highlights the need to recognise the central role played by the researcher in the generation of knowledge concerning a research topic. In adopting a constructivist position one admits that even though a researcher has tried to stay as faithful as possible to seeing the social world through the eyes of research participants, the resulting grounded theory nevertheless represents their own conceptualisation of the experiences of research informants, rather than objective truth. Given this position it is logical to assume that each individual researcher could produce a different account of the same data. Personally I do not believe this to be the case. Indeed my own experience has shown that different researchers often do independently produce noticeably similar accounts of a topic from the same raw empirical data. Furthermore, instead of seeing the researcher's foundational role in the construction of their account of criminological life as an inherent weakness of this approach to data collection and analysis, it is I would argue in fact a key strength of the constructivist position. Indeed I would say it constitutes good social science, for it points towards the important role played by relevant academic literature and so the wider academic community throughout all stages of a research project. Researchers need to be sensitive to existing concepts and theories relevant to their particular discipline so their investigations build on the work of others. Like other social researchers such as Miles and Huberman (1994) I would argue that the true value of accounts of the social world does not lie in whether or not they uncover ultimate truths concerning the nature of social reality. Rather it lies in their ability to provide insights, sensitising concepts and tentative theories about particular aspects of the social world that we may well not have everyday access to. I hold this position because, for me, the value of the social sciences lies in their ability to inform, challenge and change our existing preconceptions of the nature of the complex social world in which we live. But it is up to the reader to make up their own mind on this matter.

Theoretical sampling and theoretical saturation

Theoretical sampling is held by many to be the 'defining property of grounded theory' (Charmaz 2000: 519). Sampling strategies based on probability theory, such as random sampling, are designed to achieve statistical generalisation through being concerned with the representativeness of a given sample in relation to a larger population from which it is drawn. This approach is most associated with quantitative research. As was discussed in Chapter 3, qualitative research is typically undertaken with smaller samples than quantitative research and is concerned with making analytical as opposed to statistical generalisation through the generation of concepts that can be applied to similar phenomena beyond the research site in which they were originally developed. Theoretical sampling, alongside convenience sampling and snowball sampling, are sampling strategies often used by qualitative researchers to achieve analytical generalisation. Convenience sampling is conducted on the basis of respondent availability, and snowball sampling is conducted on the basis that a respondent provides the researcher with contact details for further possible research participants. With these two approaches there isn't necessarily an immediate link during the fieldwork stage of a project between the selection of a respondent and the empirical development of concepts. Rather a researcher identifies a group of individuals to interview and/or observe and asks questions and/or observes behaviour until they are satisfied they have collected enough data to enable them to offer an explanatory account of their chosen research topic and so answer their research question.

Although they may present their research under the qualitative grounded theory banner, in many cases researchers conduct data analysis after data collection is completed, with a researcher often dividing interview data into two parts and using the first to develop their analytical framework and the second to refine it (Charmaz 2006). This is because often researchers operate under practical constraints relating to respondent availability, while access to a research site may also be restricted. So they may only have a relatively short period of time to collect their data and not be able to engage in formal in-depth data analysis immediately after they collect data. Of course in such a situation a researcher may well use their developing impressionistic understanding of their data to refine the questions they ask research participants as fieldwork progresses, But in contrast to this, theoretical sampling requires data analysis be rigorously completed in the field every time data is collected, and as fieldwork progresses, participants are increasingly selected on the basis that they will either refine or refute emerging concepts and theory (see Box 4.2). For the grounded theory purist, cases (that is, the people, places and/or behavioural events under study) are *always* selected on the basis of conceptual development. As Glaser and Strauss (1967: 45) state: 'theoretical sampling is the process of data collection for generating theory whereby the analyst ... collects, codes, and analyses his data and decides what data to collect next and where to find them, in order to develop theory as it emerges.'

With theoretical sampling the process of data collection is controlled and directed by the researcher's conceptual understanding of their data. Hence the sampling of people, places and events under this approach is not a separate stage of project development and management: data collection and analysis are linked in an iterative backwards and forwards fashion. This can make the conduct of fieldwork highly time-intensive and mentally and physically challenging, particularly for the first-time researcher as well as researchers dealing with access-restricted research sites, such as prisons for example. Nevertheless, for the hard-line grounded theory enthusiast in-depth data analysis must occur after each interview or observation is completed before further data is collected (Corbin and Strauss 2008). Interview schedules and observational guidelines are constantly refined and new and contrasting questions asked so a researcher can, first, develop and refine emergent concepts and theory, and second, identify negative and contradictory cases to help expand the depth and scope of the analytical framework under development. This is why grounded theory is often referred to by researchers as a 'constant comparative method' with data from multiple respondents and sources being rigorously compared and contrasted 'in situ' to inductively develop and refine emergent theory throughout the fieldwork stage of a project (Glaser and Strauss 1967).

Theoretical sampling possesses the potential to be an endless exercise of theory refinement (which in itself is not such a bad thing if you are really interested in what you are studying). After all, the inductive nature of theory building used under this model of the research process logically assumes that each new instance of data collection possesses the potential to offer new insights into a topic and so could refute the researcher's current conceptual understanding of it. This is where the concept of theoretical saturation comes in. This offers a pragmatic solution to the thorny issue of when to stop collecting data. Here data collection stops once a researcher is repeatedly collecting data which supports their conceptual framework even when they are proactively searching for a negative case which contradicts it (Corbin and Strauss 2008). In other words, data collection stops once data repeatedly 'fits' concepts and no longer provide new insights into their main features and interrelationships. Grounded theorists often argue that it is possible to confirm the significance of a conceptual framework without committing the large amount of time and resources associated with quantitative research (Charmaz 2006). Although it should be noted that there are no strict guidelines concerning when theoretical saturation is likely to occur, in my experience of conducting qualitative interviews I have often found that saturation typically *begins* to occur once a researcher has completed a dozen or so interviews, although it can take at least a dozen or so more further interviews before you can feel confident enough to cease collecting data.

Box 4.2

Theoretical sampling and theoretical saturation

Theoretical sampling is a strategy associated with grounded theory that requires research participants be selected on the basis of a researcher's conceptual understanding of their topic. Under this approach data is collected from an informant and thoroughly analysed before further data is collected, which in turn directs the subsequent collection of data. As data collection and analysis progresses and the researcher's explanatory analytical framework develops, this leads to a concurrent change in the questions asked (and possibly even methods used to ask them) as

(Continued)

(Continued)

they deliberatively seek to identify contradictory as well as confirmatory data in order to achieve theoretical saturation. This approach to qualitative data collection and analysis provides a researcher with a powerful tool for generating concepts and theory, yet it is nevertheless time-intensive and is not always practically possible, particularly when research is conducted with respondents where access is limited. If you decide to adopt this approach in your research you are advised to discuss it with your supervisor as well as to consult the following recommended readings.

Recommended reading

Charmaz, K. (2006) *Constructing Grounded Theory*. Thousand Oaks, CA: Sage Publications.

Corbin, J. and Strauss, A. (2008) *Basics of Qualitative Research* (3rd edn). Thousand Oaks, CA: Sage Publications.

Conducting a Grounded Theory Analysis

Having considered matters particularly pertinent to the research design and data collection stages of project management we will now look more closely at the mechanics of how to conduct a grounded theory analysis. But it is important to begin by noting again that it is impossible to fully delineate how qualitative data is analysed. No step-by-step guidelines for conducting qualitative data analysis exist (indeed many researchers would argue that they shouldn't exist). When dealing with qualitative data the analytical process is heavily dependent on a researcher's own intuitive personal judgement and tacit understanding of the social world they are studying, as gained from their prolonged close contact with their research topic and their research informants. Consequently it is only possible to outline in broad brushstrokes the main analytical process typical to the conduct of this form of data analysis. In essence it requires a researcher to engage in a process by which they inductively condense their data by coding chunks of text to abstract conceptual themes or categories. These thematic categories are increasingly organised as analysis progresses around a core theme, or central storyline if you prefer, which Corbin and Strauss (2008) argue frames the researcher's account of 'what is going on' in relation to their topic. This core category or central thematic storyline enables the researcher to provide an answer to their research question.

In Chapter 2 we focused on how to develop a research question. In doing so we noted that academic research typically (but not always) begins in the library with a literature review. With quantitative research your literature review leads to the development of a working hypothesis regarding the potential relationship between two or more defined variables which is subsequently subject to empirical testing. In contrast to this, qualitative research typically begins with a much more exploratory research question. This is why quantitative research is often viewed as deductive and concerned with theory testing, while qualitative research is often viewed as inductive and theory building. However this does not mean that you cannot test a hypothesis using qualitative research or that existing concepts shouldn't play an important role as a researcher analyses their data (see Box 4.3). Gibbs (2007: 44) discusses how it is possible to apply pre-existing theory to qualitative data using 'concept-driven' coding, where conceptual codes 'come from the research literature' and are applied to data. This contrasts with 'data-driven' coding where a researcher '[does] not start with [such] preconceptions' but instead seeks to build concepts from data (Gibbs 2007: 45). Although qualitative research is typically associated with data-driven coding, in reality researchers tend to adopt an iterative analytical position which lies somewhere between the two extremes of pure inductive data-driven coding on the one hand and pure deductive concept-driven coding on the other hand. Indeed, they tend to start inductively before gradually moving backwards and forwards between their empirical data and the research literature surrounding their topic as data analysis progresses and they seek to refine their emerging analytical framework. The following section of the chapter outlines the main features of the data-driven coding process, to help guide you in your own analysis.

Box 4.3

Concept-driven coding and qualitative content analysis

With grounded theory analysis a researcher generates an analytical framework to help them answer their research question through adopting a 'data-driven' inductive approach towards data analysis. However, it is important to remember that the research question driving the research is usually (but not always) grounded in published academic research, and a researcher will bring this body of work and their own disciplinary and personal concerns to their analysis. Furthermore it is possible to use the existing literature to deductively drive data analysis by undertaking 'concept-driven' coding where concepts previously generated by other researchers are used in one's own research to categorise, explore and present qualitative data (this is sometimes called qualitative content analysis). For example Durkin (2009) conducted a qualitative analysis of the 'deviance disavowal' strategies adopted by men arrested by the US police for using the internet to solicit sex from children. Deviance disavowal is a concept originally developed from the body of research which emerged in response to the now classic work of Erving Goffman (1963) on stigma and negative societal reaction and labelling. Here stigma is viewed as an 'attribute that is deeply discrediting and tends to spoil the

(Continued)

(Continued)

identity of its bearer' (Goffman 1963: 3). Goffman's work was heavily influential in both mainstream social science and the sociology of deviance, inspiring researchers to look at different social groups – ranging from female body builders and transgendered individuals to drunk drivers and doctors who have sex with their patients – to examine how they cope with and respond to social stigma and the negative labelling. Durkin (2009) is concerned with looking at how individuals manage and respond to the stigma associated with their identity once they are labelled as paedophiles. Using deviance disavowal to drive the analysis of his data Durkin analysed 18 transcript recordings of police interrogations of men arrested for using the internet to solicit sex from children. He was able to identify three somewhat overlapping disavowal strategies in his data which I have summarised as follows:

1   *'I'm not a pervert or paedophile.'* Here an accused individual seeks to excuse their behaviour by claiming there has been a misunderstanding and they weren't actually going to have sex with a child, arguing as they do so that they are a good person who cares for children.
2   *'I've been stupid and made a mistake.'* Here an accused individual attributes their arrest to their having made a stupid mistake, arguing as they do so that they weren't actually going to have sex with the child in question.
3   *'We talked but I wasn't going to have sex.'* Here an accused individual admits that they did indeed have some sort of sexual conversations with a child but again claims that they were not going to have sex with them.

Durkin argues that interviewees' accounts of their behaviour show they are aware that their identity has become heavily stigmatised and soiled through their being caught having sexually explicit conversations with a child over the internet before seeking to meet them in person for sexual intercourse. Durkin states that the men interviewed used the three deviance disavowal strategies to try and manage the stigma they face through asserting that 'the current situation is not what it appears on the surface … [rather] their arrest is an unfortunate misunderstanding' (Durkin 2009: 669). In short, they are trying 'to sustain a normal definition of self despite their arrest' (Durkin 2009: 669). Durkin's insightful and informative research is a good example of how researchers can adopt a more 'concept-driven' coding approach through using concepts from the available academic corpus to shape the categorisation and presentation of rich textual data. It also highlights the key strengths and limitations and weaknesses of adopting such an approach: strengths, in terms of the rich explanatory account offered of the data and how this is clearly related to broader literature and existing analytical frameworks in such a way as to expand existing academic knowledge while also providing insight into the particular topic under study; weaknesses, in terms of how the reader can't help but feel that the rich textual data used in the analysis has somehow been 'trapped' within the concept of deviance disavowal at an early stage without alternative concepts being allowed to emerge from the data through conducting the coding process more inductively. Many researchers would argue that the primary purpose of adopting a qualitative approach is so that a research participant's own interpretations of social life and their and other people's attitudes and behaviours, can be used to inductively generate research findings rather than using existing disciplinary understandings to categorise data in a top-down manner. There is a real danger with concept-driven coding that important insights into aspects of the social world and criminological life may be left unexplored. However, researchers who use concept-driven coding argue that they do pay attention to the rich qualitative data they are working with and like Durkin their analysis does in fact include an element of induction (Neuendorf 2002). It is important to carefully weigh up the strengths and weaknesses of concept-driven coding before deciding whether or not to use it in your own research. A popular form of concept-driven coding – often referred to as 'content analysis' – is sometimes used by social scientists to analyse large amounts of qualitative data, e.g. newspaper articles covering a topic over a long period of time (Berg 1998). If you wish to find out more about this approach you might like to consult the following recommended readings.

Recommended reading

Berg, B.L. (1998) *Qualitative Research Methods for the Social Sciences*. Needham Heights, MA: Allyn and Bacon.

Durkin, K.F. (2009) There must be some type of misunderstanding, there must be some kind of mistake: the deviance disavowal strategies of men arrested in internet sex stings, *Sociological Spectrum*, 29: 661–76.

Neuendorf, K.A. (2002) *The Content Analysis Guidebook*. Thousand Oaks, CA: Sage Publications.

Coding data and theory building in grounded theory analysis

It is not always possible to begin analysing qualitative data when one wants to, even with a carefully thought-out research plan. For example, a researcher's methodological allegiance to theoretical sampling could mean they plan to systematically engage in data analysis after they collect each instance of research data, i.e. complete an interview or an observational episode. But the reality of conducting fieldwork in the real world of competing demands, tight deadlines and unforeseeable delays may well make it nigh on impossible for them to analyse their data as they originally intended until after they have collected most or even all of it. But this need not be a problem. Qualitative data analysis can occur after fieldwork is completed without necessarily having a negative impact on the quality or scope of subsequent findings (Charmaz 2006). Having said this, the fieldwork stage of research is an ideal place for a researcher to, if at all, possibly start analysing their data through beginning the process known as coding.

Coding is a central feature of qualitative data analysis. It is also a central feature of quantitative data analysis, but as we will discuss in Chapters 7 and 8 coding is approached differently by quantitative researchers. As we are concerning ourselves in this chapter with grounded theory analysis we are undertaking a form of inductive data-driven coding to produce a thematic framework to aid us in answering our research question. What theory building involves and the role coding and conceptual frameworks play in qualitative research are well summarised by Miles and Huberman (1994: 18):

> *Theory building relies on a few general constructs that subsume a mountain of particulars. Terms such as 'stress' or 'role conflict' are typically labels we put on bins containing a lot of discrete events and behaviours. When we assign a label to a bin, we may or may not know how all the contents of the bin fit together, or how this bin relates to another .... Bins come from theory and experience and (often) from the general objectives of the study envisioned. Laying out those bins, giving each a descriptive or inferential name, and getting some clarity about their interrelationships is what a conceptual framework is all about.*

Following Miles and Huberman we can define thematic coding as the process by which we tentatively generate a concept through labelling it and assigning it to our metaphorical 'bin' that contains within it events, behaviours and opinions and so on, as present within our data. This process of concept generation and refinement forms the basis on which qualitative data analysis operates. The end goal is to see how the concept bins created are thematically interrelated to one another in conceptual categories that hang together in an explanatory analytical framework which helps us to answer our research question. This is why grounded theory analysis involves the 'chunking' of text data: words, phrases, sentences and even whole paragraphs from a range of textual sources are coded to an appropriately labelled conceptual bin (Miles and Huberman 1994; Gibbs 2007).

This chunking process involves the researcher reducing data down while simultaneously and progressively engaging in abstract analysis. One should expect, as coding progresses, that some initial bins will fall by the wayside or be renamed. Others will end up fitting together into groupings as the relationships between them are identified and explored by the researcher. Corbin and Strauss (2008) hold that this data reduction and abstraction process involves three different stages of coding – open, axial and selective coding – while Charmaz (2006) prefers to use just two – open and selective coding (see Box 4.4). Regardless of which approach is adopted the shared aim is the elaboration of initial concepts into more abstract thematic categories. In grounded theory analysis categories (which are sometimes called themes) are more abstract than concepts and indeed subsume or group together concepts within them. The end aim of the analysis is to identify one category which becomes a core category around which other categories pivot. We will now turn to look at the coding process in more detail.

Box 4.4

Data collection and analysis process flow chart for grounded theory analysis

With grounded theory analysis the data collection and analysis process is often (but not always) tightly interconnected: theoretical sampling implies that a researcher will engage in data analysis after they collect data during the fieldwork stage of their research before proceeding to collect more. Not all researchers rigorously adopt this approach. While even if they do prefer it, sometimes it is not practically possible to thoroughly analyse data before collecting more. There is some disagreement between researchers over whether they should adopt a two-stage or three-stage data analysis process. The flow chart below outlines two main variations of the data collection and analysis process for grounded theory analysis, both of which are discussed in this chapter. The one on the left adopts a traditional grounded theory approach, utilising a three-stage coding process where data is collected and then analysed in a series of stages as coding progresses. The one on the right offers the researcher the choice of a broader range of sampling strategies and utilises a two-stage coding process, while data is systematically analysed after fieldwork is completed (of course this does not mean that the researcher has not engaged in informal data analysis as they collected their data). However, it should be noted that these are not mutually exclusive options and indeed many researchers will utilise a mixture of both, depending on their personal preferences, research objectives, resources, practical situation, alongside the research context and timeframe within which they must operate.

Figure 4.4.1   Grounded Theory Coding Models

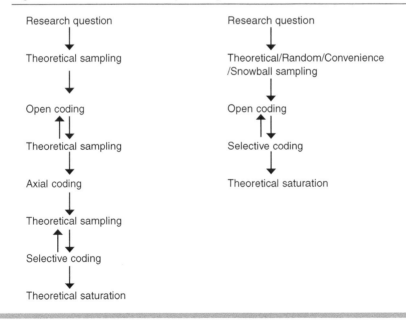

Open, axial and selective coding

Coding (which is sometimes called indexing) involves labelling chunks of text to conceptual bins. The researcher reviews their textual data and gives it labels – codes – that are of organisational and conceptual significance. As Charmaz (2006: 186) notes 'codes ... serve as shorthand devices to label, separate, compile and organize data.' Open coding is the initial process by which tentative concepts are first identified – open coding being defined as 'the process of breaking down, examining, comparing, conceptualizing and categorizing data' (Strauss and Corbin 1990: 61). In qualitative research, data analysis tends to be in a fluid state of constant revision where collected data is used to provide indicators of concepts. Schatzman and Strauss (1973) note that concrete data must provide evidence for abstract concepts but it is important to remember that this evidence is unlikely to come from a single instance but rather a number of partial instances present across a range of data sources. Evidential indicators for a concept are comparatively identified across a range of data sources as a researcher progressively collects more and more data from different informants. As Strauss (1987: 25) states '[many] indicators (behavioural actions/events) are examined comparatively by the analyst who then "codes" them, naming them as indicators of a class of events/ behavioural actions.' Because of this ongoing generative and comparative process, concepts are framed in terms of the properties that define them. Eventually this framing forms what is called a category or theme, which subsumes two or more concepts within it, and so is said to operate at a higher level of abstraction than concepts do.

It should be noted at this point that in the constructivist version of grounded theory, concepts and categories are not held to be representative of real world phenomena in a naïve inductivist sense. Rather a researcher generates them as their understanding of the meaning of their data develops in an iterative–inductive fashion over the course of conducting fieldwork and data analysis. This process very much involves the personal and disciplinary assumptions that they bring to a research topic and question. This is what Miles and Huberman (1994: 18) mean when they say that 'bins come from theory and experience and (often) from the general objectives of the study envisioned'. In practice a researcher using a grounded theory approach will increasingly move backwards and for- wards between their data and relative disciplinary academic literature as they conduct their analysis; but their analysis will nevertheless be primarily led by their data, so they must undertake a delicate balance between making sure their personal interpretation of data incorporates and synthesises what their research informants have told them, and what relevant academic literature says about their topic. This is where the craft skill of doing qualitative data analysis comes in. Qualitative data analysis can only be mastered through *doing* qualitative data analysis. Novice researchers can certainly find this delicate balancing act difficult to master at first. But I have found it helpful to view open coding as the point in data analysis where the researcher focuses solely on the data in front of them, with the academic literature and a researcher's personal preoccupations and disciplinary inclinations playing more of a role as later axial and/or selective coding phases progress.

Glaser (1992) has suggested that at the open coding stage the researcher should code their data into concepts using the following framework: Who? What? Where? When? and Why? So every time somebody speaks it is coded to 'Who?' and so on. Although this framework can certainly be useful when coding data relating to observational episodes in particular, it is seen by many to be too overly deterministic (Corbin and Strauss 2008). Charmaz (2003: 94–5) suggests that during the intensive initial open coding stage of data analysis, it is useful to first look for codes in the data bearing in mind one's research objectives and the following five key questions:

1 What is going on?
2 What are people doing?
3 What is the person saying?
4 What do these actions and statements take for granted?
5 How do structure and context serve to support, maintain, impede or change these actions and statements?

I often find it useful to begin open coding by using what can be called manifest codes (which are sometimes called 'in vivo' codes). These codes are terms used by research informants themselves and frequently reoccur as patterns in the data when topics, situations, actions and people are talked about. People who belong to particular cultural and organisational groups often use the same words and phrases when talking about people, events and why things happen the way they do. A researcher should take advantage of this when they first begin coding their data to help them begin the analytical process. Hence it is best to put one's academic reading to one side and begin open coding by undertaking an intensive line-by-line shifting-through of collected data to generate initial concepts from it. Nevertheless the level of actual chunking of the text to initial concepts may vary. Not every word, line, paragraph or even page needs to be labelled and coded to a conceptual bin. Charmaz (2002) provides a useful example of how she open-coded interview transcripts for her study of people returning to work after suffering from a chronic illness (see Box 4.5). Here she is coding this short extract from her interview, bearing in mind her own guidance concerning the questions to ask of data when beginning the process of open coding.

Box 4.5

Example of open coding

Text	Open Codes
And so I went to work on March 1st, even	Recounting the events
Though I wasn't supposed to. And then when I got	Going against medical advice
There, they had a long meeting and they said I	
could no longer rest during the day. The only time	Being informed of changed rules
I rested was at lunchtime, which was my time, we	Suffering as moral status
were closed. And she said, my supervisor, said I	Accounting for legitimate rest time
couldn't do that anymore and I said, 'Its my	Distinguishing between 'free' and work time
time, you cant tell me I cant lay down.' And they	Receiving an arbitrary order
said 'Well you're not laying down on the couch	Making a moral claim
that's in there, it bothers the rest of the staff.' So I	Finding resistance; tacit view of worth
went around and I talked to the rest of the staff,	Having a devalued moral status because
and they all said, 'No, we didn't say that, it was never	of physical suffering
brought up'. So I went back and I said, 'You know, I	Taking action
was just talking to the rest of the staff, and it seems	Learning the facts
that nobody has a problem with it but you'. And she	Making a case for legitimate rights
said, 'You aren't even here at lunchtime'. And they	Trying to establish entitlement
still put it down that I couldn't do it any longer. And	Meeting resistance
then a couple if the other staff started laying down	Comparing prerogatives of self and other
at lunchtime, and I said, you know 'This isn't fair.	Seeing injustice
She doesn't even have a disability and she's lying	
down,' so I started doing it.	Making claims to moral rights of personhood

Source: Adapted from Charmaz (2002: 677–8) Qualitative interviewing and grounded theory analysis, in J.F. Gubrium and J.A. Holstein (eds) *Handbook of Interview Research: Context and Methods*. Thousand Oaks, CA: Sage Publications.

A similar open coding strategy is advised by Miles and Huberman (1994), who suggest that a researcher's initial codes should be primarily concerned with, first, people and relations between them, second, emergent reoccurring patterns of action and talk in the data, as well as third, possible causes and explanations for these patterns. Corbin and Holt (2011) discuss open coding and how it progresses into more abstract thematic categories using the example where a researcher observes children in a playground for a project concerned with child development. The researcher observes the children and sees them 'swinging', 'building' (sandcastles, hiding places and so on), as well as 'yelling and chasing' (each other, a ball and so on). These initial open codes describe what is happening, but not why. However, it is possible to group these open-coding-stage concepts into the more abstract thematic category 'playing'. This higher-level concept explains what the children are doing when they are 'swinging', 'building' and so on. Of course 'playing' is but one thematic category and in reality it would exist alongside several other categories. Nevertheless it illustrates how often the initial open coding of concepts can be suggestive of a more abstract thematic category.

The development and fleshing-out of thematic categories can occur during the axial or selective coding stages of analysis, depending on whether one adopts a two-step or three-step coding approach. In practice I find that the division of coding into distinct axial and selective stages paints over what is in reality a more dynamic and heavily interconnected process. What is most important to remember is that in both the axial and selective coding stages the researcher begins the process of moving away from generating codes that stay close to data and towards more abstract and selective ways of conceptualising their data. As Gibbs (2007:46) notes 'it is necessary to move from description, especially those couched in terms used by participants, to more general and analytical categories'. Consequently, whereas with open coding you will tend to focus on identifying manifest codes, in axial and selective coding stages you should focus more (but certainly not exclusively) on what can be called latent codes. These are more abstract codes which point towards meanings which lie beneath the surface of the text and perhaps connect concepts together to form thematic categories.

Linking open-coded concepts to possible causes and consequences can help a researcher look for more abstract latent codes. I find it useful to remember that what you are trying to achieve in axial coding is to bring to the foreground underlying links between your open-coded concepts to tentatively establish the main themes in your data and possible relationships between its values. Hence in axial coding 'data are put together again in new ways after open coding to make connections between categories' (Strauss and Corbin 1990: 96). Axial coding has been criticised for advocating that researchers should 'close off' the conceptually rich exploratory nature of initial open coding early on after generating initial ideas and themes about what their data is telling them. First impressions can after all be misleading. It has been suggested that less-experienced researchers in particular often 'close off' possible alternative avenues too soon in favour of examining immediately apparent aspects of their data (Charmaz 2006), meaning there is a danger they will become overly focused on their immediate manifest codes and identifying apparent relationships between them. I am unsure whether or not this is indeed always the case. But I can say that in my experience I find axial coding most easy to do when I am able to deliberately seek to disprove my developing thematic understanding of my topic through conducting specifically designed interviews which enable me to frame questions in such a way that research informants use their own personal experience to answer them in either a positive, 'supporting', or negative, 'disproving', sense. I find this technique works well in helping me to confirm (or not) my developing understanding of a topic as well as flesh out the underlying meanings within my data and the dimensions of my emerging themes and their interrelationships. The example of axial coding in Box 4.6 adopts a similar approach to this, although it should be noted that one does not always need to dimensionalise in this scaled manner. However, it is certainly not necessary to collect more data to be able to do axial coding, or indeed selective coding for that matter, as you can always divide your data into two parts and use the first to engage in open coding and the second to undertake axial and/or selective coding.

Personally, when I cannot collect more data (and indeed sometimes when I can!), I prefer to adopt Charmaz's (2006) two-stage coding process. Here the first open coding phase is completed as already discussed, with data being coded in a line-by-line fashion to generate initial concepts. In the selective coding stage (which is sometimes called focused coding) only the most common and revealing codes are emphasised, with existing data being re-examined and explored to identify relationships between developing thematic categories. The aim is to identify organisational and hierarchical relationships between concepts and thematic categories. In this manner, Charmaz's (2006) two-stage coding model collapses the arguably arbitrary distinction between axial and selective coding. To my mind the two-stage coding model more readily reflects what a researcher actually does when analysing their data, that is, in terms of initially seeking to identify reoccurring patterns in their data (open coding), and attempting to identify the key features or dimensions of concepts and trying to join them together into more abstract thematic categories (axial/selective coding). Yet it is down to each researcher to develop their own way of processing qualitative data: some students find they work best with the two-stage approach and some the three-stage approach.

As the selective coding stage either begins (three-stage coding) or progresses (two-stage coding) you increasingly know what the main themes are in your data and focus more and more on confirming the relationships between them by identifying 'the core category and systematically relating it to other categories' (Strauss and Corbin 1990: 116). Regardless of whether or not a researcher formally adopts a two- or three-stage coding approach they should move through the selective coding stage until they achieve theoretical saturation. At its simplest you achieve this when the data you collect repeatedly fits your thematic framework; while as

Strauss and Corbin (1990) note, key to achieving saturation is the identification of the core theme, or central storyline, which frames the account of 'what is going on' in relation to the chosen research topic, and in doing so enables the researcher to answer their research question. Here the researcher has produced a thematic framework which could in principle be used as a sensitising device by other researchers studying similar phenomena in comparable settings. Box 4.6 provides an illustrative example of the coding process, as just discussed.

(Continued)

Acceptance related to respondents' perceptions of how accepted, loved and supported they felt at home: 'I felt welcomed and loved', or, 'I was the black sheep in the family'.

Boundaries related to respondents' perceptions of the approach to parenting adopted by their caregivers: 'I didn't know where I stood', or, 'My parents had fair ground rules'.

Emotional regulation related to the emotions felt by respondents, particularly in relation to whether they felt they could share their feelings with caregivers: 'If I was in a mood I wanted space', or, 'I would go to Mum when upset'.

Autonomy related to how much of a personal sense of separateness from others respondents felt: 'I would go exploring by myself', or, 'I was very protective of Mother'.

Self-evaluation related to respondents' perception of themselves as a child: 'I was very under-confident', or, 'I did well at school', or, 'I was a skating champ, good at archery too'.

Sexual abuse and deviation related to self-reported instances of being sexually abused: 'I blocked out a lot of early memories due to sexual abuse'.

Physical abuse related to self-reported instances of being the victim of physical violence: 'He beat the shit out of us for nothing all the time'.

Loss related to self-reported instances of loss of friends, family members, favourite pets and so on: 'Felt really cut up when Mother died'.

Conflict related to when respondents reported that the home environment was hostile, with caregivers arguing and possibly even being violent to each other: 'Home life was OK, no problems', or, 'My mother had a turbulent relationship with my stepfather'.

Safety related to the degree that participants felt their need for a sense of security was met by caregivers: 'Felt safe and secure, had no fears, nothing unpredictable happened', or, 'I never felt safe so didn't spend much time at home'.

Positive mediating interactions related to respondents reporting positive interactions with people outside of the main caregivers. No actual textual indicators are given for this concept by McCormack et al. (2010) but 'positive interactions with grandparents' is noted as an example.

Axial coding: identifying dimensions and thematic categories

As their analysis developed McCormack et al. (2010) completed two central aspects of axial coding. First, the dimensions of emergent concepts were ascertained:

The degree of *Responsiveness* ranged from a caregiver being highly responsive to a respondent's needs to completely neglecting them (responsive > neglect).

The degree of *Consistency* ranged from a caregiver being consistent in their parenting approach to being inconsistent (consistent > inconsistent).

The degree of *Acceptance* ranged from a respondent feeling they were part of a family to feeling isolated and picked on (rejection > acceptance).

The degree of *Boundaries* ranged from caregivers setting firm boundaries to setting very few (firm > lack/under control).

The degree of *Emotional regulation* respondents reported ranged from their reporting they were emotionally expressive with caregivers to feeling that they had to defend and protect themselves and their emotions from others (defended > expressive).

The degree of *Autonomy* respondents reported ranged from their reporting that they were highly autonomous to being very close to caregivers (autonomous > enmeshed).

The degree of *Self-evaluation* respondents reported ranged from their having a highly negative self-image to a highly positive one (positive > negative).

The degree of *Sexual abuse and deviation* as well as *Physical abuse* respondents reported both ranged from their experiencing none to there being sustained sexual and/or physical abuse (absent > extreme).

The degree of *Loss* respondents reported ranged from their experiencing none to their experiencing the death of a person close to them (absent > severe).

The degree of *Conflict* respondents reported ranged from it being absent to it being substantial (absent > substantial).

The degree of *Safety* respondents reported ranged from their feeling safe at home to their feeling in danger (safe > dangerous).

The degree of *Positive mediating interactions* respondents reported ranged from their reporting they had positive attachments with people to their having none (absent > substantial).

Second, as the dimensions of each concept were being ascertained they were simultaneously grouped together within broader thematic categories relating to a respondent's sense of self, parental caregiver behaviour and the context within which respondents grew up:

Responsiveness, *Consistency*, *Acceptance* and *Boundaries* were related into the broader thematic category *Caregiver relationship variables*. These are concerned with aspects of parental caregiver behaviour.

Emotional regulation, *Autonomy* and *Self-evaluation* were related into the broader thematic category *Self variables*. These are concerned with aspects of respondents' functioning within early childhood relationships.

Sexual abuse and deviation, *Physical abuse*, *Conflict*, *Loss*, *Safety* and *Positive mediating interactions* were related to the broader thematic category *Contextual variables*. This is concerned with the general aspects of the family environment and developmental context within which respondents grew up.

(Continued)

(Continued)

Selective coding: data saturation and the 'central storyline'

McCormack et al. (2010) validated the saturation of their data through repeatedly being able to code interview data to thematic categories. Respondents were drawn from four groups: offenders who had abused children ($n = 55$), offenders who had sexually assaulted adult women ($n = 30$), offenders who had been convicted of violent crime ($n = 32$) and offenders who had not been convicted of sex or violent offences ($n = 33$). Most research participants reported high levels of neglect and rejection, and low levels of consistency and responsiveness, from caregivers. They also tended to evaluate themselves negatively and to have experienced high levels of physical abuse growing up, as well as in some cases sexual abuse. McCormack et al. (2010: 91) note that '*caregiver relationship variables*' was the core thematic category around which '*contextual variables*' and '*self variables*' revolved, with research participants tending to have experienced '*negative early interpersonal experiences*'. They conclude by discussing the implications of their findings for academic research into sex and violent crime, the development of crime prevention initiatives, as well as the implementation of offender treatment programmes. McCormack et al.'s (2010) study provides an informative example of how thematic analysis can be undertaken to explore a research area and transform rich descriptive qualitative data into an explanatory analytical framework that can be used by other researchers in other contexts.

Recommended reading

Corbin, J. and Strauss, A. (2008) *Basics of Qualitative Research* (3rd edn). Thousand Oaks, CA: Sage Publications.

McCormack, J., Hudson, S. and Ward, T. (2010) Sexual offenders' perceptions of their early interpersonal relationships: an attachment perspective, *Journal of Sex Research*, 39(2): 85–93.

Think display!

Qualitative data typically involves the analysis of rich, textual data. However, one only needs to work with words for a short period of time to realise the value of using imagery to help flesh out one's emerging understanding of one's data. So when students first begin analysing their data I often advise them to sketch a visual picture of their emerging concepts and themes to help them refine their ideas about their data and its key features and relationships. Miles and Huberman (1994) similarly recommend that researchers 'think display' and represent concepts and thematic categories visually by using diagrams to help them think about their data and reflect on their emerging analytical framework. They suggest two main methods to do this – matrix displays and network diagrams. A matrix display is a table of rows and columns. Here key characteristics of the data, such as informant's age and gender, can be represented visually alongside emergent concepts and thematic categories. Table 4.1 gives an example of a matrix display concerning concepts related to two thematic categories called 'playing' and 'working'.

Matrix displays can be particularly useful when initially open-coding one's data. Network diagrams are useful for representing processes and connections within one's data and so can be used when doing axial and selective coding. Network diagrams represent relationships and hierarchies within one's data. Figure 4.1 hierarchically displays the category 'playing' with its constitutive concepts 'running', 'jumping', 'swinging' and 'skipping'. Both matrix displays and network diagrams can be highly useful methods for helping a researcher think about their data. A further approach is concept or mind maps. With mind maps you write down your hunches, ideas, concepts and categorical themes about your research on 'Post-it' notes and arrange and rearrange them on a large sheet of paper to help you think about your data, its key themes and relationships. Figure 4.2 displays a mind map showing the links between the category 'playing' and the concepts 'running', 'jumping', 'swinging' and 'skipping'. Box 4.7 contains further readings on how to use diagrams in your research. But do not think that you have to 'think display' if you don't want to: remember, there are no clear-cut rules with qualitative data analysis; it is down to each researcher to develop their own way of working with their data.

Table 4.1 Matrix display example

Category	Linked Concepts			
Playing	Running	Jumping	Swinging	Skipping
Working	Reading	Writing	Building	Drawing

Figure 4.1 Network display example (hierarchical)

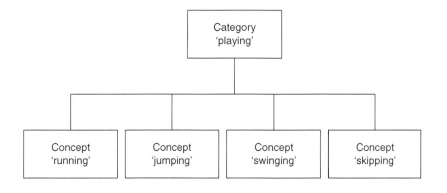

Figure 4.2 Mind map example

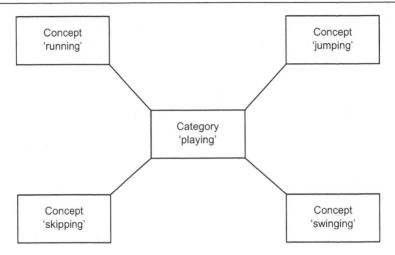

Box 4.7

'Think display'

It can be highly useful to visually represent your insights and ideas about your topic as well as your emerging concepts and thematic categories. The following recommended further readings can help you 'think display'. The aim of a thematic analysis is to produce an analytical framework which contains within it thematic categories with presumed relationships between them. Diagrams can be used to represent and track your progress in achieving this goal over time as well as to display your completed analytical framework and communicate it to others.

Recommended reading

Miles, M.B. and Huberman, A.M. (1994) *Qualitative Data Analysis: An Expanded Sourcebook*. Thousand Oaks, CA: Sage Publications.

Wheeldon, J. and Ahberg, M.L. (2011) *Visualizing Social Science Research: Maps, Methods and Meaning*. Thousand Oaks, CA: Sage Publications.

Wheeldon, J. and Faubert, J. (2009) Framing experience: concept maps, mind maps, and data collection in qualitative research, *International Journal of Qualitative Methods*, 8(3): 68–83.

Computer assisted qualitative data analysis

The process of conducting qualitative data analysis is often completed using little more than notepaper, coloured marker pens, paper files and a pair of scissors. You certainly do not need to use a computer to help you do qualitative data analysis. Indeed, many researchers prefer not to, arguing that working with the more traditional pen and paper approach allows them to work organically with their rich data. But the growth of technology and computing over the last two decades has nevertheless had a significant impact on how qualitative data analysis is undertaken. Qualitative data analysis requires a researcher to effectively organise and manage what is often a large amount of textual data as well as conduct their analysis in such a way that another researcher can follow the audit trail of their work. Computer Assisted Qualitative Data Analysis (CAQDAS) promises to make data management and leaving an audit trail of one's work both easier and more time efficient. It does not, however, conduct the analysis for the researcher.

There are several CAQDAS packages available to researchers. Although all packages have their own distinctive interface features, at their core they all essentially offer three potentially highly useful tools to support data analysis – code and retrieve, search features and data representation. Code and retrieve is exactly that; a researcher codes their data through assigning chunks of text to a concept or thematic category. When coding with pen and paper this can be a time-consuming process involving scissors, variously coloured marker pens, differently labelled paper files and multiple photocopies of an interview transcript. But when using CAQDAS a piece of text can be repeatedly coded, stored, retrieved, displayed onscreen and printed, all at the touch of a few buttons. Although this feature is clearly useful (and arguably more environmentally friendly than printing multiple paper copies of transcripts) it is perhaps the ability of CAQDAS programmes to offer search tools which sets them apart from the traditional pen and paper approach. Whereas previously a researcher would have to manually search for words and phrases, now at the touch of a button these can be identified immediately from a diverse range of texts and displayed for a researcher to analyse. Clearly text-searching features can dramatically speed up the data analysis process as well as improve its accuracy and reliability.

Finally, CAQDAS programmes offer a researcher innovative ways to display and visually represent their data in graphical form. As has already been discussed in the chapter, displaying one's data in various ways can be a highly useful tool in assisting analysis. Yet for all the benefits they offer CAQDAS has been subject to criticism. Fielding and Lee (1998) and Bazeley (2007) both note that researchers often report that they feel they lose a sense of closeness to their data when using CAQDAS. Sometimes it is also felt that CAQDAS promotes a grounded theory approach to data analysis to the detriment of alternative analysis techniques, such as narrative analysis for example. This criticism to my mind is tied up with broader methodological critiques surrounding grounded theory which we will discuss in Chapter 5 when we look at narrative analysis. Personally I think it is down to each researcher to decide if they wish to use CADQAS; the key thing to remember is that you should only use it as long as it assists you in achieving your project goals.

Box 4.8 contains further recommended readings and website resources, if you would like to find out more about CAQDAS and perhaps use a software package in your own project.

Box 4.8

Computer assisted qualitative data analysis

Computer Assisted Qualitative Data Analysis (CAQDAS) software packages can be highly useful tools for aiding the management and analysis of textual data. They can improve the accuracy, reliability and transparency of data analysis, yet some qualitative researchers prefer to use a more traditional 'pen and paper' method, and it should also be remembered that software packages do not actually do the analysis for the researcher; they are no substitute for the sustained immersion within one's textual data and the detailed reading and re-reading of transcripts. There are several different computer software packages available which researchers can use to assist them, including NVivo, MAXqda and Atlas. The following list of online resources and further readings will help you find out more about CAQDAS so you can make an informed decision about whether or not to use a software package in your own project.

Recommended readings

Bazeley, P. (2007) *Qualitative Data Analysis with NVivo*. London: Sage Publications.

Fielding, N.G. and Lee, R.M. (1998) *Computer Analysis and Qualitative Research*. London: Sage Publications.

Lewis, A. and Silver, C. (2007) *Using Software in Qualitative Research: A Step-by-Step Guide*. London: Sage Publications.

Some useful websites

CAQDAS Network Project: http://www.surrey.ac.uk/sociology/research/research centres/caqdas
Online qualitative data analysis: http://onlineqda.hud.ac.uk/index.php

---

Criticisms of Grounded Theory Analysis

Grounded theory analysis provides a general set of principles and rules of thumb to guide the research design and data collection and analysis stages of project management when dealing with qualitative data. Textual data typically brings with it a considerable degree of ambiguity, and the analytical tools discussed in this chapter can be invaluable resources for the novice researcher as they gain experiential knowledge of the art of *doing* qualitative research. Yet this approach is not without its critics. Grounded theory analysis is a form of inductive data analysis. The stated analytical aim is to build theory up from data rather than to deductively test a hypothesis. But as this and previous chapters have discussed, a researcher typically undertakes their research in such a manner that it builds on what is already known about a topic. How could they not do so, particularly as they wish to make a contribution to existing knowledge on a topic? To my mind this situation is not particularly problematic when a project is conducted in a critically self-aware manner where a researcher reflexively and openly acknowledges the role played by existing disciplinary knowledge in the creation of their resulting thematic framework.

Sometimes when one reads accounts of grounded theory research there can be a degree of ambiguity and uncertainty about how much of a determining role disciplinary academic literature has actually played in the production of what is meant to be primarily an inductively derived theoretical account of the social world (Searle 1999). Additionally this approach to data collection and analysis – particularly if theoretical sampling is used – can be very time consuming and resource heavy. When taken alongside the fact that it is difficult (but certainly not impossible) to produce a thematic framework from a handful of interviews, this can on occasion preclude it from being a viable option for relatively small-scale undergraduate research projects.

But perhaps most importantly grounded theory has been subject to sustained criticism for emphasising that the purpose of doing qualitative research is theory generation (Gibbs 2007). It is arguably guilty of underplaying the value of producing evocative, descriptive, thematic accounts of the social world and criminological life. It is by no means necessary to produce theory in order to make an original contribution to a field of academic study or garner the evidence needed to support arguments for social change. The very act of telling the story of a previously silenced voice can be enough to both empower socially disadvantaged individuals as well as influence academic thinking and governmental policy-making processes. Some commentators arguing from feminist and postmodern perspectives in particular hold that it is a matter of research ethics that the experiences and voices of research participants should not be replaced by a researcher's personal disciplinary abstractions.

In the last three decades there has been a general shift in qualitative inquiry towards emphasising multiple perspectives and viewpoints. Hence many researchers now advocate undertaking more participatory research projects where respondents are proactively involved in the collection of data and verification of a researcher's resulting account of social life. A researcher certainly needs to be sensitive to the ethics and politics of interpretation which underpin contemporary research inquiry.

Different groups of individuals often hold differing opinions on topics, and a researcher must be mindful of the potential for tension and conflict between the differing perspectives of research participants as well as between the values and goals of those being researched and those doing the research. We will touch upon such matters in Chapter 5 when we discuss narrative analysis and in Chapter 6 when we look at discourse analysis. For the moment it is enough to recognise that the analytical process outlined in this chapter brings with it assumptions about the aims of criminological inquiry that are not shared by all members of the academic community.

Yet to my mind I think it is important to remember that the production of theory remains a legitimate academic research goal in itself. Creating evocative, descriptive accounts of the world to develop our current understanding of it, or seeking to help give voice to those who have been silenced by others, are both highly laudable research aims. But so is seeking to enrich our current understanding of criminal life through attempting to engage in the systematic construction of theory. After all, a researcher has just as much right to have their experience and voice heard and listened to as the people they research. Their voice is one of the competing perspectives which when listened to in counterpoint with one another can dramatically enrich our understanding of social reality. Grounded theory analysis can be a powerful tool for exploring deviance and crime, and for all its limitations it remains an invaluable addition to the criminological toolbox.

Conclusion

This chapter has discussed the process of conducting a grounded theory analysis. The role played by theoretical sampling and coding one's data through progressive open, axial and selective stages, to generate an analytical framework that helps you answer your research question, has been discussed. The chapter also touched on how visually representing emerging thematic categories can help the analytical process of theory generation alongside the role computer software packages can play in assisting the management and analysis of qualitative data. Criticisms of this approach to data analysis have been noted, including, first, the heavy emphasis placed on producing theory from rich qualitative data and how this can lead to the experience and voice of respondents being lost; while second, on occasion researchers can underplay the actual role played by existing disciplinary concepts and theories in the generation of thematic categories and the identification of relationships between them. If you are thinking about using this approach to data collection and analysis in your research you should consult the illustrative examples, further readings and exercises provided in this chapter to assist you in applying a grounded theory analysis for your own purposes.

CHAPTER REVIEW ACTIVITIES

1 Write a short essay of no more than 1000 words comparing and contrasting the key features of objectivist and constructivist versions of grounded theory as well as how they each relate to realist and anti-realist concepts of social reality and how human beings gain knowledge of the world.

2 Using your own proposed research project to guide you, outline in no more than 1000 words how you could adopt a theoretical sampling strategy to generate an analytical framework to help you answer your research question.

3 Corbin and Strauss (2008) hold that the data reduction and abstraction process in grounded theory analysis involves three interconnected coding stages: open, axial and selective coding. Outline in no more than 1000 words the main features of all three coding stages and critically discuss why Charmaz (2006) prefers to use two coding stages: open and selective coding.

CHAPTER READING LIST

Berg, B.L. (1998) *Qualitative Research Methods for the Social Sciences*. Needham Heights, MA: Allyn and Bacon.

Bazeley, P. (2007) *Qualitative Data Analysis with Nvivo*. London: Sage Publications.

Charmaz, K. (1995) Body, identity and self: adapting to impairment, *Sociological Quarterly*, 36: 657–80.

Charmaz, K. (2000) Grounded theory: objectivist and constructivist methods. In N.K. Denzin and Y.S. Lincoln (eds) *Handbook of Qualitative Research*. Thousand Oaks, CA: Sage Publications.

Charmaz, K. (2002) Qualitative interviewing and grounded theory analysis. In J.F. Gubrium and J.A. Holstein (eds) *Handbook of Interview Research: Context and Methods*. Thousand Oaks, CA: Sage Publications.

Charmaz, K. (2003) Grounded theory. In J.A. Smith (ed.) *Qualitative Psychology: A Practical Guide to Research Analysis*. London: Sage Publications.

Charmaz, K. (2006) *Constructing Grounded Theory*. Thousand Oaks, CA: Sage Publications.

Corbin, J. and Holt, N.L. (2011) Grounded theory. In B. Somekh and C. Lewn (eds) *Theory and Methods in Social Research* (3rd edn). London: Sage Publications.

(Continued)

(Continued)

Corbin, J. and Strauss, A. (2008) *Basics of Qualitative Research* (3rd edn). Thousand Oaks, CA: Sage Publications.

Durkin, K.F. (2009) There must be some type of misunderstanding, there must be some kind of mistake: the deviance disavowal strategies of men arrested in internet sex stings, *Sociological Spectrum*, 29: 661–76.

Fielding , N.G. and Lee, R.M. (1998) *Computer Analysis and Qualitative Research*. London: Sage Publications.

Gibbs, G. (2007) *Analyzing Qualitative Data*. London: Sage Publications.

Glaser, B. (1992) *Emergence vs Forcing: Basics of Grounded Theory*. Mill Valley, CA: Sociology Press.

Glaser, B. and Strauss, A. (1967) *The Discovery of Grounded Theory*. New York: Aldine.

Goffman, E. (1963) *Stigma: Notes on the Management of Spoiled Identity*. Englewood Cliffs, NJ: Prentice Hall.

McCormack, J., Hudson, S. and Ward, T. (2010) Sexual offenders' perceptions of their early interpersonal relationships: an attachment perspective, *Journal of Sex Research*, 39(2): 85–93.

Miles, M.B. and Huberman, A.M. (1994) *Qualitative Data Analysis: An Expanded Sourcebook*. Thousand Oaks, CA: Sage Publications.

Neuendorf, K.A. (2002) *The Content Analysis Guidebook*. Thousand Oaks, CA: Sage Publications.

Potter, J. (1996) *Representing Reality: Discourse, Rhetoric and Social Construction*. London: Sage Publications.

Schatzman, L. and Strauss, A.L. (1973) *Field Research: Strategies for a Natural Sociology*. Englewood Cliffs, NJ: Prentice Hall.

Searle, C. (1999) *The Quality of Qualitative Research*. London: Sage Publications.

Strauss, A.L. (1987) *Qualitative Analysis for the Social Scientist*. Cambridge: Cambridge University Press.

Strauss, A.L. and Corbin, J. (1990) *Basics of Qualitative Research: Techniques and Procedures for Developing Grounded Theory*. Thousand Oaks, CA: Sage Publications.

Wheeldon, J. and Ahberg, M.L. (2011) *Visualizing Social Science Research: Maps, Methods and Meaning*. Thousand Oaks, CA: Sage Publications.

Wheeldon, J. and Faubert, J. (2009) Framing experience: concept maps, mind maps and data collection in qualitative research, *International Journal of Qualitative Methods*, 8(3): 68–83.

5

Narrative Analysis

CHAPTER OVERVIEW

In this chapter we will look at narrative criminology. Narrative analysis involves the collection of storied accounts and is by and large concerned with how people use narrative structure and plotting to construct a sense of personal identity and locate their lived experience within broader social processes, including crime and deviance. The chapter outlines the main principles of narrative analysis so that you can apply these as you initially design your project, as well as (perhaps most importantly), collect and analyse your own empirical data. It focuses on two approaches to the analysis of narrative content and form: first, Labov and Waletzky's (1967) 'six narrative elements', and second, a more Foucauldian (1991) approach that is concerned with the role of discursive statements in the scripting of narrative accounts, which is examined using the analytical framework developed by Agar and Hobbs (1982). Examples, further readings and exercises are provided to develop your understanding of narrative criminology and help you to apply either of these analytical approaches in your own research.

CHAPTER CONTENTS

Conducting a narrative analysis

- *Getting started: narrative content and form*
- *Focusing on narrative identity: subject positions, cultural resources and discursive statements*

Criticisms of narrative analysis
Conclusion
Chapter review activities
Chapter reading list

Introduction

Box 5.1

Seven key elements of deskwork

1 Formulating an initial research area, focusing on study skills and dealing with assessment criteria.
2 Reviewing the literature and developing a research topic with a clear question to answer.
3 **Project planning and research design.**
4 Making contacts, gaining access and obtaining ethical approval to conduct your research.
5 Managing your fieldwork: timetabling.
6 **Conducting data analysis.**
7 Writing up your findings and research dissemination.

We have already established that the consideration of which data analysis technique to use typically occurs at the research design stage of project development. Bearing this in mind, in this chapter we will look at narrative criminology as a form of qualitative research concerned with eliciting and analysing storied accounts of criminal life, considering as we do so its key features and their implications for research design and data analysis. Narrative criminologists are concerned with ensuring that the voices of marginalised and socially excluded groups are heard and with looking at storied accounts of lived experiences as interactional achievements which link personal experience to broader social context and process. Although it possesses a long history in the social sciences, narrative analysis has particularly come to the forefront of qualitative inquiry over the last three decades in response to calls for more participatory and reflexive research methodologies, as a result of the emergence of postmodernism and constructivism. We will discuss such matters in more detail shortly. For the moment it is necessary to begin by saying that narrative analysis is concerned with the collection and analysis of stories.

Human beings are natural story-tellers. We often think and speak in story form, bringing meaning to our own life and those of others through the stories we create and share. The continued popularity of myths and epic tales, poems and songs, plays and books, bears testament to the fact that the storying of lived human experience and the telling of different types of narratives about the world in which we live seem to be hardwired into human beings. Narrative analysis seeks to take advantage of this: it is interested in the stories people tell to organise and express their experience and understanding of the world alongside their place in it. Qualitative methods such as interviews or diaries are often used by narrative researchers to collect such stories. But the contemporary growth of information and communication technology and the explosion of social networking sites mean stories can now be created, shared and researched in previously unthought-of ways. In this chapter we will look at the main features of narrative criminology, highlighting its similarities and differences from grounded theory analysis as we do so, to reinforce the criminological value of listening to and thinking about stories of deviance and crime. Examples and further readings are provided to help the reader reflect on whether they would like to use this approach in their own research while at the same time developing their understanding of the principles of narrative analysis.

Narrative Analysis and Research Design

Before we move on to discuss narrative analysis in greater detail it is necessary to briefly reacquaint ourselves with realism (or positivism) and anti-realism (or constructivism). The emergence of postmodern anti-realist positions was discussed in Chapter 4 when we explored contemporary developments in grounded theory analysis. As was noted, we can picture a realist/anti-realist continuum, with realism on one end holding that reality exists independently of our beliefs and understandings of it, and anti-realism on the other end holding that reality is socially constructed and therefore does not exist independently of our beliefs about it (Denzin and Lincoln 2011). Researchers who adopt a realist or positivist position hold that value-free objective inquiry is possible and that social sciences should model their methods on those of the natural sciences as human behaviour is governed by law-like regularities (which they hope to discover). In contrast researchers who adopt an anti-realist or constructivist position argue that all inquiry is value-laden and that social sciences must use different methods from those of the natural sciences as there is no single shared reality; rather there are a variety of differing social constructions, which are created by groups of people who interact together over time. Hence there are multiple ways of knowing and understanding social reality and criminological life, depending on who you talk to as well as where and when you talk to them.

Although some researchers do adopt an extreme positivist or extreme constructivist stance, in reality many lie somewhere in the middle of these two poles in our continuum. Indeed some researchers who advocate a positivist approach recognise the existence of alternative but equally valid accounts of social reality and that different theories are grounded in different perspectives and world views which are always partial and contextually bounded. Many constructivists and positivists alike would argue that some accounts of the social world are more plausible than others and they therefore can make judgements about the applicability and usefulness of competing perspectives and theories in different circumstances. Yet at the same time it is important to begin our discussion of narrative analysis by noting that it is predominately associated with constructivism. As we will now turn to discuss, this helps us to understand the reasons behind its (re)emergence and continued relevance for helping us explore criminological life.

From early delinquent oral histories to the (re)birth of narrative analysis

Doing narrative analysis involves collection of biographical and life story material. Diaries, interviews, newspaper obituaries, journalistic articles and public records such as marriage certificates and employment files, are all narrative source materials which tell us something about a person, their life and the time in human history in which they lived. As such, they are the bread and butter on which narrative analysis operates. Indeed the use of personal life records and oral histories was bound up with the early development of criminology as an academic discipline concerned with the causes and consequences of crime. As far back as the 1850s Henry Mayhew and his colleagues were collecting delinquent oral histories from men and women involved in the English penal system in an effort to identify common pathways and turning points in offenders' life stories (Bennett 1981). This was seen to be a somewhat natural next step in the analysis of data pertaining to criminal activity obtained via court and legal records, the systematic collection and analysis of which had begun to occur across European penal systems as the nineteenth century progressed. As we discussed in Chapter 3, this focus on collecting information both about and directly from offenders was bound up with the emergence of a more empirically focused form of classical criminology. Yet it is perhaps with the Chicago school of American sociology from the early 1920s and 1930s that we first see the early systematic development of narrative forms of data collection and analysis in the social sciences in general and criminology in particular.

Chase (2005) holds that the Chicago school's focus on the use of personal records and stories to explore the effects of broader social processes on an individual's life highlighted the importance of considering power, authenticity, voice and representation in social research. Two early examples of this are Sutherland's

(1937) *The Professional Thief*, which as we discussed in Chapter 3 gave a detailed account of the life and criminal activity of Chic Conwell (the professional thief of the title), as well as Shaw's (1966) life history of 'Stanley', a petty thief and juvenile delinquent. Stanley, who was fourteen when he first met Shaw, was a jack roller, or street mugger as we would call him today. Shaw, who at the time (the 1920s) was working in the Institute for Juvenile Research in Chicago, built a close relationship with Stanley, even going so far as inviting him to his home and keeping close contact with him after the research was completed, with the two remaining close friends until Shaw's death in 1955. Shaw asked Stanley to provide an account, in his own words, of his family and personal life, delinquent activity and repeated penal convictions and institutionalisations – instructing him to give a 'detailed description of each event, the situation in which it occurred, and his personal reaction to the experience' (Shaw 1966: 23).

Written in Stanley's own words (with Shaw acting as editor and thematic organiser) what we have here is a highly evocative and powerful account of the life of a person from a poor background and broken home, living in a deprived area of Chicago, who quickly progresses from being a runaway and street beggar before his tenth birthday to shoplifting and jack rolling during his teenage years, with the result that he had nearly forty criminal convictions before his eighteenth birthday. It is therefore perhaps unsurprising that this rich account of criminal life has been said to speak to the role of social inequality, socio-economic conditions and grinding urban poverty in creating and sustaining the underlying social conditions for crime, alongside demonstrating the power of stigma and negative social labelling in co-authoring a criminal's sense of personal identity while simultaneously reinforcing the common trajectory of a criminal career (Tierney 2006). Without a doubt the early delinquent oral histories and life stories collected by the Chicago school allowed researchers to explore the complex and layered dynamics that exist between the creative social actor and the objective social structural conditions which shape and constrain their behaviour, in order to move beyond overly psychological explanations for crime and establish the sociology of deviance as a legitimate field of study (Radzinowicz 1999). Yet for all the achievements of early delinquent oral histories and life stories, at the same time it is important to remember, as was discussed in Chapter 3, that the empirical and theoretical preference during this time in the social sciences was for hard statistical data and therefore quantitative research methods. Hence although there is a long tradition of oral history and life story research in criminology it wasn't until relatively recently that narrative analysis can be said to have finally come to the foreground as a widely accepted form of qualitative inquiry.

The (re)emergence of narrative criminology is bound up with a wider constructivist turn within the social sciences. The focus of anti-realism on the social construction of reality and the concurrent emphasis placed on multiple perspectives and interpretations of the world led to a crisis of representation that challenged the legitimacy of dominant positivistic and quantitative research approaches in the social sciences which emphasised the search for singular underlying truth. Traditionally the individual account offered by a research participant was held to represent 'real life' and a researcher was therefore said to be able to obtain access to the world beyond the situation in which data was collected. In short, the realist position holds that accounts provided by research informants, such as those given by offenders of their criminal activity, could be taken to be more or less accurate representations of criminological life as it happens; that is, as long as they were carefully and rigorously collected and comparatively analysed by a researcher to allow for the ever-present possibilities of bias, error and deliberate mistruth. Such realist tendencies could perhaps be said to underpin the delinquent oral histories discussed earlier. In contrast to this some authors working within 'the narrative turn' argued from a staunchly anti-realist position that the stories people tell in fact say little about real life; rather they say more about how narratives themselves are constructed, as well as how personal identity is socially constructed and communicated in and through social interaction between the researcher and researched. As Riessman (1993: 15) notes, for narrative analysts, meaning and understanding are 'fluid and contextual, not fixed and universal, all we have is talk and texts that represent reality partially, selectively and imperfectly'; while Rosenweld and Ochburg (1992) say that 'personal stories are not merely a way of telling someone (or oneself) about one's life; they are the means by which identities may be fashioned.'

From the early 1980s onwards there was a shift in social science research away from seeking to represent social reality as if there was only one true story to discover, and towards looking at the processes by which individuals storied their lived experience in different ways as they sought to understand their own lives and the world around them. This laid the foundation stones for the cross-disciplinary growth of narrative analysis within the social sciences and humanities, including literary studies, sociology, criminology, cultural studies, education and psychology. Narrative analysis is a highly diverse movement, and although more linguistically minded approaches do exist, which by and large focus on the use of language in everyday conversation, in this chapter we will focus on how individuals use stories as reflexive social tools for giving meaning to personal experience, constructing a sense of personal identity, as well as placing life events within a broader socio-cultural context (Plummer 2001). But before we discuss narrative analysis in more detail I feel it necessary to say that to my mind it is important not to get too trapped into debates surrounding whether or not the stories we collect must be treated as total or partial fictions. Chase (2005: 651) notes that 'contemporary narrative inquiry can be characterized as an amalgam of interdisciplinary analytic lenses, diverse disciplinary approaches, and both traditional and innovative methods – all revolving around an interest in biographical particulars as narrated by the ones who live them.' There can be no doubt that narrative analysis does celebrate the fact that the stories we tell each other are creative exercises told from a particular vantage point. But to my mind it is important to remember that we are asking people to tell us about their lives for a reason. For me this means a researcher has an ethical duty to always treat the narratives they elicit from people with care, sensitivity and respect, not least of all because within criminology we are sometimes concerned with eliciting stories which contain graphic instances of physical violence, sexual abuse, mass murder and even acts of state-sponsored genocide.

1I Box 5.2 I

Narrative analysis and the social sciences

The growth of narrative analysis within the social sciences is bound up with an increasing recognition of the value of qualitative biographical, oral history and life story research methods in developing our understanding of complex social processes and dynamics, including crime and deviance. At the same time the tension between this research goal and the constructivist rejection of realism must be acknowledged and incorporated into one's research. The following further readings provide a general introduction to the historical development of this diverse approach within the social sciences.

Recommended reading

Atkinson, R. (1998) *The Life Story Interview*. London: Sage Publications.

Merrill, B. and West, L. (2005) *Using Biographical Methods in Social Research*. London: Sage Publications.

Riessman, C.K. (1993) *Narrative Analysis*. London: Sage Publications.

Collecting narratives: the long and the short of it all

Narrative analysis involves adopting an approach to data collection and analysis which is sensitive to the unfolding temporal nature of oral histories and life stories and their ability over time to reveal intersections between personal biography and collective events and understandings. Roberts (2002: 3) defines this approach to qualitative research as a methodology that 'uses stories of individuals and other "personal materials" to understand the individual life within its social context'. The story-like form people use to organise their life and express shared meaning is an ever-present feature of everyday life. As Gubrium and Holstein (1998: 14) note, human stories can be found everywhere: 'School[s], clinics, counselling centres, correctional facilities, hospitals, support groups, and self-help organisations, among many other sites for storing experience, provide narrative frameworks for conveying personal experience through time.' To this we can add the more con-temporary resources of the internet and social networking sites. The narrative analyst is now in the enviable position of being able to access people's stories and a substantial amount of historical and contemporary biographical material elec-tronically with just a few clicks of a computer mouse. Through media such as YouTube, Facebook and Twitter, alongside more specialist online multimedia oral history and life story repositories, narrative analysts can listen to, share and explore people's personal stories of key life events (see Box 5.3 for links to some general and criminology-specific sources).

Yet for all the new possibilities available for collecting stories and the supportive biographical materials new technologies bring with them, the key method remains the face-to-face interview (Atkinson 1998). This is because, at its core, narrative analysis involves a researcher listening to another person narrate their life, either in its entirety or key episodes in it. The types of life stories narrative analysts collect range from 'a fairly complete narrating of [an] entire experience of life as a whole' to shorter and more focused stories which are concerned with key aspects, episodes and turning points in a life (Atkinson 1998: 9). The former tends to produce a book-length biographical account of an individual's life while the latter tends to be used when exploring a particular topic in some detail. There is a tendency to focus on more edited narratives, based around a thematic investigative topic, within the social sciences. Shaw's (1966) *Jack Roller* and Sutherland's (1937) *The Professional Thief* are both examples of this more focused life story approach within the criminological canon. Often the decision to focus on eliciting shorter and more focused narrative accounts from people is driven by purely pragmatic concerns relating to the research topic being investigated and the resources and time available to the researcher. As Atkinson (1998) makes clear, collecting a complete account from a person of their whole life can be highly time-consuming with material being collected over numerous meetings taking place over months and even years. So for researchers working within a tight timeframe with a clear research agenda to pursue, the narrative focus can shift from asking someone to recount their whole life to looking at aspects of it which more readily link individual experience with broader social issues, such as childhood experiences of sexual abuse, domestic violence, or how a person came to be involved in a particular crim-inal activity (Goody 2000).

One only needs to look at the 'true crime' section of any high street bookshop to realise the popularity of life stories and insider accounts of criminal life. Within academic criminological research, narrative biographies and life stories tend to focus on critical incidents or significant turning-points in a life (Denzin 1989). These are used to explore an individual's relationship to crime from their own point of view while also bringing to the foreground broader social, structural issues, such as for example social mobility and class-based inequality, racism and hate crime, as well as patriarchy and gender-based violence. Hence criminologists have used victim narratives to explore issues such as rape (Bletzer and Koss 2006), childhood sexual abuse (Staller and Nelson-Gardell 2005) and domestic violence (Walklate 2004), in addition to using offender's narratives to explore the dehumanising nature of prison life (Morgan 1999), the female experience of imprisonment (Peckham 1985), life on death row (Sarat 2011), why people reoffend (Nellis 2002), organised crime (Warshow 1970), drug trafficking (Ross and Richards 2002), subcultures, drug use and dance music (Wilson 2007) and youth gang membership (Venkatesh 2008).

Prison autobiographies provide a rich vein of stimulus to the criminological imagination as it searches for insight into the causes of offending behaviour, how individuals cope with long-term imprisonment, as well as desistence from crime. Part of the attractiveness of the narrative approach for many criminologists is that it seeks to invert the traditional power relationship between the researcher and researched through requiring they take a back seat and allow a person to tell their own story in their own words in a free flowing manner. This stance is often encouraged by narrative analysts as part of a deliberate rejection of realist and positivist concerns with undertaking objective ideology-free inquiry. The fact that one's findings are always partial and from a particular perspective is something narrative analysts celebrate. The rejection of singular truth and a concurrent concern with providing a safe space within which repressed and silenced voices can come forward and be heard in a manner of their own choosing is often held to be a natural extension of the rejection of positivism.

Many narrative researchers readily acknowledge that their work is driven by a personal ethical and political commitment to improving the individual and social conditions of socially excluded and stigmatised groups. Such a stance is argued to be particularly important when dealing with sensitive topics, such as domestic violence for example. Consequently Clandinin and Connolly (2000) talk about 'living the story' with research participants so a researcher works collaboratively in a participatory fashion with both individuals and communities to engender social change. It is also often argued, given constructivism's emphasis on multiple partial perspectives, that researchers should seek to use a diverse range of alternative forms to represent and communicate their findings. This has led some to explore different dissemination strategies, including poetry, film, arts and craft, photograph displays, performative dance and community theatre (Chase 2005). Given this it is perhaps not unsurprising that narrative analysts tend to reject traditional measures for ensuring quality control in research, often advocating concepts such as 'trustworthiness', 'credibility' and 'authenticity' instead of the more traditional ones of 'validity' and 'reliability' (Riessman 1993). The further readings provided in Boxes 5.2 and 5.3 provide further guidance on such matters.

Kenyon and Randall (1997: 65) say that narrative research involves 'someone telling someone about somebody doing something'. Similarly Mattingly (1998: 7) notes that stories 'are about someone trying to do something, and what happens to her and others as a result'. This brings to the foreground a central issue in the collection and analysis of life stories; namely, that when doing narrative analysis the social interaction between the researcher and researched, as much as the resulting narrative itself, needs to be carefully considered by the researcher – because when we seek to elicit people's stories we usually end up with the telling of a sequence of events from a particular point of view which contains moral elements and judgements running through it. In other words, research participants both consciously and subconsciously seek to present themselves and their own and other people's actions in certain ways when they tell their stories. Hence when doing narrative analysis it is important to ask ourselves, 'Why are people seeking to present themselves and others in these particular ways in their stories?' By its very nature the content of a narrative interview does speak of events 'in the real world' outside of the immediate interview situation. But the fact that our stories can (and often do) vary depending on whom we are speaking to reinforces how narratives also serve multiple functions beyond providing a simple description of events. Indeed some researchers operating from a strong constructivist position go so far as to argue that it is impossible to speak of events outside of the interview situation with any certainty. Rather they focus on the interview discussion as an interactional achievement worthy of analysis in its own right. This is a viewpoint shared by many discourse analysts, which we explore in Chapter 6. But we also touch on such matters in the next section of this chapter as we look at the analysis of narrative data in more detail.

Box 5.3

Collecting narrative stories in criminology

Narrative analysis involves collecting people's stories. There are a range of ways this can be done, including using diaries, journals, video clips and interviews. Online archive resources and multimedia tools such as YouTube can also be used to create and share narrative accounts. Narrative researchers often focus on collecting narratives from research participants which are focused around a particular thematic topic, e.g. domestic violence, so they can be placed against the background of disciplinary concerns with broader social structure, i.e. patriarchy and gender-based violence. Owing to its constructivist heritage, narrative analysts seek innovative ways to quality control and disseminate research findings. Hence concepts such as narrative 'authenticity', 'creditibility' and 'trustworthiness' replace 'validity' and 'reliability'. Furthermore, in addition to more traditional dissemination practices – such as project reports, book-length biographies and journal articles – narrative analysts sometimes experiment with using poetry, film, arts and craft, photograph displays, performative dance and community theatre. The following resources provide examples of some different types of criminology-related stories available online in addition to further information on narrative analysis.

Recommended reading

Bennett, J. (1981) *Oral History and Delinquency: The Rhetoric of Criminology*. Chicago: University of Chicago Press.

Goody, J. (2000) Biographical lessons for criminology, *Theoretical Criminology*, 4 (4): 473–98.

Gubrium, J.F. and Holstein, J.A. (1998) Narrative practice and the coherence of personal stories, *Sociological Quarterly*, 39:163–87.

Plummer, K. (2001) *Documents of Life* (2nd edn). London: Sage Publications.

Pressor, L. (2009) The narratives of offenders, *Theoretical Criminology*, 13: 177–200.

Some useful websites

Centre for Narrative Research: http://www.uel.ac.uk/cnr

British Library National Sound Archive (oral history and much more): http://sounds.bl.uk

Oral History Society UK: http://www.oralhistory.org.uk

International Oral History Society: http://www.iohanet.org

BBC Oral History website: http://www.bbc.co.uk/history/trail/htd_history/oral/recording_oral_hist_01.shtml

Women's Aid website containing domestic violence survivor stories: http://www.womensaid.org.uk/page.asp?section=0001000100080014&sectionTitle=Your+stories

Hidden Hurt website containing domestic violence survivor stories: http://www.hiddenhurt.co.uk/domestic_violence_stories.html

Mencap Hate Crime website containing victims' stories: http://www.mencap.org.uk/page.asp?id=1954

Rwandan Genocide stories: http://www.rwandanstories.org/genocide.html

Conducting a Narrative Analysis

The previous section discussed how the contemporary emergence of narrative criminology is part of a broader turn towards modes of qualitative inquiry within the social sciences that share a focus on the interdisciplinary study of the generation and analysis of stories of lived experience. A narrative is a temporally ordered statement of events, as told by a protagonist; hence narrative criminology is often (but certainly not exclusively) concerned with the sequence of events surrounding some form of criminal activity as told from the perspective of offenders, victims or individuals who represent the agencies of social control (police officers, probation officers, solicitors, medical professionals and so on). In narrative criminology the collection of data requires the researcher to allow participants to take the lead in the conversation. Being a good listener and knowing when to and when not to probe for more information forms part of the craft skill of doing narrative interviews. I have found that simply telling a person you are really interested in hearing their own story in their own words about an event or topic as it happened to them is often enough to help them take the lead in the conversation. Riessman (2004) suggests using open-ended temporally and contextually aware 'what, when and where' questions, such as 'tell me what happened when …', as these require a respondent to tell an unfolding story of events.

At a broader level Atkinson (1998) and Plummer (2001) discuss the use of thematic 'life stage' structures for life story and biographic research. But however they are elicited these narratives try to be 'realist tales', in the sense that they are concerned with the telling of a person's own lived experience of 'what really happened' to them. However, no matter how authentic they may seem, they are partial representations told to achieve particular ends. An important element of the analysis of narratives involves looking at how stories are used by respondents to give shape to events, make points, as well as present their actions to others in certain ways. Narratives are used to convey information about events as well as structure a sense of self and establish and maintain social bonds and relationships between individuals. In part this is why researchers who seek to adopt this approach are critical of how grounded theory analysis 'chunks' text to generate a conceptual framework of data: it is felt to disrupt the narrative flow of the story and stop a researcher identifying narrative content and form.

Getting started: narrative content and form

We begin our discussion of narrative analysis with a similar proviso to the one given when we looked at grounded theory analysis: it is impossible to delineate the analytical process in its entirety as it is a craft skill learnt by doing. Nevertheless, at the same time it is possible to outline some of its main features. As with grounded theory analysis our analytical goal as we begin our narrative analysis is to gather together our rich qualitative data and, adopting a data-driven stance, inductively build a picture of events from it against the background of a disciplinary concern with a particular research topic and question. Hence in their research of Native American, Mexican American and Anglo American female survivors of rape in southwest America Bletzer and Koss (2006) sought to listen to the voices of their respondents, eliciting their life stories from childhood into adulthood while also focusing on incidents of sexual violence and unwanted sexual attention, with the aim of identifying personal and familial reactions to rape alongside the perceived availability of, and actual usage of, professional counselling and support services. The deeply personal stories elicited illustrated how victims from different cultural backgrounds responded in different ways to these traumatic experiences and in so doing reinforced the need to be more sensitive to the individual needs of survivors of sexual violence instead of providing generic support without regard for cultural background or personal circumstance.

The collection of stories from victims of crime in their own words frequently points to broader socio-political themes, issues and debates surrounding how the criminal justice system and society as a whole should respond to criminal acts and support victims in particular to cope with what frequently are life-altering and highly traumatic events (Walklate 2004). The act of seeking to enable previously silenced voices to have their stories heard by social elites is a worthy research goal in itself as long as it is approached with the right amount of sensitivity and methodological rigour. Yet regardless of their commitment to engendering social change the narrative criminologist also possesses personal reasons for conducting their research, and these are often directly related to disciplinary debates surrounding their topic. They may not wish to use narratives to build formal theory as is done with grounded theory analysis. But they nevertheless invariably are concerned with building on what other researchers have said about their topic so they can make a contribution to their field of study. We will discuss the role of the broader research literature in narrative analysis in a moment. For the moment let us begin by following Gibbs (2007: 63) and arguing that a researcher should begin their analysis inductively and by looking at the content and form of their narratives to identify:

- Events – what happened?
- Experiences – images, feelings, reactions, meanings.
- Accounts, explanations, excuses.
- Narrative – the linguistic and rhetorical form of telling the events, including how the narrator and audience (the researcher) interact; temporal sequencing, characters, emplotment and imagery.

The first three of these – events, experiences and accounts, explanations and excuses – relate to the immediate content of a story while simultaneously pointing towards the fourth element – how the narrative form is structured linguistically and rhetorically to achieve certain goals. I find it useful to focus on content at the beginning of the analytical process to build up a descriptive account of my data with a view to subsequently identifying narrative form. Earthy and Cronin (2008: 433) note that a concern with the content of a narrative includes both 'the surface content (what happened? who was present? how did different parties react?) and the underlying latent content (what were the motives or intentions of participants? what might particular items symbolise for the narrator or others? what is the meaning and importance of this story for the narrator?)'. Focusing on content can feel very much like the open coding stage in grounded theory analysis where a researcher is looking for common patterns within the data across different respondents' accounts in order to build an initial generic picture of events (Lieblich et al. 1998). However, a key difference between narrative analysis and grounded theory analysis is that by refusing to become overly concerned with the thematic 'chunking data' to abstract concepts, and instead focusing on the unfolding content of a story as it is told, we can begin to become aware of narrative form and 'how the plot is structured, events are sequenced and language is used. For example particular words or phrases may have the effect of making the story seem more convincing or protecting the narrator from being criticised' (Earthy and Cronin 2008: 433). What this means is that whereas a focus on narrative content enables us to generate a rich, descriptive account of what our respondents say, focusing on narrative form helps us to identify how the way things are said enables the speaker to achieve certain interactional goals. Consequently as we begin our analysis it is important to identify linear order, perspective and voice, causality and plot, within respondents' stories (see Box 5.4). The goal is to produce a rich, descriptive account of the narrative content of our source material as well as move towards looking more closely at narrative form and so how a story is being told and for what ends. In the rest of this chapter we will look at two common methods used in narrative analysis to achieve this goal: first, Labov and Waletzky's (1967) 'six narrative elements', and second, a more Foucauldian (1991) approach which focuses on the role of 'discursive statements' in the production of narrative accounts.

Box 5.4

Narrative content and form

The analysis of respondents' stories focuses on what we refer to as narrative content and narrative form. Identifying narrative content enables a researcher to build a rich, descriptive account of what our respondents are saying, while focusing on narrative form enables them to see how respondents use plot, characterisation and language to produce a convincing story, persuade their audience, argue a point or protect themselves from criticism. The process of identifying content and form requires a researcher to consider the following aspects of narrative construction:

Linear order – people's stories of events should possess a beginning, middle and end. Focus on identifying a common sequence of events that is shared by respondents' narratives alongside key variations within this. Such sequences will contain both the narrator and other people as events unfold over time. For example, when listening to the stories about the immediate aftermath of a street mugging we might identify that most respondents phone a friend or family member for help and support but some phone the police before seeking to walk home by themselves.

Perspective and voice – people narrate their stories and there should be an identifiable voice in the story. This will possess a stable and predictable identity with judgements, assumptions, opinions, values and reasons for actions. For example, when relating their stories about the aftermath of street mugging, respondents may voice reasons why they didn't immediately phone the police and instead phoned a family member based on their opinion about the likelihood of their attacker being subsequently caught and their possessions being returned to them.

Causality and plot – people give their stories a sense of causality through plotting them and giving them characters in the form of a protagonist, antagonist and witnesses (which include both people in the story as it happened and the interviewer as a witness the story is being told to). Plots may well possess a linguistic style or genre: they might be comical, ironic, tragic, mythical, romantic and so on. For example, when relating how they came to be mugged in the street on their way home from work, respondents may focus on the ironic or even comic nature of their story as they knew they shouldn't walk down that particular street because they had just read a newspaper article that morning which talked about it being a well-known 'mugging hot-spot'.

Analytical focus of chapter

In this chapter we will look at two approaches to the analysis of narrative content and form. Labov and Waletzky's (1967) 'six narrative elements' and a more Foucauldian (1991) approach that focuses on the role of discursive statements in the production of narrative accounts, which we will explore using the analytical approach of Agar and Hobbs (1982). Examples of both approaches along with further readings are provided to help you use either (or even both) of these approaches in your research.

The initial analytical goal is to get to grips with our data and build up a thick, descriptive account of its content. As we familiarise ourselves with narrative content we also get a feel for narrative form. We are all familiar with genre as a form of narrative structuring used in dramatic plays, TV programmes and Hollywood movies. One only needs to hear the term 'chick flick' to know we are talking about a romantic movie with a female lead looking for love, and to be able to imagine how the plot may unfold, possible comic incidents and twists in the tale, what the main characters may be like, and so on. Often the stories people tell about everyday life events they have experienced fall into recognisable genres, each of which possesses its own particular associated narrative form and imagery. For White (1987) the genre of story plots may be tragic, comic, romantic or satirical, while for Frye (1988) they can be ironic, mythical, romantic, tragic or comic. Hence a story may be romantic in that our hero must face and successfully overcome a series of challenges to achieve a goal and secure victory. Or it may be tragic, with our hero being defeated by enemies or betrayed by friends with the result that they become ostracised from society. Such classic story forms are useful tools for capturing the key elements of a narrative.

One popular method used in narrative analysis was developed by Labov (1972, 1982) and Labov and Waletzky (1967). This argues that all narrative stories possess similar core elements. As for all forms of qualitative data analysis, narrative analysis needs to be able to reduce large amounts of textual data down to more manageable proportions for comparative and analytical purposes. The aim of using Labov and Waletzky's (1967) narrative elements is to take a story and create a shorter, more focused snapshot of it with the aim of identifying key content and form so that different research respondents' stories can be compared and contrasted for key similarities and differences (see Box 5.5). Labov and Waletzky (1967) argued that there were five elements present in all narratives, to which they added a sixth, the *abstract*. This summarises the main features of the story and its meaning. It is followed by the *orientation* which outlines who is involved in the story, when it takes place and in what location. This in turn is followed by a *complicating action*, which outlines the main elements of the story and what happened: Was it a turning point? A crisis? A problem? It also outlines how the narrator handled the issue. This is followed by an *evaluation* of the significance of what happened for the narrator alongside a *resolution* which details how the problem or issue was resolved. Finally, a *coda* brings the story back to the present moment. Completing this exercise can reveal how the narrative form is structured rhetorically to achieve certain goals. This in turn helps a researcher to focus on the role of the narrator and how they are using their story creatively for a purpose.

When compared across several different respondents' narratives, the analytical approach proposed by Labov and Waletzky (1967) can enable a researcher to produce a rich, descriptive report of findings. However, for some narrative researchers a key analytical goal is to locate the position of the narrator in the story and how they draw on broader social discourse to establish a sense of personal identity, make points and voice opinions, as they story aspects of their lived experience with their audience in mind. As we will now turn to discuss, here the overlap between narrative analysis and discourse analysis becomes readily apparent.

Box 5.5

Labov and Waletzky's (1967) six narrative elements

Abstract – This tells us what the story is about and summarises the key point of the narrative.

Orientation of the story – This tells us the time, the place, the situation and the participants in the story. It tells us the who? what? when? where? and how? of the story.

Complicating action sequence – This tells us the central story. These often are placed in the past tense and involve a crisis, a problem, a situation or turning-point and how the narrator dealt with it.

Evaluation – This tells us the significance and meaning of the actions as well as the attitudes and opinions of the narrator: Why is it important?

Resolution – This tells us what finally happened and what the key outcomes of the events were from the perspective of the narrator.

Coda – This is an optional element and represents a return to the present through moving on to other events, perhaps even shifting the conversation to another orientation and complicating action.

This analytic structure can be used to help manage narrative data through highlighting key elements of a story. Reducing narrative content in this manner can also help to highlight narrative form: the rhetorical purpose of the account. Not all stories fit this structure exactly, but I find that most do fit quite well into it. The evaluation element is particularly important as this focuses on how the narrator feels about the event and how they now see themselves in relation to it. This can be useful for establishing what the narrator is trying to achieve in telling their story in this particular way. The following example shows how Labov and Waletzky's (1967) six narrative elements have been applied to 'John's story' to compress it down from a much larger interview transcript into a smaller snapshot format that still effectively communicates how he decided to seek counselling to help him stop reoffending. Here we can see that the evaluation element of the narrative shows that John believes he has changed his behaviour and will now stop offending.

Example: 'Breaking the cycle: John's story'

Abstract

'Well, I've been in and out of prison all my adult life for doing stupid things and it had to stop … I'd be inside then come out, promise everybody I'd go straight, but I'd get bored and drink and get into trouble … I think I was finally growing up … I didn't want to lose my new girlfriend … I just kinda came to a point in my life where I knew it was down to me and if I wanted to change only I could help myself.'

Orientation of the story

'What I thought was, "Well you've been in and out of prison for, like, nearly ten years of your life and things have got to change" … People had said in the past I needed to get some counselling and advice if I really wanted to change … Even

(Continued)

(Continued)

had to talk to a psychiatrist a few times because you get sent to them on the inside when you hit someone [in prison] [laughs] … but I didn't really say much … I suppose there was all this stuff to do with my family growing up I hadn't really got around to talking about really …'

Complicating action

'Well, after I came out [of prison] last time I just felt different, I'd really had had enough … I was just so angry all the time and I couldn't work out why … so I talked to my probation officer and she sent me to see this counsellor fella and we just talked for an hour or so every few weeks … It was hard at first … One time we talked about the match the night before [a football match between local rival teams] and he supported ['bluetown'] too, just like me … after that we kind of just got along, you know? … We talked about everything and I told him what had happened to me when I was younger … we talked a lot about being frustrated and angry and losing control … what I could do differently … I saw him for about a year all in all.'

Evaluation

'It didn't happen overnight but I can say now that I feel like a new person … I'm more in control of myself now. I don't drink [laughs], well, I still have a pint or two occasionally, but I keep a lid on it … I know my triggers and I stop myself from doing things now … It's like I can see what I am doing and stop myself before it gets too far.'

Resolution

'I'm glad I did it [got the counselling] … I know I made the right choices. I ain't going back inside [prison].'

Coda

'Ellen [his fiancée] knows everything about me and what I've done in the past and what I'm trying to do now … I think we really can make a future together. I feel like I've changed for the better.'

Recommended reading

Labov, W. (1972) *Language in the Inner City*. Philadelphia: University of Pennsylvania Press.

Labov, W. (1982) Speech actions and reactions in personal narrative. In D. Tannen (ed.) *Analysing Discourse: Text and Talk*. Washington, DC: Georgetown University Press.

Labov, W. and Waletsky, J. (1967) Narrative analysis and versions of personal experience. In J. Helm (ed.) *Essays on the Verbal and Visual Arts*. Seattle, WA: University of Washington Press.

Focusing on narrative identity: subject positions, cultural resources and discursive statements _____

As we look at linear order, perspective, voice, causality and plot in our narratives, using Labov and Waletzky's (1967) six narrative elements to help us do so, we begin to see narrative form and the functions the story performs. John's story in Box 5.5 serves as an example of a 'redemptive tale' where he knew only *he* could change his behaviour, but he needed the help of a counsellor to do it as he felt *he* couldn't control himself and stop being violent towards others without professional help, because he had unresolved childhood trauma to deal with. In telling his story in this manner John is able to present a version of his self to his audience – the narrative researcher – which acknowledges his past wrongdoings while simultaneously using his story to show himself in a positive light with a hopeful future. This is in no small part due to his voiced recognition of the need to change and his personal determining role in making this change, but also through highlighting the need to address underlying causes for his criminal behaviour which he hints at being rooted in early childhood trauma. Hence the underpinning narrative form of John's story is that he is trying to portray himself as to some extent a victim of circumstances beyond his control. But the goal here is not to engage in normative value judgements concerning John's story. Rather, the aim is to focus on how stories are reflexive social tools for giving meaning to personal experience, constructing a sense of personal identity, as well as placing particular life events within a broader context.

Examining storied accounts in this manner to look at the presentation of a self through focusing on narrative form and its rhetorical elements requires that we move away from seeing a narrative as *the* authentic story of the narrator and the life events they bear witness to. Instead, we move towards seeing narrative accounts as the outcome of a situated negotiation in which the researcher plays a collaborative role in co-authoring the resulting story. For example, in her study of male masculinity and 'doing gender' Pressor (2005) relates how the men she interviewed sought to enact a form of 'chivalrous masculinity' in their narratives through using personalised 'story vignettes' to offer her advice on men, dating and relationships, as part of the broader interview discussion of male behaviour and masculinity. Furthermore, she notes that she positioned herself in gendered ways in the interviews to present herself as vulnerable, non-threatening and feminine. She did this so as to establish rapport with her interviewees and not challenge the narrative flow of informants' storied accounts of how men should enact their masculinity in what they personally saw as being gender-appropriate ways. The person telling the story is aware of their audience, namely, the researcher; hence the very real possibility that a story of life events may vary considerably depending on to whom a person is speaking. Far from being a point of concern this fact allows us to critically reflect on how shared cultural practices and resources are used by social actors in particular situations to achieve certain ends. In Pressor's case this involves her presenting both her empirical findings and her reflections on how she and her informants together drew on cultural expectations and resources concerning appropriate gender roles to build rapport, present a self, as well as situate their interview discussion within a broader concern with 'doing gender' and questions surrounding what are appropriate masculine and feminine identities in the eyes of research participants.

Narrative identities then do not emerge in a vacuum. A story-teller draws on a variety of cultural resources to construct a narrative self-identity that they have acquired the use of as members of particular social groups possess common ways of thinking and doing. The cultural resources at play in people's narratives include 'the myths, scientific theories, common sense and folk beliefs, technologies, artwork and values that underpin socio-cultural institutions and structure everyday human activity' (Ward and Marshall 2007: 289). Here we are touching on the overlaps between narrative analysis and discourse analysis (indeed some researchers use the terms interchangeably); we look at discourse analysis in Chapter 6. For the moment it is enough to touch on the work of the French philosopher Michel Foucault (1991) and how he argued that individual subjectivities – that is, a person's sense of self – are neither fixed nor stable, but rather are constituted in and through a spiral of power/knowledge discourses, as generated by political objectives, institutional regimes and expert disciplines, whose primary aim is to produce knowable and governable individuals.

From the end of eighteenth century onwards there was a steady growth in new scientific disciplines, such as psychiatry, sexology, sociology and medicine. Foucault holds that a key outcome of the rise of these new sciences was the more intensive use of 'dividing practices' to objectify an individual and their body via systems of notation, classification and standardisation. Foucault argues that through their examination and assessment techniques experts produced normative classifications for subject positions (normal, mad, bad, sexually deviant, etc.) which increasingly became inscribed within the disciplinary regimes of society's organisational and institutional structures, including the criminal justice system and the agencies of social control (Foucault 1991). A particular concern for some Foucauldian-inspired narrative criminologists lies with exploring the stories people tell to examine the role played by 'discursive statements' within their narratives as individuals seek to construct a sense of self and act to achieve certain ends, within social situations. Box 5.6 outlines this more discursively-minded approach to narrative analysis, utilising the analytical approach of Agar and Hobbs (1982). In doing so it shows how focusing on narrative form can bring to the foreground the complex ways in which stories can help to shape an individual's sense of self and what they see as appropriate forms of behaviour. Furthermore, it also reinforces how a researcher develops their own theoretical 'interpretive spin' on a story which is grounded in their reading of broader disciplinary literature.

Riessman (1993) argues that although they do seek to work inductively with their data a narrative analyst nevertheless always approaches a topic through a disciplinary lens which aids their analysis, and this must be made explicit when presenting findings. For narrative researchers the task of reporting 'singular truth' in a value-neutral and impartial manner is no longer held to be a viable research goal. All accounts of social reality and criminological life are partial and open to contestation. They are situated in local circumstances and involve the presentation of particular points of view. This does not mean, however, that the narrative analyst does not seek to generalise from collected data. Although they tend not to be overly concerned with analytical generalisation, that is, as described in our discussion of grounded theory analysis in Chapter 4, they nevertheless do seek to draw broader inferences from their data while simultaneously acknowledging they are engaged in an ongoing disciplinary project as a member of an academic community. In practice this means that a researcher will outline their findings in such a way that they acknowledge their limitations but at the same time highlight the contribution made to current academic discussion surrounding their research topic.

There are some postmodern narrative researchers in particular who argue that participants' own narratives should be presented with little or no theoretical sophistication and allowed to 'speak for themselves'. Although I do think this is a valid point when dealing with highly sensitive topics where voices have been silenced by others, such as in the case of childhood experiences of sexual abuse for example, I also think it is important to recognise that a researcher possesses a right to make their own voice heard. That is, as long as they do so while at the same time providing a suitable cautionary note that their analysis represents just one possible interpretation of the narratives presented. We are members of an academic community which is collectively seeking to enrich current understanding of criminal life while working within an ethical practice framework that privileges research participants' personal safety and right to confidentiality and anonymity. We will touch on such matters again when we look at discourse analysis. For the moment, having outlined the main features of two ways of doing narrative analysis, we can conclude our discussion by considering some criticisms of this approach to qualitative data analysis.

Box 5.6

Foucault, discursive statements and narrative identities: hegemonic masculinities and crime

Using Labov and Waletzky's (1967) six narrative elements to analyse multiple respondent stories first, we begin to, inductively build a compact but rich picture of narrative content, and second, we begin to see narrative form and the functions

(Continued)

(Continued)

a story performs. Comparing and contrasting respondent stories using this approach can help a researcher to produce an analytically rich account of their topic. However, some narrative researchers utilising a more Foucauldian (1991) focus seek to examine narrative form and function to specifically locate the subject position of a narrator in the story and how they draw on broader cultural resources and discursive practices to establish a sense of personal identity, make points and voice opinions, as they story aspects of their lived experience within a social situation with their audience in mind. As fully paid-up members of society, individuals possess cultural resources and discursive ways of thinking and doing. Discourse consists of relatively coherent groups of statements that define different kinds of speaking and writing – such as legal, medical, racist or ageist forms of discourse – using language to convey meaning and create subject positions for social actors to internalise and use as scripts to inform their behaviour. Discourse is defined as 'a system of statements which construct an object' (Parker 1994: 61). The analytical concern is with the regulative underpinnings of dominant discursive vocabularies that constrain the way in which we think about and act in the world. From this perspective language is structured to reflect dominant power relations and sustain social inequalities. Discourse shapes how we act in social situations. It provides scripted subject positions and social roles with behavioural expectations. Hence researchers using this approach in their analysis are concerned with how 'discourses facilitate and limit, enable and constrain, what can be said (by whom, where and when)' (Parker 1994: xiii). This approach can be criticised for viewing individuals and human agency as being somewhat reducible to 'figures' in the discourse. Also, to some extent adopting this approach does imply a researcher will prioritise a theoretical standpoint over that of their research participants regarding the meaning and interpretation of a story. This does on the surface seem to contravene the purpose of narrative criminology in collecting life stories to capture and prioritise the voice of an individual or group of people (Goody 2000). Nevertheless, it is arguable that such an approach more readily acknowledges the role played by existing academic material in constructing a seemingly inductive account of social reality and criminological life. It also can result in a more reflexive 'polyvocal text' where a researcher's personal reading of the meaning of a narrative account sits alongside that of research participants, with both perspectives being accorded equal voice and legitimacy (Atkinson 1999).

Foucauldian narrative analysis has been fruitfully applied to explore the relationship between gender and crime. One such example is the concept of 'hegemonic masculinities'. In summary, Connell (1990) argued that there were dominant and submissive forms of masculinity within western nations, which were, respectively, ideal types of 'accredited' and 'discredited' models of manliness.

Hegemonic forms of masculinity provide the dominant culturally approved model against which men create and model themselves as men. It is argued that within western nation-states a particular form of hegemonic masculinity has emerged to cultural dominance that subordinates homosexuality and other forms of masculinity (and femininity) in favour of competitive individualism, independence, aggression, a capacity for violence, and heterosexuality. Hence men, to be 'real men', must avoid all things feminine, restrict emotions severely, show toughness and aggression, exhibit self-reliance, strive for achievement and social status, and actively engage in homophobia (Connell 1990). This provides a discursive framework in which men can locate their sense of self, *do* gender and construct a masculine identity in social situations. But it does not mean that all men act this way all the time or that there is not a multiplicity of ways to enact 'maleness'.

Messerschmidt (1993: 84) applied Connell's framework to crime, analysing as he did so how 'for many men, crime serves as a "resource" for doing gender'. This signalled the beginning of a fruitful, theoretically informed research agenda looking at crime to examine why it is a predominately male activity (albeit with the proviso that masculinities are not the whole story when it comes to crime). One example of this approach is the work of Evans and Wallace (2008) and their study of the masculinity narratives of nine male prisoners from a London prison in the United Kingdom. The men were encouraged to tell their life stories, looking at how they grew up and if there was a right or wrong way to be a 'proper man', especially within the prison environment. These stories were analysed with a focus on narrative content and form to identify how a unified, meaningful and coherent story was rhetorically put together by research participants. Following Agar and Hobbs's (1982) analytical framework for discourse analysis, discursive statements relating to the ways masculinity and doing gender were talked about and enacted within respondents' stories were framed in three ways to identify narrative coherence as related to an overarching 'metanarrative':

Local coherence – This is concerned with how the temporal flow and causal relations within the narrative accounts tie together:

> There were several themes ... the most interesting in terms of reflecting on masculine identity followed a sequence: through thinking about growing up (particularly the relationship with father) and moving the story forward in time to think about the relationship with sons (either real or imagined).

(Evans and Wallace 2008: 491)

(Continued)

(Continued)

Global coherence – This is concerned with parts of the narratives that serve to move the whole story forward:

> [There were] ... two streams of global coherence ... key to the overall point of the story: first, one about being in prison and its effect on them as men, second, an individual stream that illustrated something unique about them. These ranged from violence, emotions and role models to race and physicality.

(Evans and Wallace 2008: 491)

Thematic coherence – This is concerned with parts of narratives that express cultural norms and values:

> The thematic coherence section sets out these excerpts that express participants' general cultural themes or values, that is, their personal philosophy about being male and how they project it to other men.

(Evans and Wallace 2008: 491)

Metanarrative

The metanarrative draws together the three levels of analysis within the stories people tell, and places them within the broader discourse which shapes and scripts them. In the case of looking at the masculinity of offenders this is 'the expression of the life script of the individual about being male' (Evans and Wallace 2008: 492). Summarising their metanarrative of hegemonic masculinity Evans and Wallace identify how men narrate their subject positions, that is, their sense of self as being a man, in one of three ways in relation to this dominant discursive script of how 'real men' should behave: they either reject it, accept it or seek to transform it. The first of these groups emphasised how they had experienced close and loving paternal relationships, and although they see the presence of an aggressive and assertive form of hegemonic masculinity within the relationships between male prisoners around them, they do not enact it themselves and consequently felt a sense of difference from other prisoners. The second of these groups had experienced a very negative and/or abusive paternal relationship but 'despite the fact that they often expressed huge dislike for their fathers, they too lived predominately from within the hegemonic masculinity codes' (Evans and Wallace 2008: 499). Finally, the third group may also have experienced a negative and/or abusive paternal relationship, as well as initially internalising the hegemonic masculinity codes, but had through certain 'turning-points' in their lives 'begun to evaluate the codes and move beyond them toward a more balanced view of their own masculinity' (Evans and Wallace 2008: 499). The implications of these findings are discussed by Evans and Wallace in relation to offender counselling and rehabilitation programme provision, the criminological study of prison life, as well as the links which exist between crime and masculinity. They provide an insightful example of how Foucauldian narrative criminologists can utilise Agar and Hobbs's (1982) analytical approach towards discourse analysis to produce theoretically informed accounts of criminal life that also possess strong practical social policy implications. The following recommended readings will help you to apply this approach in your own research. We also discuss discourse analysis in Chapter 6.

Recommended reading

Agar, M. and Hobbs, J.R. (1982) Interpreting discourse: coherence and the analysis of ethnographic interviews, *Discourse Processes*, 5: 1–32.

Atkinson, P. (1999) Voiced and unvoiced, *Sociology*, 33(1): 191–6.

Evans, T. and Wallace, P. (2008) A prison within a prison: the masculinity narratives of male prisoners, *Men and Masculinities*, 10: 484–97.

Parker, I. (1990) Discourse: definitions and contradictions, *Philosophical Psychology*, 3 (2): 189–204.

Parker, I. (1994) Discourse analysis. In P. Banister, E. Burman, I. Parker, M. Taylor and C. Tindall (eds) *Qualitative Methods in Psychology*. Buckingham: Open University Press.

Criticisms of Narrative Analysis

Narrative analysis undoubtedly possesses a great deal of potential as a research tool that recognises, first, how human beings story the world around them and their place in it, and second, how analysing these stories can reveal the complex and layered dynamics that exist between the life biography of the creative social actor and the social structural conditions which often act to shape and constrain their behaviour. Yet it has been subject to criticism for by and large refusing to engage in formal theory generation and testing as found in experimental and survey forms of quantitative research. It is certainly the case that some narrative researchers argue participants' own narratives should be presented with little or no theoretical sophistication and allowed to speak for themselves owing to their concern for bringing to the foreground silenced, stigmatised and excluded voices. But as we have discussed in this chapter, more theoretically informed approaches to narrative criminology do exist, including in the form of a Foucauldian (1991) approach which focuses on the role of power, entrenched interests and discursive statements in the scripting of narrative accounts.

The constructivist underpinnings to narrative analysis make it inherently wary of attempts at theory testing in a purist empirical sense. Rather it readily acknowledges the partial nature of storied accounts of criminal life. As this chapter discussed, such matters are not in themselves held to be inherently problematic, not least of all because narrative researchers tend to operate from a different value-framework to their more positivistic and realist-minded cousins. For most narrative criminologists a focus on 'polyvocal texts' means that multiple (and even contradictory) interpretations can sit alongside each other and be accorded equal legitimacy (Atkinson 1999). Indeed, it is arguable that the contemporary turn to constructivist strategies in qualitative research more generally has led to the use of more diverse forms of dissemination strategies which possess the potential to enhance the impact of social science research. However, perhaps a fair criticism of narrative criminology is that there can be a tendency for narrative analysts to treat the stories they are told relatively uncritically (Bury 2001). It is important that narrative researchers follow Pressor (2005) and examine their own role in the co-production of a respondent's story, especially as they analyse its form and what the author achieves when they narrate their personal experience in particular ways. After all, we all like to cast ourselves in a positive light when narrating our life stories.

Conclusion

The chapter has provided an introduction to narrative analysis and the role the collection and analysis of stories can play in enhancing our understanding of crime and deviance. It has focused on how narrative criminologists sometimes work with groups of individuals who are marginalised or stigmatised in some way to gather evidence and tell the story of silenced or socially excluded voices. The stories people tell can be powerful tools for engendering social change. The chapter looked at how stories can be viewed as interactional achievements and in doing so outlined two different approaches to the analysis of narrative content and form: first, Labov and Waletzky's (1967) 'six narrative elements', and second, a more Foucauldian (1991) approach that focuses on the role of discursive statements in the scripting of narrative accounts, which we examined using the analytical framework developed by Agar and Hobbs (1982). If you are thinking of using either (or even both) these approaches in your research you should consult the illustrative examples, further readings and exercises that have been provided in the chapter to help you apply narrative analysis for your own purposes. The chapter also noted overlaps between narrative analysis and discourse analysis, which we examine in more detail in Chapter 6.

CHAPTER REVIEW ACTIVITIES

1 The types of life stories that narrative criminologists collect range from complete biographical accounts of a life to shorter and more focused stories that are concerned with key aspects, episodes and turning-points in a life. Write a 1000-word essay detailing the strengths and weaknesses of these two approaches in generating accounts of criminological life. As part of this discussion, consider how each approach could be used to answer your own proposed research question.

2 Write a 1000-word essay detailing how you could use e-resources such as online archives, YouTube and social networking sites to generate narratives for a project concerned with young people's experience of either: a) domestic violence, b) homophobia, or c) illegal drug use. Make sure you consider as part of your discussion how you could disseminate your research findings online as well as in a more traditional report format.

3 Conduct a short interview (10 to 15 minutes) with a friend, asking them to tell you a story about a key event in their life that changed their behaviour and attitude towards someone close to them. Make sure you record the interview and transcribe it fully. Using Labov and Waletzky's (1967) 'six narrative elements' break down your transcript of their story into a shorter narrative snapshot. What does completing this process tell you about the content, form and purpose of the narrative?

CHAPTER READING LIST

Agar, M. and Hobbs, J.R. (1982) Interpreting discourse: coherence and the analysis of ethnographic interviews, *Discourse Processes*, 5: 1–32.

Atkinson, R. (1998) *The Life Story Interview*. London: Sage Publications.

Atkinson, P. (1999) Voiced and unvoiced, *Sociology*, 33(1): 191–6.

Bennett, J. (1981) *Oral History and Delinquency: The Rhetoric of Criminology*. Chicago: University of Chicago Press.

Bletzer, K.V. and Koss, M.P. (2006) After-rape among three populations in the southwest: a time for mourning, a time for recovery, *Violence Against Women*, 12: 5–29.

Bury, M. (2001) Illness narratives: fact or fiction?, *Sociology of Health and Illness*, 23: 263–85.

Chase, D. (2005) Narrative inquiry: multiple lenses, approaches, voices. In N.K. Denzin and Y.S. Lincoln (2011) *The Sage Handbook of Qualitative Research*, Thousand Oaks, CA: Sage Publications.

(Continued)

(Continued)

Clandinin, D.J. and Connolly, F.M. (2000) *Narrative Inquiry: Experience and Story in Qualitative Research.* San Francisco, CA: Jossey Bass.

Connell, R.W. (1990) *Masculinities.* Cambridge: Polity Press.

Denzin, N.K. (1989) *Interpretive Biography.* London: Sage Publications.

Denzin, N.K. and Lincoln Y.S. (2011) *The Sage Handbook of Qualitative Research.* Thousand Oaks, CA: Sage Publications.

Earthy, S. and Cronin, A. (2008) Narrative analysis. In N. Gilbert (ed.) *Researching Social Life* (3rd edn). London: Sage Publications.

Evans, T. and Wallace, P. (2008) A prison within a prison: the masculinity narratives of male prisoners, *Men and Masculinities,* 10: 484–97.

Foucault, M. (1991) Governmentality. In G. Burchell, C. Gordon and P. Miller (eds) *The Foucault Effect: Studies in Governmentality.* London: Harvester Wheatsheaf.

Frye, N. (1988) *On Education.* Toronto: Fitzhenry and Whiteside.

Gibbs, G. (2007) *Analyzing Qualitative Data.* London: Sage Publications.

Goody, J. (2000) Biographical lessons for criminology, *Theoretical Criminology,* 4(4): 473–98.

Gubrium, J.F. and Holstein, J.A. (1998) Narrative practice and the coherence of personal stories, *Sociological Quarterly,* 39: 163–87.

Kenyon, G.M. and Randall, W. (1997) *Restorying our Lives: Personal Growth through Autobiographical Reflection.* Westport, CN: Praeger.

Labov, W. (1972) *Language in the Inner City.* Philadelphia: University of Pennsylvania Press.

Labov, W. (1982) Speech actions and reactions in personal narrative. In D. Tannen (ed.) *Analysing Discourse: Text and Talk.* Washington, DC: Georgetown University Press.

Labov, W. and Waletsky, J. (1967) Narrative analysis and versions of personal experience. In J. Helm (ed.) *Essays on the Verbal and Visual Arts.* Seattle, WA: University of Washington Press.

Lieblich, A., Tuval-Mashiach, R. and Zilber, T. (1998) *Narrative Research: Reading Analysis and Interpretation.* Thousand Oaks, CA: Sage Publications.

Mattingly, C. (1998) *Healing Dramas and Clinical Plots: The Narrative Structure of Experience.* Cambridge: Cambridge University Press.

Merrill, B. and West, L. (2005) *Using Biographical Methods in Social Research.* London: Sage Publications.

Messerschmidt, J. (1993) *Masculinities and Crime.* Boston: Rowman and Littlefield.

Morgan, S. (1999) Prison lives: critical issues in reading prisoner autobiography, *The Howard Journal of Criminal Justice,* 38(3): 23–45.

Nellis, M. (2002) Prose and cons: offender auto/biographies, penal reform and probation training, *The Howard Journal of Criminal Justice,* 41(5): 32–48.

Parker, I. (1990) Discourse: definitions and contradictions, *Philosophical Psychology,* 3(2): 189–204.

Parker, I. (1994) Discourse analysis. In P. Banister, E. Burman, I. Parker, M. Taylor and C. Tindall (eds) *Qualitative Methods in Psychology.* Buckingham: Open University Press.

Peckham, A. (1985) *A Woman in Custody: A Personal Account of One Nightmare Journey Through the English Penal System.* London: Fontana.

Pressor, L. (2005) Negotiating power and narrative in research: implications for feminist methodology, *Signs,* 30(4): 2067–90.

Plummer, K. (2001) *Documents of Life* (2nd edn). London: Sage Publications.

Radzinowicz, L. (1999) *Adventures in Criminology.* London: Routledge.

Riessman, C.K. (1993) *Narrative Analysis.* London: Sage Publications.

Riessman, C.K. (2004) Narrative interviewing. In M.S. Lewis-Beck, A. Bryman, A. and T.F. Liao (eds) *The Sage Encyclopedia of Social Science Research Methods.* Thousand Oaks, CA: Sage Publications.

Roberts, B. (2002) *Biographical Research.* Milton Keynes: Open University Press.

Rosenweld, D.L. and Ochburg, R.L. (1992) *Storied Lives: The Cultural Politics of Self-understanding.* New Haven, CT: Yale University Press.

Ross, J. and Richards, S. (2002) *Convict Criminology.* Belmont, CA: Wadsworth Publishing.

Sarat, A. (2011) *Is the Death Penalty Dying? European and American Perspectives.* Cambridge: Cambridge University Press.

Shaw, C. (1966) *The Jack Roller: A Delinquent Boy's Own Story.* Chicago: University of Chicago Press.

Staller, K.M. and Nelson-Gardell, D. (2005) A burden in your heart: lessons of disclosure from female preadolescent and adolescent survivors of sexual abuse, *Child Abuse and Neglect,* 29: 1415–32.

Sutherland, E.H. (1937) *The Professional Thief: By a Professional Thief. Annotated and Interpreted by Edwin H. Sutherland.* Chicago: University of Chicago Press.

Tierney, J. (2006) *Criminology: Theory and Context* (2nd edn). Harlow, Essex: Pearson Education.

Venkatesh, S. (2008) *Gang Leader for a Day.* London: Penguin.

Walklate, S. (2004) *Gender, Crime and Criminal Justice* (2nd edn). Cullompton, Devon: Willan Publishing.

Ward, T. and Marshall, B. (2007) Narrative identity and offender rehabilitation, *International Journal of Offender Therapy and Comparative Criminology,* 51: 279–97.

Warshow, R. (1970) The gangster as tragic hero. In R. Warshow (ed.) *The Immediate Experience: Movies, Comics, Theatre And Other Aspects Of Popular Culture.* New York: Atheneum.

White, H. (1987) *The Content of the Form: Narrative Discourse and Historical Representation.* Baltimore: John Hopkins University Press.

Wilson, A. (2007) *Northern Soul: Music, Drugs and Subcultural Identity.* Cullompton, Devon: Willan Publishing.

6

Discourse Analysis

CHAPTER OVERVIEW

Chapter 6 looks at discourse analysis. The starting point for conducting a discourse analysis is the recognition that language is constitutive of reality: the system of our language is absolutely fundamental to the construction of our thoughts about ourselves and the world around us. Furthermore, language systems are socio-culturally bounded and historically located. The ways we talk and think about the world we live in change over time and are heavily dependent on shared cultural reference points and commonly held norms and values. The chapter discusses one analytical tool used by criminologists and other social scientists to discursively analyse language systems within a social-cultural context, namely, interpretive repertoires. This analytical concept was first introduced by Gilbert and Mulkay (1984) and subsequently developed by Potter and Wetherell (1995). Interpretive repertoires and subject positions can be used to discursively examine the identity work involved in constructing people in different ways. The chapter outlines the historical development of discourse analysis within the social sciences through examining the emergence of postmodernism and its influence in contemporary forms of criminology concerned with how different forms of 'crime-speak' are valued more than others. This state of affairs is held to reflect and reinforce social inequalities based around class, gender, race and sexuality. The chapter notes that this approach is bound up with the qualitative 'narrative turn' within criminology and discusses the similarities between interpretive repertoires and the Foucauldian approach to discourse analysis outlined in Chapter 5. The main features of doing a discourse analysis utilising interpretive repertoires are outlined so you can apply these in your own research and collect and analyse empirical data. Examples, further readings and exercises are also provided to develop your understanding of discourse analysis and help you to apply this analytical approach in your own research.

Introduction

Box 6.1

Seven key elements of deskwork

1   Formulating an initial research area, focusing on study skills and dealing with assessment criteria.
2   Reviewing the literature and developing a research topic with a clear question to answer.
3   **Project planning and research design.**
4   Making contacts, gaining access and obtaining ethical approval to conduct your research.
5   Managing your fieldwork: timetabling.
6   **Conducting data analysis.**
7   Writing up your findings and research dissemination.

In this chapter we examine discourse analysis. As Chapter 5 discussed, discourse analysis and narrative analysis are closely interrelated; together they form part of what has been referred to as the qualitative turn within the social sciences. There are several different approaches to discourse analysis, including the Foucauldian-inspired approach of Agar and Hobbs (1982) outlined in Chapter 5. This focuses on the discursive statements, cultural practices and subject positions employed by individuals as they story accounts of lived experience to highlight the role played in their creation by power, culture, social inequality and entrenched social-structural interests. In this chapter we will look at a form of discourse analysis closely related to this approach. Discourse analysis is a very broad church that includes linguistics, socio-linguists and conversational analysis approaches on one hand, and more interpretive, socio-cultural and social-psychological approaches on the other hand. The shared point of interest lies in the constitutive and situated role of language. That is, language is held to create what it refers to, rather than simply describe it, and is held to operate within a social situation; hence, the common discursive focus on social interaction and language in-use.

Perhaps the key difference between the two ends of the discursive analytic spectrum is that the more linguistic approaches tend to focus on speech acts and the sequencing of verbal (and sometimes non-verbal) communication within social interaction, while socio-cultural and social-psychological approaches tend to focus on language use that may well be situated but which nevertheless also takes place against a broader socio-cultural and historical context. Here discourse analysis studies the ways 'social power abuse, dominance and inequality are enacted, reproduced and resisted by text and talk in the social and political context' (van Dijk 2001: 352). In this chapter we are concerned with this latter form of discourse analysis and to this end we will look at a sociological/social-psychological analytical approach which focuses on the analysis of what are termed 'interpretive repertoires'. As we shall discuss, interpretive repertoires are more or less coherent ways of describing ourselves and the world around us: they provide ready-made explanations and subject positions which we can creatively use when talking within a social situation.

A key difference between interpretive repertoires and more Foucauldian forms of analysis is that they tend to make more room for human agency and the creative use of discourse by individuals as they seek to achieve particular ends. Nevertheless, at the same time it is important to remember that interpretive repertoires impinge on individuals, stifling their human agency and self-determination, and even construct them in particular ways to make them more amenable to social categorisation and administrative control by criminal justice agencies and the legal system (Carlen 2010). Certainly within criminology, discourse analysis is often conducted as a result of a concern with social inequality and a concurrent recognition that the language of the criminal justice and legal systems institutionalises the domination of the individual and frequently enforces a limited, punitive, exclusive and non-pluralistic view of individuals accused of deviance and criminality.

The emphasis placed by discourse analysis on language as constitutive of social reality means it adopts an anti-realist social constructivist position. We looked at social constructivism when we discussed narrative analysis in Chapter 5, while our discussion of grounded theory analysis in Chapter 4 also revealed how attempts have been made by social scientists to incorporate social constructivism within contemporary developments in grounded theory. But what distinguishes discourse analysis from grounded theory analysis in particular is that it adopts what can be termed a 'strong constructivist' anti-realist position. Discourse analysts tend to argue that language is wholly constitutive of reality and lived human experience: nothing exists outside of 'the text'. This position, as we shall see, brings with it some interesting consequences for the conduct of criminological research which employs a discourse analytic approach. In this chapter we will look at the main features of discourse analysis to reinforce the criminological value of this approach to the analysis of criminal life. Further readings and examples are provided to help the reader reflect on if they would like to use this approach in their own research while at the same time developing their understanding of the key principles of discourse analysis.

Discourse Analysis and Research Design

Discourse analysis has emerged in the social sciences in the last three decades through a process of cross-fertilisation involving a range of academic disciplines, including linguistics, sociology, psychology, gender studies, philosophy, criminology, literary theory, communication studies and cultural studies. It is important to begin our discussion by stating that, first, in this chapter we are *not* concerning ourselves with linguistic and conversational forms of discourse analysis, and second, that discourse analysis is an umbrella term covering a range of analytical positions and theoretical perspectives, which although they may share in common a concern with language in-use can and do differ from each other in many ways, including perhaps most importantly how they go about analysing empirical data. Edley (2001: 189) notes that 'there is no simple way of defining discourse analysis. It has become an ever broadening church, an umbrella term for a wide variety of analytic principles and practice.'

This variety in analytic principle and practice noted by Edley is perhaps to be expected as the term 'discourse' is itself typically quite broadly defined to encompass both spoken and written language (and sometimes visual and textual forms of communication as well). For example, Potter and Wetherell (1987: 7) define discourse as 'all forms of spoken interaction, formal and informal, and written texts of all kinds'. Bearing this in mind, we shall define discourse analysis as the examination of language and its associated culturally grounded assumptions and meanings, which act to structure ways of talking about a topic, in order to reveal the socio-political functions discourse serves. A concern with ignored, silenced and excluded discursive positions lies at the heart of much postmodern criminology (Henry and Milovanovic 2003). From this point of view language is not value-neutral. It is inherently structured to reflect power relations and broader socio-economic and cultural inequalities within society. Hence, the definition above points to the frequently critical and overtly politicised nature of discourse analysis. As we shall shortly discuss, its intellectual development lies with the emergence of postmodernism; hence, it is highly critical of methodological claims to objectivity and value-free research. Indeed at its most critically engaged, discourse analysis aims to reveal 'the role of discourse in the (re) production and challenge of dominance' (van Dijk 1993: 249) with some researchers going so far as advocating that discursive research should intervene 'on the side of dominated and oppressed groups against dominating groups' (Fairclough and Wodak 1997: 259). In the rest of this section we will briefly (and selectively, given the possibly enormous range of our topic) examine the postmodern origins of discourse analysis in relation to criminology so we can move on to discuss key design issues a researcher must bear in mind when considering whether they wish to utilise this approach in their research. In doing so we also provide a necessary background for the later discussion of how to use the concept of interpretive repertoires as an analytical tool to discursively examine data.

Postmodernity, the linguistic turn and criminological deconstructions of 'crime-speak'

The intellectual roots of discourse analysis lie in the emergence of postmodernism and the resultant social constructivist perspectives regarding the nature of knowledge of social reality and how this is obtained. Postmodernism emerged in the latter part of the twentieth century through the writings of French scholars such as Lacan, Baudrillard, Foucault, Derrida and Lyotard. One of the key features of postmodernism is its rejection of what are termed 'grand narratives', i.e. theories of the physical and social worlds which allow us to apprehend 'Truth' and so explain, control and alter them to our will. In the broadest terms we can say that there are three interconnected themes running through postmodernism. First, there is a critique and rejection of modernism and the philosophical principles which underpinned the emergence of the Enlightenment period in the eighteenth and nineteenth centuries and saw the development of modern scientific forms of inquiry.

Enlightenment modernism heralded the emergence of the belief that progress could be made towards a utopian social order through controlling the physical and social worlds via the application of scientific rationality. It was held that, as scientific forms of knowledge developed so would our ability to solve common social problems such as hunger, disease, crime and poverty. Positivism, in the form of quantitative research and experimental criminology, as discussed in Chapter 3, can be thought of as the methodological outcome of this Enlightenment belief. From a postmodernist perspective such faith in progress, science and reason was, at best, naïve, at worst, deliberately misleading. Yes, technological and scientific developments have over the last 150 years dramatically improved human life expectancy and the general standard of living for *some* of the world's population.

However, such developments have not only brought with them new hazards and risks, such as global warming, but also remarkably expanded our ability to engage in war and kill each other, while on a global scale, social problems such as poverty and hunger remain largely unresolved. Indeed, if anything the gap between the rich and the poor, the haves and the have-nots, appears to be widening.

Second, over the last 50 years we have seen the emergence of a radically different form of media-saturated globalisation driven by the information and communication technological revolutions. Today's rapidly changing social conditions are characterised by a mixture of liberalist ideology, consumer-driven lifestyle engineering, as well as the increasing questioning of traditional forms of political and religious authority. This has brought about the somewhat paradoxical result that although we have arguably seen a growth in the number of liberal democratic nation-states in the last 50 years, we have also seen the increasing questioning of individuals, organisations and political parties who claim to protect such values. Third, it is argued that the intensification and speeding up of social life – as symbolised by the maxim 'think local, act global' – reinforces that there has been a paradigm shift towards an age of uncertainty and an ever-growing public awareness of risk and its mismanagement. There is growing public scepticism of the ability of experts to manage social problems and eliminate risk. Day after day we are bombarded with media images of natural and man-made disasters which reinforce our inability to survey and control dangerousness and risk. This has led to the radical questioning of all forms of knowledge, including scientific forms of knowledge with their claims to objectivity and value-neutrality, just at the point in human history when we are more dependent on scientific and other forms of expertise than ever before. We will return later in this chapter to the consequences of contemporary social changes, as encapsulated by postmodernism in relation to conceptions of human nature, when we examine how subject positions relate to interpretive repertoires.

One of postmodernism's core tenets is a deep scepticism about knowledge claims and the rejection of the idea that rationality, reason, science and technology lead to progress. The material and social worlds are chaotic and unpredictable. Modernists argue that the world can be ordered, scrutinised, predicted and controlled, that is, as long as you use the right research methodology. Postmodernists, in contrast, argue that such a project is fundamentally flawed: it is an illusion created by the nature of language itself. Postmodernists argue that modernists claim we can obtain knowledge of the world because the language we use to explore and explain it reflects the nature of things as they are; that is, language is held to transmit reality and is therefore viewed as a value-neutral information-carrying device. Hence a modernist researcher can obtain knowledge of the world and how it works, including its underlying causal relationships, so they can make predictions which can form the basis for an intervention to change what is happening in the future. Such knowledge is not only generalisable to other contexts; it is also value-free and objective and so is free from researcher bias. Although they may admit there is truth to the claim that language is an information-carrying device – how could you be reading this book and understand its contents if language does not transmit information and shared meanings? – postmodernists nevertheless hold that language is constitutive: it is a site where meanings are created, manipulated and destroyed.

Language is not transparent and value-neutral. It is encoded with the power to create reality. In addition to the French postmodernists, the linguistic turn within the social sciences can in part be traced back to the linguistic philosophers Wittgenstein and Winch, as well as the sociologists Berger and Luckmann, who together laid the foundations for an anti-realist social constructivist view of reality whereby accounts of the world are said not to exist independently of the social actor and the language they use to describe the world around them (see Philips and Hardy 2002). We discussed social constructivism and anti-realism in Chapter 4 when we talked about grounded theory analysis and in Chapter 5 when we talked about narrative analysis. The key starting assumption of discourse analysis is staunchly anti-realist: language constructs the world instead of representing it.

A key outcome of the recognition of the constitutive role of language is that it problematises the research process: the neutrality, objectivity and independence of the researcher are all called into question. We shall return to this point shortly when we discuss research design. At this point in our discussion it is important to further consider the idea that the words used to give meaning to the world do not in fact create a real and true understanding of it. For this brings to the foreground the point that language can 'create bodies of knowledge that in effect exclude other, alternative, though equally valid, bodies of knowledge … the process of constructing a meaningful social world is, therefore, an expression of power and domination' (Tierney 2006: 321). What this means is that when we say what something is we also imply what it is not: good and bad, male and female, criminal and non-criminal, and so on. From a postmodernist position, texts need to be deconstructed to reveal the entrenched interests that guide and underpin them, which may be political, racist, sexist or homophobic in nature. Within criminology this means recognising that meanings attached to criminal activity (and attempts to prevent it) are co-produced by those who engage in crime, those who try to stop them, those who seek to report it or to otherwise dramatise it for mass consumption, as well as those who seek to study it.

Postmodern criminologists seek to deconstruct the social processes and meanings connected to crime and criminal justice by political parties, policy-makers and policy-enforcers, the media, the criminological academic community, as well as members of the general public. They do this to reveal underlying assumptions, hidden values and hierarchical relationships of power and control, which it is claimed are discursively embedded within 'crime-speak'. Postmodern criminological deconstructions of crime-speak aim to reveal how certain conversations are valued over others, how the media and politicians often perpetuate conventional cultural meanings surrounding who breaks the law and why, as well as how in doing so they frequently deny the possibility of alternative or replacement explanations for crime, criminal behaviour and criminal law. As the postmodern criminologist Arrigo (2003: 48) argues:

> *Deconstruction or 'trashing' entails a careful reading and de-coding of a text (written or spoken). The purpose of deconstructing the text is to unveil the implicit assumptions and hidden values (i.e. often inconsistent, contradictory beliefs about social phenomena) embedded within a particular narrative. Deconstruction shows us how certain truth claims are privileged within a given story, while certain others are disguised or dismissed altogether. Because deconstruction focuses on the actual words people use to convey their thoughts, it attempts to uncover the unconscious intent behind the grammar people employ when writing and speaking. Thus, language or entire systems of communication are put under the microscope for closer inspection. In a sense, then, trashing a text entails reading between the lines to ascertain meaning (i.e. ideology) given preferred status in a particular language system.*

Following Arrigo (2003) we can say that a key element of the deconstructive process of discursive analysis within criminology involves 'trashing' or myth busting commonly held beliefs, assumptions and ways of talking about the social problem that is crime; such as, for example, that it is primarily committed by 'bad people', 'the underclass', 'youth gangs', 'immigrants and ethnic minorities', or some other stigmatised and socially excluded group. This concern with myth busting is particularly important to postmodern criminology in the forms of cultural criminology and constitutive criminology. These theoretical approaches to the analysis of criminal life have emerged within criminology over the last two decades as a result of a postmodern turn within the social sciences. They share in common a concern with how power and inequality impact on rule-making, law enforcement and media images of crime. Hence, they are concerned with how some forms of crime-speak are given more credence than others for no other reason than that they come from people who occupy positions of power (Ferrell et al. 2008).

Constitutive criminology in particular is preoccupied with how the deconstruction of dominant discursive understandings of crime can open up space for the creation of what are termed 'replacement discourses'. These are forms of crime-speak which have been dismissed, neglected or deliberately silenced, not because they are inaccurate or are deliberate untruths, but because they do not 'fit' with dominant ways of talking about a topic, or perhaps they offer unpalatable or even morally unacceptable alternative viewpoints to mainstream explanations for crime and criminal behaviour. Replacement discourses seek to address this state of affairs and are 'designed to displace harmful moments in the exercise of power with discourses that tell different stories about the world' (Henry and Milovanovic 2003: 67). Consequently, postmodern forms of criminology emphasise qualitative research methods and the need to collect the life stories and other textual resources (e.g. newspaper articles or personal diaries and related biographical materials), of the silenced and socially excluded, in addition to those belonging to individuals who possess authority and power.

Chapter 5 looked at the development of narrative life story research within criminology. It also explored the links which exist between narrative analysis and discourse analysis when it introduced Foucauldian approaches to the analysis of life stories. Here it was noted that discourse acts to shape how people participate in social life. It provides subject positions which people can utilise in everyday spoken interaction to achieve certain ends. Subject positions can be thought of as 'locations' within a conversation: they are socially recognised identities made relevant by specific ways of talking about a topic (Edley 2001). But the subject positions attached to discursive statements are double-edged – the social actor may adopt them to express agency and personal creativity during a social interaction but they also can act to constrain their behaviour and label it in different ways. Furthermore, institutionalised forms of surveillance and control, such as criminal justice agencies like the police, utilise discursive statements and attached subject positions so they can come to know an individual and manipulate and control them, if need be. For example, Foucault (1972: 46) noted in his study of the history of madness, and the development of modern medical methods to treat it, that 'psychiatric discourse finds a way of limiting its domain, of defining what it is talking about, of giving it the status of an object – and therefore of making it manifest, nameable, and describable.'

Influenced by the work of Foucault, postmodernist criminology explores how the media, social institutions and specialist forms of expertise, act to discursively construct individuals as a locatable object of scrutiny through the different ways 'crime-speak' is enacted for different purposes in different situations (Henry and Milovanovic 1999). Consequently, the analytical concern is to examine the discursive resources people draw on, how these came to be culturally available to use, as well as what kinds of subject positions and social identities they make available and at the same time close off, deny or otherwise silence. The identification of different interpretive repertoires forms part of this analytical process as these help to 'construct discourse and enable the performance of particular action' (Potter and Wetherell 1995: 49). We will discuss how to undertake a discourse analysis utilising the analytical concept of interpretive repertoire in the next section of this chapter. First it is necessary to consider some key research design issues in light of the preceding discussion of the grounding of discourse analysis within postmodernism. Box 6.2 contains further recommended readings concerning postmodernism and its influence within contemporary criminology.

Box 6.2

Postmodernism and criminology: recommended readings

Postmodernism is a complex concept which emerged in the latter half of the twentieth century within the social sciences through the work of French scholars such as Lacan, Baudrillard, Foucault, Derrida and Lyotard. The writings of these authors heralded the beginning of a contemporary critique of modernism in the form of western Enlightenment ideals pertaining to the role of science and technology in promoting social good and engineering positive social change for the betterment of humankind. Underpinning this critique is the viewpoint that language is not a value-neutral tool and does not enable us to access reality as it exists separately from the words used to describe it. Postmodernists deny that it is possible to speak of the world as if it exists independently of human apprehension of it. Some postmodernists, such as Foucault, argue that language serves the interests of entrenched interests of political and social elites within society. Postmodern sociologists and criminologists tend to focus on how certain ways of talking about social problems, such as crime, are valued more than others, as well as how these can reflect and reinforce social inequalities based around class, race, gender and sexuality. One of the key aims of discourse analysis is to open up such instances for closer inspection, critical appraisal and public debate. The following recommended readings provide further information on postmodernism and its impact in criminology through the development of constitutive criminology and cultural criminology.

Recommended reading

Butler, C. (2002) *Postmodernism: A Very Short Introduction*. Oxford: Oxford Paperbacks.

Ferrell, J., Hayward, K. and Young, J. (2008) *Cultural Criminology: An Invitation*. London: Sage Publications.

Henry, S. and Milovanovic, D. (2003) Constitutive Criminology. In M.D. Schwartz and S.E. Hatty (eds) *Controversies in Critical Criminology*. Cincinnati, OH: Anderson Publishing.

Lea, J. (1998) Criminology and postmodernity. In P. Walton and J. Young (eds) *The New Criminology Revisited*. Basingstoke: Macmillan.

Getting started: key research design considerations

The preceding discussion highlighted several key points which must be borne in mind when designing a discourse analysis study. To begin with, it is important to remember that the critical focus of discourse analysis is typically on analysing 'dialogical struggle (or struggles) as reflected in the privileging of a particular discourse and the marginalization of others' (Keenoy et al. 1997: 150). In practice, this means a discourse analyst is concerned with deconstructing how a research topic is constructed by social actors through drawing on particular discursive resources which set up a variety of subject positions and social identities for the speaker while at the same time closing off, marginalising or silencing others. Furthermore, discourse analysts are often interested in the 'why now?' question – why are these particular discursive resources being drawn on at this point in time? – not least of all because this helps the analyst to reflect on whose interests are being served when a topic is talked about in particular ways. It is futile to undertake a discourse analysis if one does not share this research focus. As Potter (2004: 607) argues, 'to attempt to ask a question formulated in more traditional terms ("what are the factors that lead to condom use among HIV+ gay males?") and then use discourse analytic methods to answer it is a recipe for incoherence.' Consideration of your research question and whether it is appropriate for a discourse analysis approach is an issue you must consider carefully and talk through with your research supervisor. The further readings provided in Box 6.3 will also help you at the project development stage.

Let us assume that your research goal is sympathetic to the adoption of a discursive approach. The next point to bear in mind is that the emergence of discourse analysis within the postmodern turn in the social sciences means there is a tendency to reject deductive hypothesis-testing models of research practice which claim to be able to obtain value-neutral knowledge of social reality. As has been discussed, the idea that scientific rationality somehow confers privileged access to reality is rejected outright by postmodernists. This rejection implies that a researcher must accept that all knowledge is partial, incomplete and fallible. Recognition of the constitutive role of language inherently problematises the research process: the neutrality, objectivity and independence of the researcher are all called into question. Consequently, the discursive criminological researcher, much like their counterparts in other social science disciplines, must face head-on the dual crisis of representation and legitimation (Denzin and Lincoln 2011).

The crisis of representation relates to the fact that if we accept the constructivist claim that objective knowledge is impossible, then we also have to accept that all accounts of criminological life are partial and biased. The extreme conclusion to draw from this is that it is only ever possible to read a piece of research as if it is solely an account of the world view of the person who conducted the study, rather than the people they collected their data from. The crisis of legitimation is bound up with the crisis of representation, as it is concerned with the issue of how we can develop and apply procedures to evaluate the quality of the research findings presented when it is impossible to use objective reality as a construct from which to guide one's conclusions (Wetherell et al. 2001a). As we discussed in Chapter 3, traditionally the concepts of validity, reliability and generalisation have been used to guide the design and quality control of empirical research within the social sciences. However, as Searle (1999: 41) notes, these are 'rooted in a realist view of a single external reality knowable through language'. Without the commonsensical realist notion of a single stable reality, as governed by predictable processes which operate regardless of whether we are personally around or not, we enter into a relativistic postmodern world of partial truth and inherent uncertainty and unpredictability.

We are in much the same social constructivist territory here that we entered when we explored narrative analysis in Chapter 5. Some researchers of a strong anti-realist bent reject outright the ability of social science research to capture truths about the nature of social reality, not least of all because they may refuse to privilege academic research over other forms of inquiry and shared understanding. Other researchers are in favour of adopting a more pragmatic 'critical realist' approach when seeking to navigate the social constructivist terrain (Wetherell et al. 2001b). Here we must recognise we can't obtain a definitive and objective account of criminological life and acknowledge that different and even contradictory accounts can sit alongside each other and be accorded equal legitimacy. But at the same time we also need to bear in mind that while all accounts of criminological life are partial, some nevertheless reveal the truth of events more than others, particularly when the research process is well conducted and involves listening to the voices of the disempowered, the silenced and socially excluded. However, we must accept and even celebrate the role played by a researcher in co-producing the resultant account of their topic – the concept of reflexivity, which was discussed in Chapter 3, is foundational to narrative and discursive forms of analysis.

The value of social constructivism arguably lies in how it frees the researcher to speak of the research process as a complex *lived* experience, rather than offering the traditional sanitised version of it. Just as the real world is messy, chaotic, serendipitous and full of conflicting information, opinions and experiences, so too is the process of *doing* criminological research. Hence accounts of criminological life should be viewed as creative endeavours which involve the researcher and their research participants co-creating a coherent shared story about some aspect of the world they happen to share an interest in. Yet, the process of collecting, analysing and communicating such shared stories to others – be it in the form of a written report, a verbal presentation, a piece of poetry, or even as a short dramatic play – necessarily involves a process of selection, editing and the general bringing-together of a diverse and often disjointed range of materials in such a manner that they coalesce into a coherent narrative whole. Even when they seek to present the words of others without offering their own interpretation, a researcher is implicated in the research process through the manner in which they provide a structural framework to enable others to make their voices heard and the reader to access their stories.

In the final analysis, it is difficult to shake off the argument that the research report presented by a researcher does not in fact enable us to directly access the experiences and viewpoints of research participants, and indeed, only offers one possible interpretation of events – namely, the one belonging to the researcher. Furthermore, the role of the academic community must not be ignored, for they too are implicated in the research process via the influence they exert in the form of 'the literature' conversation surrounding a topic. What this means in practice is that accounts of criminal life are partial and situated truths which are creatively constructed by a researcher in lieu of their personal interpretation of what their research respondents tell them as well as what the broader academic community they belong to is saying about their topic. The picture becomes even more complicated when policy-makers, the media and general public are also considered as possible research stakeholders and dissemination audiences – particularly as they may possess oppositional experiences and viewpoints concerning the topic under investigation.

Given the considerations just outlined, some narrative and discursively minded researchers, such as Riessman (1993), have offered different criteria to use to evaluate research instead of the more traditional concerns with validity and reliability: namely, 'persuasiveness', 'correspondence', 'coherence' and 'pragmatic use'. Here research accounts are judged on their ability to provide a coherent and persuasive account of a topic, with pragmatic use referring to its ability to stimulate both old and new research avenues for other researchers, so recognising the role of the academic and policy-making communities in influencing a researcher's thinking about their topic. The notion of correspondence reinforces the need to engage in a process of respondent validation of the resulting research account through seeking feedback from research participants to verify that it captures their lived experiences and world views. One can imagine here a researcher moving backwards and forwards between their own and their research respondents' interpretations of their findings, to ensure respondents feel their voices have been recognised and fully heard, as well as to add new analytical insights learned as a result of the respondent validation process – before a final project report is made ready for publication. Furthermore, respondent validation is arguably central to the conduct of criminological discourse analysis, given its propensity to emphasise obtaining narratives with the goal of bringing to the foreground the voices of socially excluded, stigmatised, unheard and disempowered groups. As van Dijk (1996: 84) argues, discourse analysis 'should describe and explain how power abuse is enacted, reproduced or legitimated by the talk and text of dominant groups and institutions'.

Certainly, from a criminological perspective, discourse analysis reinforces the importance of exploring how some ways of talking about crime are more stable and privileged than others. The motivation for undertaking discourse analysis often comes from a researcher's personal concern with social inequality and a concurrent recognition that the language of the criminal justice and legal systems institutionalise the domination of the individual and frequently enforce a limited, punitive, exclusive and non-pluralistic view of individuals accused of deviance or criminality, and in some circumstances, this state of affairs holds true for victims of crime as well (Carlen 2010). Discourse analysts can find themselves working closely alongside vulnerable groups, including victims of domestic violence, childhood sexual abuse, miscarriages of justice or racially motivated hate crime. Of course, not all discursive research involves working with such topics, or requires a researcher to become proactively involved within social movements pursuing political reform objectives, such as the victims' rights movement or the prison abolitionist movement. Such involvement is certainly not a prerequisite for engaging in discourse analysis, and the nature and level of any researcher engagement in more ethically and politically sensitive research can and does vary considerably.

There are no hard and fast rules to guide the novice researcher who finds themselves involved with such research topics. That is, aside from the need to maintain an awareness of the politicised nature of their topic as well as to make sure they adhere to ethical guidelines relating to the need to ensure informed consent is sought and gained from potential research participants, before they are included in a research study. Each researcher, under guidance of their supervisor, must decide for themselves how to go about pursuing a topic and address any pertinent ethical and political issues involved. This said, the further readings in Box 6.3 should help novice researchers explore in greater detail the issues discussed in this section of the chapter.

Box 6.3

Designing a discourse analysis study: recommended readings

There are several key issues to consider at the research design stage of a discourse analysis study. It is important to ensure that you are asking a research question for which a discursive approach to data analysis is appropriate. The strong anti-realist underpinnings to discourse analysis mean the concepts of validity, reliability and generalisation need to be carefully thought through and justified, as these research design and quality control tools are arguably inappropriate for this approach: what alternative criteria should you apply, why, and how will you justify your choice? The tendency for discourse analysis to examine how language use is structured by hierarchical power relations, as based around broader social inequalities relating to class, gender, race and so on, means that sometimes political-interest and ethical-practice considerations need to be accounted for by a researcher at the research design, data collection and analytical stages of a project. The following recommended readings provide further guidance on the design of discourse analysis research within the social sciences.

(Continued)

(Continued)

Recommended reading

Carlen, P. (2010) *A Criminological Imagination: Essays on Justice, Punishment and Discourse*. London: Ashgate Publishing.

Jaworsk, A. and Coupland, N. (eds) (1999) *The Discourse Reader*. London: Routledge.

Philips, N. and Hardy, C. (2002) *Discourse Analysis: Investigating Processes of Social Construction*. London: Sage Publications.

van Dijk, T. (1993) Principles of critical discourse analysis, *Discourse and Society*, 4: 249–83.

van Dijk, T. (2008) *Discourse and Power: Contributions to Critical Discourse Studies*. Houndsmills: Palgrave Macmillan.

Weiss, G. and Wodak, R. (eds) (2001) *Critical Discourse Analysis: Theory and Interdisciplinarity*. London: Palgrave Macmillan.

Wetherell, M., Taylor, S. and Yates, S.J.E. (eds) (2001a) *Discourse as Data: A Guide for Analysis*. London: Sage Publications.

Wetherell, M., Taylor, S. and Yates, S.J.E. (eds) (2001b) *Discourse Theory and Practice: A Reader*. London: Sage Publications.

Doing a Discourse Analysis

It is important to begin our discussion of how to undertake a discourse analysis as we did when we outlined grounded theory and narrative forms of analysis, by acknowledging that it is a craft skill developed by each individual researcher over time through the act of engaging with research data and *doing* analysis. Unlike the statistical techniques associated with quantitative forms of data analysis, qualitative forms of data analysis do not follow an agreed, set, analytical protocol. Of course, this does not mean that a novice researcher shouldn't seek guidance from their supervisor, relevant textbooks and/or published discourse analysis studies, to gain tips and insights into how to apply a discursive approach in their own research. But it does mean it is important to bear in mind that there are no set procedures for doing a discourse analysis which can be applied in a step-by-step fashion to obtain a given end result. Furthermore, the diversity of different discursive analytical approaches available across the social science disciplines further complicates matters and if a researcher is not careful they can quickly feel overwhelmed by the diversity of guidance available. Potter (2004: 611) sums up the situation well when he says that:

> There is no single recipe for doing discourse analysis. Different kinds of studies involve different procedures, sometimes working intensively with a single transcript, other times drawing on a large corpus. Analysis is a craft that can be developed with different degrees of skill. It can be thought of as the development of a sensitivity to the occasioned and action-oriented, situated and constructed nature of discourse. Nevertheless, there are a number of ingredients which, when combined together, are likely to produce something satisfying.

In this section of the chapter we will look at two key ingredients – namely, interpretive repertoires and subject positions – that when applied as analytical orienting tools for textual analysis can be highly useful in helping a researcher deconstruct how a research topic under investigation is constructed by the social actors involved, by drawing on particular discursive resources which set up a variety of subject positions and social identities for the speaker, while at the same time closing off, marginalising or silencing others. Here, as we shall see, it is important to bear in mind what Potter (2004) says about developing one's sensitivity to the action-oriented, situated and constructed nature of discourse, while at a practical level it is equally important to recognise that, as with all forms of qualitative research, discourse analysis requires a mixture of tenacity, time and patience. Discursive data analysis cannot be completed after reading a text a couple of times. One must be prepared to inductively 'work up' one's analysis from intensively reading and re-reading discursive data over a prolonged period of time. There are no easy options and quick fixes when it comes to engaging in qualitative research. Nevertheless, the guidance in this chapter should make the experience of doing a discourse analysis easier for the first-time novice researcher who feels their research is best suited to this approach.

Interpretive repertoires

When beginning a discourse analysis it is important to remember that the key analytical concern is to examine the discursive resources people draw on, how these came to be culturally available to use, as well as what kinds of subject positions and associated social identities they make available and at the same time close off, deny or otherwise silence. The origins of the concept of interpretive repertoires of reinforces the value of adopting this analytical approach when a researcher is exploring how people talk about a topic, an event, an activity or a person, particularly when they are trying to explain or justify an opinion or point of view. The concept of interpretive repertoires first appeared in the work of two sociologists, Gilbert and Mulkay (1984), who were examining the way scientists work together as part of a community of practitioners to advance human knowledge and understanding of a scientific problem. In particular, they examined an area of biochemistry concerned with the ways energy is stored in cell structures to explore how scientists involved in this research area understand and present their work in different contexts. They collected together a broad range of discursive materials, including journal articles, laboratory reports, newspaper pieces, scientist-to-scientist correspondence, as well as perhaps most importantly, interviews with 34 key experts belonging to the field of study known as oxidative phosphorylation.

When Gilbert and Mulkay examined their textual data they identified that there wasn't a single common definition of how scientific work progressed; rather, there seemed to be two distinctive ways of talking about scientific activity. They termed these ways of talking 'interpretive repertoires'. The first way of talking about the conduct of research was frequently found in scientific articles and research papers. Here the scientific endeavour was discussed in the form of an experimental research methodology whose procedures were described as being conducted in an objective, value-neutral manner. Hence, they could be replicated by other scientists. The second way of talking about the conduct of research, which tended to dominate the more informal face-to-face interviews completed by Gilbert and Mulkay for their study, emphasised the creative and personal nature of the scientific process and the need for researchers to gain experience and master the practical skills of experimental design through 'getting the feel' for research design and data analysis. Gilbert and Mulkay argued that the first, formal, way of talking about the scientific process formed what they termed an *empiricist interpretive repertoire*. Gilbert and Mulkay observed that 'the texts of experimental papers display certain recurrent stylistic, grammatical and lexical features which appear to be coherently related' (1984: 55–6). These, they argued, possessed an impersonal writing style and distanced the identity and person of the author – the research scientist – from the research process to reinforce its objective nature. In contrast to this, the second way of talking about the scientific process was termed a *contingent interpretive repertoire*. Here scientists 'presented their actions and beliefs as heavily dependent on speculative insights, prior intellectual commitments, personal characteristics, indescribable skills, social ties, and group memberships' (Gilbert and Mulkay 1984: 56). Importantly, Gilbert and Mulkay identified that research participants could alternate between each repertoire, adopting different discursive positions depending on the context in which they were talking and to what end. So when a scientist talked about their own research they emphasised the empiricist repertoire, while when they talked about the research of other scientists, particularly those they were in competition with, they emphasised the contingent repertoire, to reinforce the prejudices, biases and experimental problems with their work. Gilbert and Mulkay argued that their study revealed how social scientists were mistaken to hold that they could use techniques such as interviews to access an accurate and stable picture of the social world as perceived through the eyes of their informants. Rather, the contextual variability present in their research participants' accounts of how scientific work is undertaken reinforced that people use language in social situations as a positioning device to provide accounts of beliefs and actions and portray themselves and others in certain ways. This recognition led to the increasing focus within the social sciences, but within sociology and social psychology in particular, on making the interview situation itself – specifically, the social interaction between the interviewer and interviewee – the focus of inquiry. That is, the analytical focus became the language used by the interviewee when 'in-conversation' with an interviewer, instead of using the interview situation in the more traditional manner as a tool to gain access to what an interviewee thinks about a topic, or what their behaviour is, or why they believe what they do, or choose to act in such a way.

The work of Gilbert and Mulkay reinforces that language is a tool people use to achieve certain ends, including, most importantly, getting an argument across, attributing blame and presenting oneself in a particular way. The use of language in this manner is context dependent. So just like the scientists in Gilbert and Mulkay's study, the reasons why you say something – e.g. why you applied to attend a particular university and study a particular course there – will vary depending on who you are talking to and in what situation – i.e. to a university admissions officer during an entry interview, to your parents over dinner as you weigh up your options, or to your friends when chatting over a beer in the pub on a Friday night. This is why discourse analysts pay close attention to the rhetorical nature of discourse and how it is used by people in particular situations to establish one version of the world in the face of competing alternative versions.

The concept of interpretive repertoire was further developed by the social psychologists Potter and Wetherell (1987), who following Gilbert and Mulkay defined them as 'recurrently used systems of terms used for characterising and evaluating actions, events and other phenomena often characterised by certain metaphors or figures of speech' (1987: 149). For Potter and Wetherell interpretive repertoires are identifiable in the form of common words and turns of phrase which are used by people when they are trying to achieve something when speaking. Hence, the analytical focus is on identifying relatively coherent ways of talking about a topic which can be used as a resource by a speaker during everyday social interaction. What is more, interpretive repertoires are held to be communally shared and so are part and parcel of the metaphors, cultural idioms and 'folk ways' of a society, a social organisation, a public institution, a neighbourhood, or a group of people who share something in common. They are shared social tools and not the personal inventions of particular individuals.

Think here for a moment about how 'in-group' ways of expressing oneself are often based around the use of 'in-house' slang that provides culturally familiar and habitual lines of argument composed of recognisable themes and narrative imagery, which capture shared points of view and ways of understanding within a group, while at the same time serving to separate its members somewhat from 'outsiders'. Edley (2001: 198) puts is succinctly when he says that:

> interpretive repertoires are part and parcel of any community's common sense, providing a basis for shared social understanding. They can be usefully thought of as books on the shelves of a public library; permanently available for borrowing. Indeed, this metaphor captures nicely the point ... that when people talk (or think) about things, they invariable do so in terms already provided for them by history. Much of it is a rehearsal or recital. This is not to say, of course, that there can never be such a thing as an original or novel conversation. Indeed, there is often no telling how conversations will turn out. What it does mean, however, is that conversations are usually made up of a patchwork of 'quotations' from various interpretive repertoires. Or, in terms of a quite different metaphor, interpretive repertoires are like the pre-figured steps that can be flexibly and creatively strung together in the improvisation of dance.

The focus by Edley here on the 'historical' and 'patchworked' nature of interpretive repertoires brings us to a central issue for discourse analysis, namely, the extent to which discourse seeks to determine and subjectify individuals by acting to curtail or shape their agency. Foucauldian forms of discursive analysis emphasise how language constructs social institutions (e.g. the criminal justice system), specialist forms of expertise (e.g. lawyers and other professionals who work in the criminal justice system) and individuals (e.g. criminals and victims) through the hierarchal and ideological operation of 'discourse statements' which seek to position people in certain ways as particular social subjects to better enable surveillance and social control. We discussed in Chapter 5 how discursive statements act to constrain human agency through 'scripting' narrative accounts of lived experience. The Foucauldian analysis of discourse holds that they act to position social actors to enable surveillance and control. That is, different discourses (i.e. the medical, the psychiatric, the legal and so on) position individuals in different ways and in doing so enable political and cultural elites to survey and control populations through making them knowable and governable. The analytical focus is on examining how discursive statements as things said privilege particular ways of seeing and codifying certain social action over others. The concept of interpretive repertoires shares much in common with this Foucauldian approach to discourse. Both view language as constitutive of social reality and hold that after human beings are born one of the first things they do is become indoctrinated into particular ways of understanding the world around them through learning the 'local language' from parents, immediate members of family and other nurturing caregivers. However, arguably the value of the concept of interpretive repertoires lies in that it tends to seek to avoid an overly deterministic view of the relationship between discourse and human agency (Potter and Wetherell 1995; Potter 2004). Instead, the flexible nature of discourse is emphasised: language is viewed as a tool that can be used to both constrain and free human thought and action.

People are held to possess a creative ability to rhetorically draw on different interpretive repertoires as they seek to achieve something within a social interaction. In part, this is because interpretive repertoires are fragmented and are often used flexibly by people when they talk. So they are unlikely to leap off the page fully grown into the lap of the discursive researcher. The researcher must be patient and meticulous in their search for reoccurring images, figures of speech and metaphors when different people talk about a topic, an event, a thing, people and actions (Edley 2001). Nevertheless, in the final analysis the ability of discourse to shape and constrain human agency cannot be ignored. A key interest for discourse analysts is how interpretive repertoires act to shape human agency through fashioning a patchwork of subject positions and social identities for individuals to call on, as needed, within social situations, as well as how in so doing they rhetorically close off, deny or otherwise silence alternative points of view. Remember here that in discourse analysis, language is held to be constitutive of social reality. This implies that the discourse analyst − whether they are adopting a Foucauldian or an interpretive repertoire approach − has accepted that there *are* limits to the extent an individual can creatively resist the power of discursive frameworks to define them.

A key difference between the Foucauldian and the interpretive repertoire approaches is the extent to which they respectively emphasise the possibility of resistance: the latter tends to allow more room to manoeuvre in this regard than the former. Box 6.4 contains guidance on analysing textual data for interpretive repertoires. An important feature of the analytical process is the identification of the subject position of the speaker, as implied by the identity work involved when a particular interpretive repertoire is adopted. We shall look at subject positions in more detail before moving on to explore an example of a discourse analysis which looks at the identity work involved in the adoption of certain subject positions through the utilisation of two contrasting forms of interpretive repertoire in Box 6.5.

Box 6.4

Interpretive repertoires

Interpretive repertoires can be defined as being 'broadly discernible clusters of terms, descriptions, and figures of speech often assembled around metaphors and vivid images' (Potter and Wetherell 1995: 89). So, for example, when the media and politicians discuss terrorism they often write and talk about it using the language of war and battle: 'the war on terror', 'the enemy within', 'the theatre of war', 'the potential threat', 'needless slaughter', and so on. In purely linguistic terms we can think of interpretive repertoires as coherent ways of talking about objectives and events in the world; however, they are more accurately viewed as a shared social resource which is used by people who hold in common a language and culture. They are commonplace sets of taken-for-granted knowledge and so are bound

(Continued)

(Continued)

up with a community's commonsense ways of reasoning. Hence Burr (1995: 117) describes them as a 'tool-kit of resources for people to use for their purposes, representing a consistency that is not available at the level of the individual speaker'. This reinforces that it is important not to view interpretive repertoires as the creations of individual social actors. Rather, they are social products which are culturally and historically located in a particular time and place (Edley 2001). An important feature of interpretive repertoires is that they can be used in contrasting ways in different contexts: the discourse analyst must not expect their research participants to always use a particular interpretive repertoire. Repertoires are used creatively by people in different ways in different situations to achieve different ends. Speakers often seek to rhetorically use an interpretive repertoire to establish a particular version of events as being more objective and true than competing versions. This reinforces their utility as rhetorical and ideological tools for legitimising or discrediting social, cultural and political practices. Consequently, an important analytical concern for discourse analysts is the effects of a particular interpretive repertoire when it is used in a particular situation: whose voice and point of view is being promoted and whose is being contradicted, ignored or silenced? This links to the concern with 'replacement discourses' discussed earlier in the chapter when the development of postmodern forms of criminological analysis was considered.

The identification of an interpretive repertoire is very much a craft skill, even more so than with grounded theory and narrative forms of analysis. Unlike with grounded theory analysis and some forms of narrative analysis, there are no set, agreed analytical procedures and data-coding frameworks to guide the novice discursive researcher. Indeed, many discourse analysts would refuse point blank to accept that it is possible to provide guidance because they would argue that providing prescriptive methodological and analytical guidance smacks of positivism and underplays the central role of the researcher within the research process. However, it is possible to delineate some basic analytical principles. It is particularly important to develop one's sensitivity to the action-oriented, situated and constructed nature of discourse (Potter, 2004). In other words, the focus is on what people are trying to achieve when they use language in particular ways in particular situations. Depending on their topic a discourse analyst will collect together their discursive materials in the form of research interviews, recordings of everyday social interactions, personal biographic documents, alongside more public documents such as newspaper articles, medical files, social policy legislative records and political pamphlets. In this regard discourse analysis forms part of the narrative turn within criminology and the social sciences more generally, as already discussed in Chapter 5. The beginning of data analysis involves developing one's familiarity with one's data. This means undertaking an intensive line-by-line reading of it – focusing on reoccurring expressions, thematic patterns of speech, imagery, metaphors and rhetorical stances. The aim is to gain insight into the ways accounts are organised through the use of certain sets of descriptive practices which construct and justify a particular way of looking at events, objects, people and behaviours, in contrast to other possible ways of viewing them. Sometimes these alternative ways of seeing will be directly referred to and criticised, other times they are implied or left unsaid. This is where the skill and craft of doing a discourse analysis comes in. I often find it helpful here to focus on not just the content of the discourse but also its author and who they are (e.g. a teacher, a housewife, a member of a girl gang, a sex offender), the grounds on which they say what they do (e.g. their justification for what they say, as related to who they are, who their audience is and what the topic of conversation is), about whom or what are they saying it (e.g. their pupil, their husband, another gang member, or a victim of child abuse), and their objective in saying it (e.g. to justify a grade, to make the point they feel they aren't listened to by their partner, to explain why they carry a knife, or to blame their victim in some way for their actions). This analytical focus on the rhetorical and persuasive use of language for a purpose is reiterated by Potter (2004: 608) who argues that the discursive researcher should focus on answering the following basic discourse-analytic questions when examining their data:

- What is this discourse doing?
- How is this discourse constructed to make this happen?
- What resources are available to perform this activity?

These questions reinforce the active nature of language and how the speaker constructs the elements of what they say using different linguistic resources in the form of visual references, figures of speech and metaphors to achieve certain effects. When taken together these questions point the researcher towards the identification of the interpretive repertoires at work within the discourse they are examining. Potter (2004) advises the researcher to focus on variation in accounts – different descriptions of objects and events, choices of words and stylistic variations – and to use these as an 'analytic lever' for examining discourse. He highlights the importance of paying close attention to the detail of what is said, the rhetoric at work in the organisation of arguments and the undermining of alternative positions, as well as the sense of personal accountability offered when there is a concern with justifying the rational, ethical and sensible nature of a position. He also notes the need to pay close attention to the personal stake and interest a person possesses in what they say, not least of all because this often reveals how people view themselves and so what their sense of personal identity is. This, in turn, reinforces the importance of paying attention to who and what type of person – the subject position – is implied by an interpretive repertoire. The further readings and short example of an analysis below should help you get a clearer idea of how to apply this approach in your own research.

Are criminals born or made?
An interpretive repertoire analysis

Imagine that you are interested in how people talk about criminality and those who commit crime: you are interested in identifying the interpretive repertoires

(Continued)

(Continued)

people employ when they talk about the reasons why people commit crime. So you set up a project whereby you create an online webpage that contains a news article summarising a recent criminological research study which purports to have established a statistically significant association between behavioural difficulties, an affinity for juvenile delinquency and a particular variation of the dopamine transporter gene (NB: this is an imaginary study but there has been some fruitful research into genetic markers and aggressive behaviour in recent years). The news article summary you create concludes with the question, 'So, are criminals born or made?' It then invites readers to answer this question in light of what they have read. The following four short extracts typify the kinds of response you obtain:

Extract response 1

This is just another excuse for people to blame anybody else but themselves for their actions. What about personal choice and responsibility? Genes don't determine who we are, just like our upbringing doesn't determine who we are. No matter what the bleeding heart liberals like to think, it's about some people choosing to act a certain way because they don't care about others, not because they had hard childhoods, or whatever else excuse they come up with. I grew up in a deprived area without much and I turned out OK; lots of my friends did too. The ones who didn't, chose to act the way they did. You always have a choice no matter what your circumstances, and I'd like to see people take on more, not less, responsibility for their actions.

Extract response 2

Criminals are made, not born. Society plays a key role in making us who we are. When the nurturing and growing needs of a child aren't met to help them grow up properly, then that's when problems start, and I think it's amazing how parents in particular seem to just abdicate responsibility for their kids these days. Children have it hard enough growing up these days as it is, without Mum and Dad adding to the problem by not showing them how to behave. If you have no sense of stability and belonging at home and grow up in a deprived area and perhaps don't do too well at school or aren't motivated to learn, which let's face it, really limits your options, then it's not surprising that you start acting up. We all know that if you fall in with the wrong people then minor things like standing on street corners and drinking and smoking can quickly progress to joining gangs and getting involved in drugs and stuff. So I think it's things like poor family relationships and other social and economic factors like deprivation and poverty that lead into criminal activities, not genetics.

Extract response 3

I'm not sure it's down to genetics. I know the scientists will say that some genes seem to be linked to aggression, which I think may well be true, but I think we need to remember when it comes to human beings, what is most important is how you are brought up. Aggressive instincts in humans can be controlled. I mean, I have a bad temper but I don't go around showing it all the time: I choose to control it. Children need to be brought up properly by parents who know right from wrong and are prepared to discipline them properly. Too many people these days bring up children who have no idea how to behave, no respect for anything or anyone, and above all, no fear of doing wrong. But you also can't just blame the parents. It's also about the choices you make as a person. Part of being an adult is being grown up enough to not blame everybody else for your problems. You have choices and you make them. And I don't buy into this idea that just because people live in a bad area they are more likely to behave badly.

Extract response 4

This is brilliant!!! I've finally got a scientific excuse to blame someone or something else, rather than take responsibility for my own actions, so I'm off now to rob the local shop. Bye!! Sorry for the sarcasm, but come on – how long will it be before people start talking about trying to eradicate this gene instead of looking at the real social problems that's behind most crime? Poverty and poor life chances have been linked time and time again to social problems like crime, mental health issues, drug and alcohol abuse and lowered life expectancy. The politicians and media barons who control how we see things and what the police do have a vested interest in keeping a social order and economic system designed to make sure the rich keep getting rich and the poorer stay where they are at the bottom of the social ladder. As long as we have this unequal society we have, you are going to have crime.

Discussion

From these few brief extracts we can clearly see that while some people may talk as if they accept that genetics can play a role in influencing human behaviour they nevertheless reject a genetically deterministic view of criminality. Indeed, two distinctive interpretive repertoires seem to be being used by research participants when they talk about why people break the law. On one hand emphasis is placed on personal responsibility, individual choice and free will (as epitomised by extract responses 1 and 3), while on the other hand, emphasis is placed on psychological or social factors which may be at play in influencing criminal behaviour, such as a person's upbringing, social circumstances or vested political interests for example (as epitomised by extract responses 2 and 4). With further analysis and data collection a researcher may well be able to subdivide the second repertoire into distinctive yet somewhat overlapping 'psychological', 'socio-economic', 'cultural' and 'vested interest' interpretive repertoires. We can also see common phrases and expressions emerging, such as 'bleeding heart liberals' and 'bad seeds' – which need further exploration and critical reflection. Nevertheless, the brief examples we do have reinforce that the image of 'the criminal type' portrayed by our two interpretive repertoires is quite layered and complex and they clearly

(Continued)

(Continued)

could be used in a variety of situations for a number of different purposes – from justifying a personal action (e.g. how one raises one's child) to advocating a social policy (e.g. the use of physical punishment as a deterrent for criminal behaviour). The extracts also reinforce how differences between repertoires are sometimes not clear-cut, and most importantly, how speakers can creatively 'mix and match' repertoires when making points. We can perhaps see this most clearly in extract response 3. Here the speaker draws on elements of both repertoires when making their points, using talk about social factors to rhetorically argue against a genetic viewpoint before switching to emphasising personal choice as the key factor influencing criminal behaviour. Importantly, we can also see that in talking about the topic in one way or another the various speakers position themselves in particular ways which rhetorically reinforce the limitations of what can be said about the 'self' and 'other'. So when personal choice and responsibility is talked about in relation to crime a certain type of image of *both* speaker and offender is portrayed and communicated to others; namely, that the speaker is a moral person who possesses a sense of personal responsibility while a criminal is a person who selfishly seeks their own benefit and could have chosen otherwise, but didn't (extract 1 epitomises this 'positioning' activity by the speaker). Such a portrayal enables a punitive position to be argued that an offender deserves to be punished as they have finally got what is coming to them. This reinforces the need to attend to the subject positions associated with an interpretive repertoire. Because people are positioned as certain types of individuals by repertoires, such constructions can be powerful rhetorical devices for making arguments which silence alternative viewpoints, and in doing so they could sustain economic and cultural inequalities based around key social categories such as race, gender, class and sexuality. The discursive researcher needs to be mindful of this as they conduct their analysis. The following recommended readings will help you further explore how to use interpretive repertoires as an 'analytical lever' in your own research, as will the practical example in Box 6.5.

Recommended reading

Edley, N. (2001) Analysing masculinity: interpretative repertoires, ideological dilemmas and subject positions. In M. Wetherell, S. Taylor and S.J.E. Yates (eds) *Discourse as Data: A Guide for Analysis*. London: Sage Publications.

Gilbert, N. and Mulkay, M. (1984) *Opening Pandora's Box: A Sociological Analysis of Scientists' Discourse*. Cambridge: Cambridge University Press.

Potter, J. (2004) Discourse analysis. In M. Hardy and A. Bryman (eds) *Handbook of Data Analysis*. London: Sage Publications.

Potter, J. and Wetherell, M. (1987) *Discourse and Social Psychology: Beyond Attitudes and Behaviour*. London: Sage Publications.

Potter, J. and Wetherell, M. (1995) Discourse analysis. In J. Smith, R. Harré and I. van Langenhove (eds) *Rethinking Methods in Psychology*. London: Sage Publications.

Subject positions and identity work

The concept of subject positions is bound up with the discursive analysis of interpretive repertoires. This is because emphasis is placed by discourse analysis on examining the representational practices at work in relation to the presentation of a version of oneself and other people within a social exchange through utilising different forms of talk and commonly held cultural meanings. We saw in Box 6.4 how individuals sought to position themselves and other people in particular ways when talking about the question of genetics and why people break the law. The concept of subject position is important as it is bound up with the postmodernist underpinnings to discourse analysis. On a day-to-day level we commonly think of ourselves as possessing a relatively stable sense of personal identity. Yet a key element of postmodernism is its rejection of the idea that people possess a single, stable, consistent and defined sense of self. The idea that people possess a stable and coherent sense of who they are, which is sometimes called 'possessive individualism', emerged in the seventeenth and eighteenth centuries, through the works of a variety of Enlightenment modernist writers, such as Thomas Hobbes, John Stuart Mill, Adam Smith, John Locke, Jeremy Bentham and Herbert Spencer (Macpherson 1962).

Yet the postmodernist argument goes further than saying that the notion of having a stable personal identity is wrong and instead people possess a fluid and fragmented sense of self. Rather, it is pointed out that our sense of self is linked to how others see us and the social roles we play out as a member of society, i.e. daughter, friend, employee, student and so on. Furthermore, it is argued that to a certain degree this notion of possessive individualism was bound up with the relatively stable socio-economic and cultural circumstances in which people lived up until the middle of the twentieth century. In other words, an individual's sense of self and personal identity is seen to be tightly bound up with their social identity which until relatively recently is held to have possessed distinctive and stable social norms based around class, gender, race and so on; e.g. a nineteenth-century farm labourer is held to possess a very different notion of who they are and what their position in the world is compared to an aristocratic lord of the time. Indeed, it is argued that over the latter part of the twentieth century, people became increasingly 'free from the social forms of industrial society – class, stratification, family [and] gender status' (Beck 1992: 87). Here, lives stopped being mapped out for people. Who a person is, and who she could possibly be, is no longer defined by her locality, her occupation, her gender, or even her religious affiliation. This does not mean that inequalities no longer exist; only that they can no longer be so easily attributed to the traditional sociological categories of class, race, age or gender. So a person's identity is fluid and negotiable, detached from traditional social structures and cultural mores; she is able to construct her life biography as she sees fit. She is in a very real sense the creative artist of her life. Postmodernism, as Williams (2000: 71–2) puts it:

invokes the contemporary presence and growth of new kinds of individuals without singular identities, or indeed any of the conventional attributes of stable subjectivities. Such individuals are portrayed as the product of their own autonomous actions chosen without regard to consistency, alignment with collectivities or attachment to moral values.

Of course, such arguments can be overstated; many people do align themselves with social groups, indeed it is arguable that most if not all human behaviour is social and collective, while most people would say they do possess shared moral values with other members of such groups, i.e. people in their friendship circle, members of their family, work colleagues and so on. While it is also clear that although some progress has been made over the last half century, social inequalities do still exist and many individuals are still limited and defined by their social circumstances and traditional social categories such as gender, class and race. Indeed, criminological discursive analysis is often engaged in highlighting how such categories continue to shape the ways crime is perceived and responded to. Nevertheless, the important point to bear in mind here is the need to accept the truism that 'rather than having one fixed version of who we are, we all move between multiple identities' (Silverman 2007: 1–2), because this brings to the foreground that people can and do shift between different versions of themselves as they talk with different people in different situations about a particular topic, event, person or behaviour. Social interaction is the location where people construct and negotiate accounts of themselves in interaction with others, and for the discourse analyst such accounts are held to be fluid and contingent rather than stable and everlasting. This is why people are not seen to possess interpretive repertoires in the same way they have been traditionally seen to hold an attitude or belief beyond a particular social interaction – e.g. an interview – by social scientists who adopt a more thematic 'chunking' approach to data analysis.

Subject positions are personal but nevertheless social identities made relevant by specific ways of talking (Edley 2001). Following Foucault, discourse can be said to position people in particular social categories such as gender, race and ethnicity, age, disability, mental health. For example, shared culturally gendered notions surrounding what it is to be male or female are internalised by individuals so they talk and act in particular gendered ways in social situations. Discourse offers us images, metaphors and ways of talking which we can become intellectually and emotionally committed to so we feel they are a natural and normal part of us and how we express ourselves as individuals. However, this should not be taken to mean that a person's sense of self and personal identity wholly flows from discourse: people are not wholly powerless to resist the flow of the discursive stream. They are creative beings and are both the products and producers of discourse. Indeed, the creative identity work at play in terms of how people use discourse in the form of interpretive repertoires as a resource to construct identities in social situations and achieve certain ends is an important element of doing discourse analysis. Hence when analysing social interaction – as it occurs in an interview situation or everyday social life – it is important to pay attention to how different subject positions are offered, accepted or resisted within discursive exchanges between people.

Yet it must be remembered that, as a socially shared resource, discourse is ultimately held to shape and direct individuals: language is constitutive of social reality and there are limits to the agency and creative freedom a person possesses. The social actor can only resist and swim against the discursive stream for so long. This is where consideration of power and social inequalities come to the foreground for discourse analysts. Box 6.5 contains an example of a research study, concerned with the topic of child abuse, which uses the concept of interpretive repertoires to explore the identity work involved in the discursive presentation of self to claim an identity when the idea is discussed that maltreated children are likely to become abusive parents.

Box 6.5

Interpretive repertoires, subject positions and identity work

Consideration of identity work and the subject positions implied by an interpretive repertoire is central to the analysis of discourse. An individual's sense of self and personal identity is often bound up with the words they use when they talk about a topic. In other words, they possess a stake in what they say and this stake must be claimed and justified in social exchanges with other people. It is important to recognise that the deployment of interpretive repertoires and the adoption of subject positions do not happen independently of the social situation in which they are employed. Indeed, they emerge and develop as part of an unfolding exchange between two or more social actors who may possess different positions, goals and viewpoints. Consequently a central feature of discursive analysis is the examination of how different subject positions are offered, accepted or resisted within discursive exchanges between two or more people. One example of the use of interpretive repertoires to explore the identity work involved in the discursive presentation of self to claim an identity (in this case 'the good parent') is the work of Croghan and Miell (1999) concerning child abuse.

Croghan and Miell begin by noting that victims of childhood sexual abuse suffer well-documented long-term effects, including self-harm, drug and/or alcohol abuse, suicide, behavioural problems and social isolation. They also note that an association is often made by the media and experts such as psychiatrists between childhood sexual abuse and later abuse – this is the so-called 'intergenerational hypothesis' or 'cycle of abuse' theory that maltreated children can become abusive parents. Croghan and Miell note that the intergenerational hypothesis has been criticised for focusing on psychological factors and the 'abnormal individual' rather than the cultural and socio-political factors relating to child abuse and the operation of power in the context of dominant gender relations within western societies. Yet they also recognise

(Continued)

(Continued)

that the general acceptance of the intergenerational hypothesis by social and political elites does mean that it is potentially a powerful tool for social surveillance and control; both formally via health and social care providers, and more informally via everyday social interaction. Croghan and Miell note that a person who identifies themself as having been a victim of childhood abuse in social interaction with other people adopts a discursively risky positioning move as it invites negative assumptions and inferences that are potentially highly damaging, including that the person in question may well be, at best, a poor parent, or at worst, a danger to their own and possibly other people's children. In other words by admitting they were abused themselves as children, individuals can put their parenting 'credentials' at risk: they may be discursively positioned as victims of a heinous crime but they are also positioned as *potentially* abusive parents themselves.

Croghan and Miell are concerned with the identity work involved when a person talks about childhood abuse, and they utilise the analytical concepts of interpretive repertoires and subject positions to discursively examine identity constructions in the wake of what they term the 'semi-deterministic' discourse of the intergenerational hypothesis. Croghan and Miell collected data using semi-structured interviews with 65 mothers who had been abused during childhood. Two interpretive repertoires were identified in the data relating to how victims of childhood abuse sought to discursively position themselves. The first is a '*repertoire of conscious assimilation*'. Here participants employ words, phrases and terms associated with socialisation and social learning to position themselves 'as assimilating a pattern outside the norm – that is, outside what is commonly defined as normal which becomes "their" norm, which means that they need to be "re-taught" since … their norms are not based in "reality" so that the abused have to "start again and invent being a parent" for themselves' (Croghan and Miell 1999: 319). Here then the interviewee is discursively positioning themselves as having learnt inappropriate behaviours which must be replaced with a correct normative framework to guide behaviour so they can learn how to be a good parent. The emphasis is on the conscious recognition of the need to 'break the cycle' and gaining expert help to 're-programme' oneself into appropriate behaviours. The implication here is that they weren't aware (at least at first) that the abuse was not normal behaviour. In contrast to this, in the second repertoire, '*repertoire of unconscious assimilation*' the interviewee was aware the abusive behaviour was inappropriate but there nevertheless is a recognition that they somehow may have assimilated certain behaviours and they therefore need to 'face the abuse' and talk about it to help break the cycle and stop themselves from 'repeating the pattern'.

This focus on the conscious rejection of abusive behaviour as unacceptable, but at the same time that somehow abusive behaviour has been assimilated and could be enacted via unconscious triggers in particular situations, means that 'escape from this tendency is not presented as simply a resolution not to abuse but as "effective therapy": that is, through the reliance on expert intervention in order to help the abused to gain access to their own experience' (Croghan and Miell 1999: 320).

Croghan and Miell go on to detail how both these interpretive repertoires carry with them the implication that an abused person's identity is damaged by childhood sexual experience, and that the identity work in operation during social interactions seeks to repair this through verbalising the need for expert help and discursively lay claim to an appropriate subject position whereby they are able to present themselves as 'able to avoid passing on abuse to their children' (1999: 329). Croghan and Miell provided detailed summaries of each repertoire as different forms and frequencies of childhood abuse are discussed; these cannot be reproduced here for reasons of space (discourse analysis studies are typically not amenable to summaries) but you may like to look at them to help guide your own research (see recommended reading below). Croghan and Miell's study provides an interesting and informative example of how individuals seek to discursively manage a damaged identity. Importantly, they note that individuals are discursively positioned by the intergenerational hypothesis surrounding child abuse, and they must creatively resist this positioning if they are to lay claim to the identity of 'good parent'. This brings to the foreground that

> those positioned in this way incurred the risk of the failure to establish common ground between account maker and audience, and of failing to establish maternal credibility. This was likely to have grave consequences for women so positioning, particularly in terms of their relationship with welfare professionals engaged in the assessment of the risk they presented to their child.

> (Croghan and Miell 1999: 332)

It is important to recognise the power of discourse to enable the surveillance, categorisation and social control of individuals by experts and state-endorsed agents, particularly if individuals do not have the necessary discursive resources available to appropriately articulate and lay claim to a culturally acceptable identity. Individuals accused of deviance and crime arguably possess spoiled and damaged identities; and a key element of doing a criminological discourse analysis can be said to involve the examination of the types of discursive positioning employed by institutions of social control, such as the police or courts, as well as how such positioning is responded to and resisted (or not) by offenders in and through the forms of identity work associated with the particular interpretive repertoires they employ in a range of social situations – not least of all because this reflects a broader disciplinary concern with social justice and humane social policy.

Recommended reading

Croghan, R. and Miell, D. (1999) Born to abuse? Negotiating identity within an interpretative repertoire of impairment, *British Journal of Social Psychology*, 38: 315–35.

Wetherell, M. (1998) Positioning and interpretative repertoires: conversation analysis and post-structuralism in dialogue, *Discourse and Society*, 9: 387–99.

Criticisms of Discourse Analysis

Discourse analysis is an important addition to the criminological analytical toolbox. It enables a researcher to deconstruct the role of language and power in the construction of crime-speak. But the lack of clear analytical procedures for doing a discourse analysis – unlike the shift from open to axial and selective coding with grounded theory analysis, for example – is held to be problematic by some researchers. Yet for others it opens up the opportunity to place the researcher at the centre of the analytical stage and to celebrate the co-produced nature of accounts of criminal life. Discourse analysis has also been subject to criticism for its emphasis on anti-realism and rejection of a theory-building approach to criminological research. Indeed, postmodernism in general has been heavily criticised for its extreme anti-realist relativist stance and apparent inability to 'develop progressive ideas and policies that can change the social world for the better' (Tierney 2006: 322).

To some extent I feel such arguments are overstated and involve a lot of unnecessary academic posturing. Most criminologists, postmodernist or otherwise, would agree that criminological deconstructions of crime-speak, like all forms of academic analysis, should try to impact positively in the world and serve to somehow help minimise the very real risks, dangers, harms, pains and sufferings which exist within it. The fact of the matter is that, as we discussed when we examined narrative analysis in Chapter 5, the broader academic community, in the form of the literature review undertaken around a research topic, plays an essential role in shaping our research endeavours. When done well the grounding of one's research project within the literature surrounding a topic can do much to bolster the analytical process and increase the relevance of the research findings presented beyond the immediate context in which they were generated. Recognising this does not imply that a researcher prefers a hypothesis testing approach to research design. Or that they can somehow obtain privileged access to a definitive account of criminological life. Rather the concern here is with acknowledging the inherent value of participating within the broader academic conversation that surrounds a research topic under investigation, that is, if we are to address social problems and influence policy development. This reinforces the need to carefully balance the anti-realist social constructivist foundations of discourse analysis with a broader commitment to pursuing social change and justice. The practical and ethical implications of this balancing act must be carefully thought through at all stages of a discursive project. The further readings provided in this chapter will help you reflect on this issue as you pursue your own research.

Conclusion

This chapter has provided an introduction to discourse analysis. It has focused on how criminologists analyse discourse to examine the ways in which some forms of crime-speak are privileged more than others. Discursive analysis is often conducted as a result of a concern with social inequality and a concurrent recognition that the language of the criminal justice and legal systems institutionalises the domination of the individual and frequently enforces a limited, punitive, exclusive and non-pluralistic view of individuals accused of deviance and criminality. This brings to the foreground the idea that different forms of discourse surrounding crime and criminality make people more amenable to social categorisation and administrative control by criminal justice agencies and the legal system, and it is the purpose of discourse analysis to deconstruct such processes. The chapter discussed the work of Gilbert and Mulkay (1984) and how the analytical concepts of interpretive repertoires and subject positions can be used to discursively examine the identity work involved in constructing people in different ways. If you are thinking about using this approach in your own research you should consult the illustrative examples, further readings and exercises that have been provided in the chapter to help you apply discourse analysis for your own purposes.

CHAPTER REVIEW ACTIVITIES

1 The development of discourse analysis is bound up with the emergence of post-modernism and the linguistic turn within the social sciences. Of particular concern for discursive criminologists is the identification of how particular ways of talking about crime can exclude or silence individuals and groups. Write a 750-word essay reflecting on the political and ethical factors which may arise from undertaking discursive research to identify 'replacement discourses' with social groups who are struggling to make sure their voices are heard.

2 'Traditional research design and quality assurance measures such as validity, reliability and generalisation are inappropriate for discourse analysis.' Critically evaluate this statement in no more than 1000 words.

3 Conduct a short interview (10–20 minutes) with one male and one female friend, asking them to talk about why they think men commit more crime than women. Analyse the verbal exchange between your interviewees, looking for interpretive repertoires and associated forms of identity work. What does completing this process tell you about how discourse can shape the ways people talk about crime in relation to gender while at the same time being used creatively by individuals in social situations to construct a sense of self and personal identity in relation to a topic under discussion?

CHAPTER READING LIST

Agar, M. and Hobbs, J.R. (1982) Interpreting discourse: coherence and the analysis of ethnographic interviews, *Discourse Processes*, 5: 1–32.

Arrigo, B.A. (2003) Postmodern justice and critical criminology: positional, relational and provisional justice. In M.D. Schwartz and S.E. Hatty (eds) *Controversies in Critical Criminology*. Cincinnati, OH: Anderson Publishing.

Beck, U. (1992) *Risk Society: Towards a New Modernity*. London: Sage Publications.

Burr, V. (1995) *An Introduction to Social Constructivism*. London: Routledge.

Butler, C. (2002) *Postmodernism: A Very Short Introduction*. Oxford: Oxford Paperbacks.

Carlen, P. (2010) *A Criminological Imagination: Essays on Justice, Punishment and Discourse*. London: Ashgate Publishing.

Croghan, R. and Miell, D. (1999) Born to abuse? Negotiating identity within an interpretative repertoire of impairment, *British Journal of Social Psychology*, 38: 315–35.

Denzin, N.K. and Lincoln, Y.S. (2011) *The Sage Handbook of Qualitative Research*. Thousand Oaks, CA: Sage Publications.

Edley, N. (2001) Analysing masculinity: interpretative repertoires, ideological dilemmas and subject positions. In M. Wetherell, S. Taylor and S.J.E. Yates (eds) *Discourse as Data: A Guide for Analysis*. London: Sage Publications.

Fairclough, N. and Wodak, R. (1997) Critical discourse analysis. In T. van Dijk (ed.) *Discourse Studies: A Multidisciplinary Introduction, Volume 2*. London: Sage Publications.

Ferrell, J., Hayward, K. and Young, J. (2008) *Cultural Criminology: An Invitation*. London: Sage Publications.

Foucault, M. (1972) *The Archaeology of Knowledge*. New York: Pantheon Books.

Gilbert, N. and Mulkay, M. (1984) *Opening Pandora's Box: A Sociological Analysis of Scientists' Discourse*. Cambridge: Cambridge University Press.

Henry, S. and Milovanovic, D. (1993) Back to basics: a postmodern redefinition of crime, *The Critical Criminologist*, 5: 12.

Henry, S. and Milovanovic, D. (1999) *Constitutive Criminology at Work: Applications to Crime and Justice*. New York: State University of New York Press.

Henry, S. and Milovanovic, D. (2003) Constitutive criminology. In M.D. Schwartz and S.E. Hatty (eds) *Controversies in Critical Criminology*. Cincinnati, OH: Anderson Publishing.

Jaworsk, A. and Coupland, N. (eds) (1999) *The Discourse Reader*. London: Routledge.

Keenoy, T., Oswick, C. and Grant, D. (1997) Organizational discourses: text and Context, *Organization*, 2: 147–58.

Lea, J. (1998) Criminology and postmodernity. In P. Walton and J. Young (eds) *The New Criminology Revisited*. Basingstoke: Macmillan.

Macpherson, A. (1962) *The Political Theory of Possessive Individualism*. Oxford: Clarendon Press.

Philips, N. and Hardy, C. (2002) *Discourse Analysis: Investigating Processes of Social Construction*. London: Sage Publications.

Potter, J. (2004) Discourse analysis. In M. Hardy and A. Bryman (eds) *Handbook of Data Analysis*. London: Sage Publications.

Potter, J. and Wetherell, M. (1987) *Discourse and Social Psychology: Beyond Attitudes and Behaviour*. London: Sage Publications.

Potter, J. and Wetherell, M. (1995) Discourse analysis. In J. Smith, R. Harré and I. van Langenhove (eds) *Rethinking Methods in Psychology*. London: Sage publications.

Riessman, C.K. (1993) *Narrative Analysis*. London: Sage Publications.

Searle, A. (1999) *Introducing Research and Data in Psychology: A Guide to Methods and Analysis*. London: Routledge.

Silverman, D. (2007) *A Very Short, Fairly Interesting, and Reasonably Cheap Book about Qualitative Research*. London: Sage Publications.

Tierney, J. (2006) *Criminology: Theory and Context* (2nd edn). Harlow, Essex: Pearson Education.

van Dijk, T. (1993) Principles of critical discourse analysis, *Discourse and Society*, 4: 249–83.

van Dijk, T. (1996) Discourse, power and access. In C.R. Caldas-Coulthard and M. Coulthard (eds) *Text and Practices*. London: Routledge.

van Dijk, T. (2001) Principles of critical discourse analysis. In M. Wetherell, S. Taylor and S.J.E. Yates (eds) *Discourse Theory and Practice: A Reader*. London: Sage Publications.

van Dijk, T. (2008) *Discourse and Power: Contributions to Critical Discourse Studies*. Houndmills: Palgrave Macmillan.

Wetherell, M. (1998) Positioning and interpretative repertoires: conversation analysis and post-structuralism in dialogue, *Discourse and Society*, 9: 387–99.

Wetherell, M., Taylor, S. and Yates, S.J.E. (eds) (2001a) *Discourse as Data: A Guide for Analysis*. London: Sage Publications.

Wetherell, M., Taylor, S. and Yates, S.J.E. (eds) (2001b) *Discourse Theory and Practice: A Reader*. London: Sage Publications.

Weiss, G. and Wodak, R. (eds) (2001) *Critical Discourse Analysis: Theory and Interdisciplinarity*. London: Palgrave Macmillan.

Williams, A. (2000) *Musicology and Postmodernism*. London: Blackwell Publishing.

7

Univariate Analysis

CHAPTER OVERVIEW

Chapter 7 provides an introduction to univariate quantitative data analysis. This is the analysis of single variables. The chapter discusses how criminologists use quantitative research design in the form of experimental and survey research to explore a topic as well as test a hypothesis concerning an assumed association between two or more variables, such as gender and fear of crime. The chapter outlines key univariate statistics, including levels of measurement, measures of central tendency, measures of dispersion, as well as discussing different ways to graphically display data. Examples, further readings and exercises are provided to develop your understanding of univariate analysis and help you apply this approach in your own research. Often due to practical limitations students will find themselves engaging in secondary data analysis – that is, they will analyse data which has been collected by others, such as the Crime Survey for England and Wales – and Chapters 7 and 8 both provide relevant examples for this approach in addition to outlining key data analysis principles and procedures regardless of whether students are working with their own data or not.

CHAPTER CONTENTS

Introduction

Box 7.1

Seven key elements of deskwork

1 Formulating an initial research area, focusing on study skills and dealing with assessment criteria.
2 Reviewing the literature and developing a research topic with a clear question to answer.
3 **Project planning and research design.**
4 Making contacts, gaining access and obtaining ethical approval to conduct your research.
5 Managing your fieldwork: timetabling.
6 **Conducting data analysis.**
7 Writing up your findings and research dissemination.

Taken together, Chapters 7 and 8 provide an introduction to data analysis techniques used in quantitative research by criminologists. As was discussed in Chapter 3, quantitative research comes in two main forms: survey research and experimental research. Both of these utilise univariate and bivariate analysis. Univariate analysis is concerned with the key features of single variables, i.e. age, gender, fear of crime, and so on. Bivariate analysis is concerned with ascertaining whether there is a relationship between two variables, e.g. gender and fear of crime. Bivariate analysis encapsulates a key feature of quantitative research: the analysis of variables and presumed relationships between them as stated in the form of an empirically testable hypothesis, e.g. that women are more afraid of being a victim of crime than men. Being able to conduct a univariate and bivariate analysis of one's data enables a criminologist to explore criminal life in a theoretically aware manner grounded in current academic discourse.

More complicated statistical analysis techniques beyond bivariate analysis include multivariate analysis which looks at the relationships between three or more variables, e.g. fear of crime in relation to both gender and age. Multivariate analysis is not discussed in this book as it aims to provide an introduction to the basics of doing criminological research, and multivariate analysis is generally seen as being a more advanced topic which the majority of social science students will not get to grips with until they undertake postgraduate research. The focus of this book is on helping the beginning researcher master the art of conducting basic statistical techniques bearing in mind the academic form in which quantitative research is often conducted within the social sciences. Once you feel you have mastered this then the further readings provided will help you move towards expanding your understanding to include the more advanced statistical techniques.

In this chapter we will look at how to do univariate analysis against the background of academic conventions pertaining to the conduct of quantitative research. The chapter begins by discussing the deductive hypothesis testing model which arguably predominates in quantitative research, focusing as it does so on the key role played by broader academic literature in helping a researcher identify a research question, define variables and research instruments, as well as interpret findings. Against this background the chapter outlines the main features of doing univariate analysis so that you can apply these in your own research. The chapter looks at the different types of variable data that quantitative researchers deal with, in the form of levels of measurement, as well as key univariate statistical tests, including measures of central tendency and measures of dispersion. The different ways data can be represented graphically are also outlined. Completing a univariate analysis of one's data allows a researcher to come to certain conclusions regarding its key features, either as an end goal in itself or as a necessary prelude to completing a bivariate analysis. But before looking at such matters let us start our discussion with the academic form in which quantitative research is typically undertaken.

Quantitative Research and Research Design

As was discussed in Chapter 3, quantitative research comes in two basic forms – surveys and experimental research. Both criminology surveys and experimental research utilise a mixture of descriptive statistics and analytical statistics where correlation tests are applied to two (or more) variables in order to test a hypothesis. Descriptive statistics involve univariate analysis, e.g. we might ask a group of people their experience of different types of crime (street robbery, physical and sexual assault, burglary, fraud and so on) from which we use univariate statistics to build a rich, descriptive picture of their responses. This approach can be used to answer a research question, e.g. 'What is the student experience of different types of crime within "Yellow Town"?' Analytical statistics involves bivariate analysis, i.e. we look at different types of crime and compare them to our respondents' age, gender, occupation, or some other aspect of our data-set, to identify if there is a relationship (correlation) between these variables. This approach can be used to test a research hypothesis, e.g. that gender influences the student experience of certain types of crime.

Analytical statistics are discussed in Chapter 8 when we look at bivariate analysis. For the moment it is enough to preface our discussion of univariate analysis by noting that the design of quantitative research built around the application of descriptive and analytical statistics follows a generic form which demonstrates the role of existing published research in the formation of a research question and/or hypothesis to guide analysis (see Box 7.2). Once the research question or hypothesis is defined a researcher can either design their own research instrument typically a questionnaire or research experiment to generate their own data (this is called primary data analysis), or use existing data for their own purposes (which is called secondary data analysis). Chapter 3 discussed how criminologists often engage in secondary data analysis and use existing governmental data-sets, such as the Crime Survey for England and Wales in the United Kingdom or the National Crime Victimization Survey in the United States. Indeed, given the range of data made freely available by governmental departments and bodies, secondary data analysis is undoubtedly a highly versatile criminological investigative tool.

Social science students often find themselves working with secondary data, owing to practical limitations pertaining to the collection of large-scale data-sets. But whether one is working with primary or secondary data, quantitative data analysis is typically undertaken with the assistance of a software computer package. One of the most widely used packages is called SPSS (Statistical Package for the Social Sciences). This is a relatively straightforward software package that comes with its own embedded help guide. Box 7.2 contains recommended readings that provide further specific guidance on how to use SPSS. All the statistical techniques detailed in this book can be completed in SPSS with a few clicks of the mouse. However, you are advised to familiarise yourself thoroughly with the contents of this and the next chapter before you use SPSS, because – as is the case with qualitative data analysis software packages – with quantitative data analysis it is down to the researcher to apply the right tests, interpret what the results mean, as well as place their findings in a broader context. It is undoubtedly true that students 'learn by doing' but it is equally true that considerable time can be saved by doing the right thing in the first place. This is particularly true when it comes to statistical analysis. It is all well and good to know which buttons to click to generate a graph using SPSS but before you start doing this it is important to bear in mind that which graph you use to present your data is determined by the level of measurement of your data.

The following discussion of quantitative research design represents an idealised model of the research process. This is particularly the case when we are looking at analytical statistics where the focus is on testing hypothesis. Selecting out two variables to look at in closer detail can be highly useful for exploring a research topic, testing underlying assumptions found in other people's research, or to confirm what other researchers say they have found. But the real world is inherently complex and contingent. So the idea that a researcher can set out a formalised relationship between two variables does need to be approached with some caution. There will always be intervening variables when we analyse the relationship between two variables. The identification of the range of variables involved in a topic takes place during the literature review stage of a project. For example, a mixture of common sense and a cursory review of academic research may lead us to conclude that there is a relationship between a person's gender and their fear of crime. However, it is equally important to recognise that this literature will also reinforce that there are a range of other variables involved as well: a person's age, socio-economic status, personal relationships and lifestyle choices, geographical location, race and ethnicity, and cultural background will all play a role in influencing their fear of crime (and that is before we consider certain types of crime as opposed to others). Hence, even if a statistical relationship between gender and fear of crime is found, it is necessary to acknowledge the limitations of one's research and the possibility that these other factors could also be influential. Consequently we should approach the models of the research process discussed in this chapter (see Box 7.2) with an open mind and the recognition that a good part of their value lies in their use as educational tools for introducing new researchers to the main features of how research in the social sciences should be undertaken.

Within quantitative research the research process typically follows a hypothetico-deductive model. This involves five analytical stages: first, the collection of current information on a topic to clarify its key variables and identify possible relationships; second, the generation of a research question to fill a gap in our current knowledge on a topic or the generation of a hypothesis which explains the relationship that exists between the variables identified; third, the devising of a method to answer the question or to test the hypothesis and refute or accept it; fourth, the analysis of one's data to answer the question or accept or reject the hypothesis; and fifth, discussion of contribution to the existing literature given the findings outlined, as well as critical consideration of the limitations of the research presented. Typically research limitations will include consideration of the strengths and weaknesses of the research method used to collect data, the relative size of the research sample given the total study population, as well as the statistical results obtained.

(As we will discuss when we look at bivariate analysis in Chapter 8, the strength of the association we identify can vary.)

The process of hypothesis generation and testing often involves the identification of an independent and dependent variable. Variation in the independent variable causes variation in the dependent variable. Once formulated a hypothesis must be tested. This can be done through either designing a questionnaire or experiment (primary data analysis) or using existing data (secondary data analysis). The testing of the hypothesis leads to it being accepted or rejected. But regardless of whether the focus is on answering a research question descriptively or seeing if a hypothesis is accepted or refuted, the result leads the researcher back to the academic literature surrounding their topic. This is an important point. Finding out that one has to reject what we thought should happen given our review of the existing academic literature surrounding a topic is just as important (indeed in many ways more so) than finding out that what we thought would happen has indeed happened. It is important to remember that you are involved in an ongoing conversation concerning a topic of shared interest within the broader academic and policy-making communities. As critical criminologists, even when we do accept a hypothesis we do so tentatively, ever mindful of the limitations of our contribution and the inherent complexity and uncertainty present in research conducted with human beings. Hence our research forms but one small part of the broader and ever-evolving disciplinary discourse surrounding our topic.

Box 7.2

Quantitative research design: descriptive and analytical models

As was discussed in Chapter 3, quantitative research comes in two basic forms: surveys and experimental research. Criminology surveys and experimental research utilise a mixture of descriptive statistics (univariate analysis) and analytical statistics (bivariate analysis) where correlation tests are applied to two variables in order to test a hypothesis.

The research cycle for univariate analysis (descriptive model for survey research)

With descriptive surveys the focus is on building up a rich account of a topic given the research question one is asking. Hence if we have reviewed the literature, and our research question was 'What are the main types of crime students experience during their university studies?' we could develop a questionnaire for distribution which contains a battery of questions to ask students about their experience (if any) of different types of crime. From this we could come to certain conclusions regarding students' self-reported experience of crime which could be used by criminal justice agencies and educational providers to inform crime prevention policy and practice, or even as a basis from which to develop a formal hypothesis to test.

(Continued)

(Continued)

Figure 7.2.1 Univariate Research Cycle

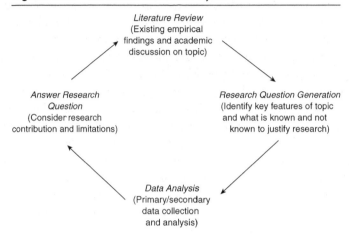

The research cycle for bivariate analysis (analytical model for survey/experimental research)

Surveys and experimental research can be used to apply analytical statistics to a research question. With analytical statistics, correlation tests are applied to two (or more) variables in order to test a hypothesis. Hence although the main features of the research cycle remain the same the focus shifts to the acceptance or rejection of the hypothesis.

Figure 7.2.2 Bivariate Research Cycle

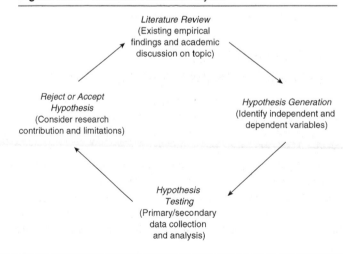

Doing criminological research:
an example exploring gender and fear of crime

Imagine you are interested in the relationship between gender and crime. In particular you wish to look at the difference (if any) between men and women in relation to fear of crime. Remember that being afraid of crime is not the same as actually having been the victim of crime. So you may here have a broader concern with the role played by the media portrayal of crime in 'broken Britain', not least of all because you are aware that there is criminological literature available that argues that while women may fear violent crime more than men they nevertheless are less likely to be victims of violent crime than men. You think that the media constantly remind women of their vulnerability to violent sexual assault in certain social situations, for example, at a nightclub or on the way home from work in the dark during winter. Therefore you think that female fear of crime is mediated not just by their personal experience – or the experience of women close to them – of intimidating and/or violent sexual behaviour, but media discourse as well. Additionally, you think that current research does not recognise enough that the socialisation of the genders may make women feel more able to openly admit their fear of crime than men. You therefore plan to conduct mixed-methods research using a mixture of interviews and a questionnaire to explore perceptions and experiences of violent crime alongside male and female reporting of it. However, before you do this you feel it would be useful to make use of the statistical data on respondents' self-reported fear of crime that are available to you via the Crime Survey for England and Wales (CSEW). There may be several reasons why you feel doing this may be beneficial; including because you think it will help your background review of your topic, or perhaps because you plan on applying for research funding and recognise that you will therefore need some hard statistical evidence to back up your assertions and research plan. Regardless of the exact reasons, the important thing to remember is that your reading of the literature has led you to develop the hypothesis, to be tested via the CSEW data-set, that women fear being attacked more than men. Your independent variable is therefore gender and your dependent variable is fear of being attacked. According to your hypothesis, change in your independent variable – if a respondent is a man or a woman – is associated with change in your dependent variable – fear of being attacked. But whether or not you find there is a relationship between fear of being attacked and gender the results of your analysis will inform your subsequent research and engagement with relevant literature surrounding your topic. This is how social science works as an accumulative disciplinary project. Your research goal is to make some small but nevertheless important contribution to this ongoing exercise. We will return to this exploration of gender and fear of crime at the end of Chapter 8, after we have outlined the main features of bivariate analysis, so we can look again at the process of doing quantitative research in criminology more closely.

(Continued)

Recommended readings

The following further reading provides a good introduction to quantitative research in criminology:

Bushway, S. and Westburd, D. (2005) *Quantitative Methods in Criminology*. Aldershot: Ashgate Publishing.

The following further readings provide a good introductory guide to the computer assisted statistical analysis package SPSS:

Bryman, A. and Cramer, D. (2011) *Quantitative Data Analysis with SPSS 17, 18 and 19: A Guide for Social Scientists*. London: Routledge.

Wagnar, R. (2010) *Using SPSS for Social Statistics and Research Methods*. London: Sage Publications

Doing a Univariate Analysis

Univariate analysis can be conducted as an end in itself or as a stepping stone before conducting a bivariate analysis. Sometimes the focus of survey-based research is to answer a research question, e.g. how afraid are students of being attacked? In such cases we want to focus on how best to summarise and describe our data-set, bearing in mind that it is a sample selected from a larger population, e.g. we may sample 1000 students from a total student campus population of 10,000 students. Other times we are concerned with using our survey data-set to test a hypothesis so we can analyse the relationships within the data collected, e.g. students' gender and their fear of being attacked, while in experimental research we deliberately seek to manipulate the independent variable to see if it causes a change in the dependent variable. No matter which of these approaches we are using, our starting focus is with exploring and summarising data. It is important to begin our discussion of univariate analysis by stating the importance of knowing the level of measurement of each of your variables. Everything you do is dictated by the level of measurement. It even dictates what graphs you should use to visually display your data, as well as (when the time comes) what bivariate statistical tests to conduct.

Levels of measurement

What is a variable? The simple definition is that it is something which varies. Criminologists ask lots of questions to which a person's response can vary: What is you gender? What is your age? Have you been a victim of crime? How afraid are you of being burgled? When we talk about levels of measurement we are concerned with different types of variation in response that a question can elicit. These can be placed under one of three headings.

Nominal variables

Nominal variables are also known as categorical variables. Nominal variables are typically obtained by asking respondents to select a response from a list of items. Most importantly, there is no real difference (numeric or otherwise) between the possible responses and they therefore cannot be ordered and ranked. Some nominal variables are dichotomous in that there are only two possible categories of response (e.g. they elicit a yes or no response). Examples of questionnaire items which produce nominal data include:

'Are you male or female?'

'Has your home been broken into in the last twelve months?'

Ordinal variables

Ordinal variables are similar to nominal variables in that they are typically obtained by asking a respondent to select an answer from a list of items. However, unlike with nominal variables the categorical responses can be ordered and ranked. In other words, it is possible to argue that there are real differences between the responses. Examples of questionnaire items which produce ordinal data include:

'All convicted criminals should serve their entire prison sentence without time off for good behaviour: Strongly agree, Agree, Neutral, Disagree, Strongly disagree.'

'What is your occupation? Higher professional, Lower professional, Routine white collar, Skilled manual, Semi-unskilled manual.'

Interval/ratio variables

Interval variables operate on a continuous scale and there are clear measurable differences between each item on the scale. With ordinal variables we can say, for example, that 'strongly disagree' and 'agree' represent a degree of difference in attitude towards a question; however, one person's 'agree' may well be another person's 'strongly agree'. Unlike with nominal variables the differences in ordinal data can be somewhat qualitative. Nevertheless they *are* differences in the responses elicited. In contrast to this, with interval data the differences between items are equal and measurable throughout the scale. Examples include temperature, height, length, weight and age. Responses can be ordered and ranked and the differences between the ranks is universally consistent and can be calculated mathematically. So if I am 2 centimetres taller than you the difference in height between us is the same as the difference in height between you and your friend who happens to be 2 centimetres shorter than you. Interval variables with an absolute zero point on the item scale, such as age, height and weight, are also called ratio variables. Hence temperature is not a ratio variable because it can have a minus value. Examples of questionnaire items which produce interval data include:

'What is your age?'

'How many people live in your house?'

'What was the length of your prison sentence?'

Box 7.3

The hierarchy of levels of measurement

When you define the questions you are asking a respondent, you are also defining the level of measurement of their response. There are three types of level of measurement – nominal, ordinal and interval. The univariate and bivariate statistics you can use to summarise and explore your data are dependent on the level of measurement: if you apply an inappropriate test given the level of measurement of your data the resulting analysis will be fundamentally flawed. Levels of measure-ment can be placed into a hierarchical order relating to the presence (or lack thereof) of measurable differences in the types of response elicited. Nominal varia-bles are the lowest as there is no real numeric or qualitative difference between the response categories elicited. Ordinal variables are in the middle as it is possible to identify differences between the responses elicited; however, these tend to be more qualitative than numeric. Interval variables are the highest as they are pure numeric differences in responses elicited. As you define your questions you should consider the type of data you are seeking to obtain, to ensure you can answer your research question and test a hypothesis. Additionally, an important factor to consider is the appropriateness of your question, given the context in which it is being asked; e.g. it might be preferable to obtain exact numeric (and so interval) figures relating to how many times your respondents have engaged in criminal activity compared to how many times they have been caught committing a criminal offence, but they may well feel uncomfortable providing such specific information, so it may be preferable to structure your questions so they elicit more open and general responses.

Frequencies

Once we know the level of measurement of our data we know which descriptive statistical tests we can apply to help us summarise, explore and describe our findings. The starting point for this is to produce a frequency table for each variable we have in our data-set. A frequency table summarises all the responses we have for each variable. It gives a count of the total number of responses for each variable and its possible responses as well as providing three percentage breakdowns. The first is for the total sample size (which is always 100%), the second is for the number of valid cases (which is always 100% unless they are missing responses), and the third is for the cumulative percentage (which is the sum of the valid percentages as you move down the possible responses). Table 7.1 provides an example of a frequency table for gender in a sample of 170 respondents. We can see that there are no missing responses: there are 170 responses in total in column one, 74 male and 96 female. Column two shows us the relative percentage breakdown for the frequency of responses: we can see that 43.5% of our sample is male and 56.5% female. Column three shows us the valid percentages: there are no missing responses. Column four shows us the cumulative percentage: this is the sum of the responses as we move down the categories. As there are only two possible responses and no missing variables the cumulative percentages are the same as the valid percentages.

Table 7.1 Gender frequency table

		Frequency	Percent	Valid Percent	Cumulative Percent
Valid	Male	74	43.5	43.5	43.5
	Female	96	56.5	56.5	100.0
	Total	170	100.0	100.0	

Table 7.2 shows an example of a frequency table relating to ethnicity in a sample of 70 responses. Again, we can see that there are no missing responses. There are 70 responses in total in column one, 36 white/European, 18 Asian, 14 West-Indian and 2 African. Column two shows us the relative percentage breakdown for the frequency of responses: we can see that 51.4% of our sample is white/European, 25.7% Asian, 20% West-Indian and 2% African. Column three shows us the valid percentages; there are no missing responses. Column four shows us the cumulative percentage: this is the sum of the responses as we move down the categories. So we can see that 51.4% of our sample is white/European, 77.1% is white/European AND Asian, while 97.1% is white/European, Asian AND West-Indian.

Table 7.2 Ethnicity frequency table

		Frequency	Percent	Valid Percent	Cumulative Percent
Valid	White/European	36	51.4	51.4	51.4
	Asian	18	25.7	25.7	77.1
	West-Indian	14	20.0	20.0	97.1
	African	2	2.9	2.9	100.0
	Total	70	100.0	100.0	

Measures of central tendency

Producing frequency tables for each variable in the data-set allows us to build up an initial picture of our responses so we can begin to tell the story about what we have found. Frequency tables are limited as they do not allow a researcher to make comparisons between responses. However they are invaluable tools for initially identifying the main features of the frequency of responses for each question asked. The next stage in our univariate analysis is to look at measures of central tendency. These are useful for beginning to look at the distribution of a variable from the minimum to the maximum, and come in three forms. Each is concerned with the 'average' or 'most frequent' value in a distribution of responses. In other words, they are concerned with identifying the middle point in the data.

Mode

The mode is the simplest measure of central tendency to calculate. It is the only measure appropriate for nominal, ordinal and interval data. The mode is the value which occurs most frequently in the distribution of the data. For example, if respondents' ages were 18, 19, 18, 20, 18, 20, 18, 19, 18, 23, 24, 24, 18, then the mode would be 18 as it occurs six times. When two responses occur with the same frequency this is called bimodal when three or more responses occur with the same frequency this is called multimodal.

Median

The median is appropriate for ordinal and interval/ratio data only. The responses are placed in order of size, and the median is the middle value in the distribution. For example, if respondents' ages were 17, 18, 18, 19, 20, 20, 21, then the median would be 19 as this splits the distribution into two with three ages below and above it. The median helps to account for extreme variables. So for example if we were to add a very young person to our sample, say a 5-year-old instead of the 17-year-old, then the median would still be 19 as the distribution is now 5, 18, 18, 19,

20, 20, 21. To calculate the median of the distribution when you have an even number of results you take the two middle values and calculate the average of them to give you the median. So for example if we were to have a distribution of 5, 18, 18, 19, 20, 20, 20, 21, we would take the two middle values of 19 and 20 and calculate their average by adding them together and dividing them by 2 – which in this case gives the result of 19.5 – so our median would be 19.5 (which some may argue should be rounded up to 20).

Mean

The mean is appropriate for interval/ratio data only. It is the most familiar measure of central tendency and most people will equate it with what is meant when they are told to calculate the average. To calculate the average you add up all the responses and divide it by the number of responses. For example, if our respondents' ages were 17, 18, 18, 19, 20, 20, 21, then when we add up responses we get 133 and when we divide this by the number of responses (7) we get a mean age of 19. The problem with the mean is that it can vary considerably and indeed be more than a little misleading if we have extreme values in our distribution. So it would only take the addition of one 60-year-old respondent to make our mean value 24 instead of 19, even though 7 of our 8 respondents are 21 years old or less. In such circumstances it is recommended that you consider using the median instead to describe your data.

Box 7.4

What do we achieve by using measures of central tendency?

Which measure of central tendency you use is dictated by the level of measurement of your data. With interval/ratio data you should use the mean or the median; sometimes even the mode can be useful, but the preference is for the mean. Just remember to be careful if you have extreme values (sometimes referred to as outliers) in your data as you may be better off using the median rather than the mean. Knowing the mean can be very important when it comes to describing your data: we may wish to know the average number of times members of our sample have been the victim of crime or have committed a criminal offence. With ordinal data the ranking order of the median value makes it an extremely useful measure of central tendency, particularly when you are using attitudinal scales: is the most frequent response to our question strongly disagree, disagree, neutral, agree or

(Continued)

strongly agree? Knowing which of these it is helps us to summarise and explore our data so we can draw conclusions about what the shared attitudes of our respondents are towards an issue. Finally, for nominal data the mode is the only appropriate measure of central tendency. Knowing the most frequent response in our data is particularly useful when it comes to nominal variables: do we have more students in our sample who have been a victim of crime than students who haven't been a victim of crime? Constructing frequency tables and identifying measures of central tendency undoubtedly help a criminologist summarise and explore their data in a meaningful way. However, it is all well and good knowing what the minimum, maximum and average values are, but we also want to know about its distribution in between these points. To do this we next need to look at measures of dispersion.

Measures of dispersion

Measures of dispersion provide us with information relating to how dispersed or spread out our data is. It is necessary to begin by saying that measures of dispersion are not appropriate for nominal data, while when we are dealing with ordinal data we can only use the range and interquartile range (although the interquartile range is often the most appropriate, particularly when dealing with attitudinal scales). The standard deviation is only appropriate for interval/ratio data.

Range

The range is the most straightforward measure of dispersion (see Table 7.3). It is simply the maximum minus the minimum value. For example, in a sample of 1000 victims of crime, if the lowest age of respondents is 17 and the highest age 68, then the range of our data is 68 (maximum) − 17 (minimum) = 51 years. The range is of most use for defining the spread of interval/ratio data. However, it is dependent on the two extreme points in the data, which can be distorting if there is a large difference between these and the rest of the data-set. For example, our lowest age of respondents may be 17 and the highest age 68, making the range 51, but on closer inspection we may see that only a handful of our 1000 respondents fall into these two points, with the majority being clustered around the 25 to 40 age range. The range doesn't tell us anything about what the most typical value is or how the values are distributed between the minimum and maximum, hence the value of using the interquartile range.

Table 7.3 Range

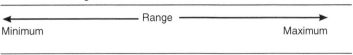

Minimum	Range	Maximum

Interquartile range

The interquartile range tells us about how the values are distributed along the range of the values. It seeks to eliminate the extreme scores from the distribution to overcome the limitations of the range. The interquartile range is calculated by placing the data in order from lowest to the highest then dividing it into four equal parts (quartiles) and focusing on the middle 50% of the distribution (quartiles 2 and 3). The interquartile range is the central half of the data. It can be used with interval and ordinal data. If you are using the median as a measure of central tendency then the interquartile range is the appropriate measure of dispersion to use (see Table 7.4).

Table 7.4 Interquartile range

Quartile 1	Quartile 2	Quartile 3	Quartile 4
Minimum			Maximum

Variance/standard deviation

The standard deviation is the most widely used measure of dispersion but can only be used with interval/ratio data. If you are using the mean as a measure of central tendency then the standard deviation is the appropriate measure of dispersion to use. Sometimes variance is calculated by subtracting the mean, from each unit of data then squaring each of the differences from the mean before adding them all together and dividing them by the total number of observations minus 1. However, as this result is not measured in the same units as the original value it can be highly confusing. The standard deviation is more straightforward and meaningful as it is calculated using the square root of the variance of data from the mean. It focuses on the spread or dispersion of the data as based around the mean, and is then essentially the average amount of variation around the mean. If the data is closely concentrated around the mean then the variance will be small, while a large variance suggests a more even spread. For example, if our mean age was 19 and our standard deviation was 4 we would know that the majority of our data is clustered between the 15 and 23 age range (although the minimum age could be much lower and our maximum age much higher). Because it is calculated like the mean, using all available data, it can produce a distorted picture if extreme low and high responses exist. Consequently it is best to check for extreme low or high values before employing this measure of dispersion (see Table 7.5).

Table 7.5 Standard deviation

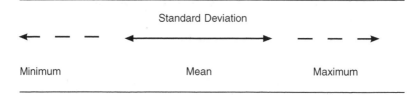

	Standard Deviation	
Minimum	Mean	Maximum

Box 7.5

What do we achieve by using measures of dispersion?

Measures of dispersion are the next step in exploring and summarising the main features of your data. Which measures of dispersion to use is dictated by the level of measurement of your data. You cannot use measures of dispersion with nominal data. For ordinal data you should use the interquartile range and for interval/ratio data the standard deviation (although you can also use the interquartile range although if you wish). Through using measures of dispersion we are able to identify the spread of our data and so the distribution of the responses to our questions. A measure of dispersion that is small indicates that our responses are clustered around a central point: the data is very similar so everybody seems to be saying much the same thing. A measure of dispersion that is large indicates that our responses are more diverse: the data is more fractured so our respondents possess a more divergent range of opinions or experiences. Either way, knowing the result helps us to summarise the main features of our data-set and come to conclusions regarding what our data is telling us.

Representing data graphically

It is useful to be able to represent our data in graphical form both as we initially explore its main features and subsequently when we are seeking to communicate our findings to others. When dealing with nominal and ordinal data the easiest methods to use are bar graphs and pie charts. Figure 7.1 displays a bar chart. When displaying data on an axis like this we refer to x as the horizontal and y as the vertical. In univariate analysis when we are dealing with single variables the y-axis of the bar chart typically gives the total count or frequency for each possible response category of the variable as displayed on the x-axis. Figure 7.1 clearly shows that we have more men ($n = 55$) than women ($n = 45$) in our sample. Pie charts such as the one in Figure 7.2 also display the total count or frequency for each possible response category, but they do so in slices, which is useful for visually representing the relative size of responses. Figures 7.3 and 7.4 show the value of using bar charts and pie charts to display ordinal data, particularly when we are eliciting attitudes from people. Here our sample clearly agrees that they are more afraid of having their home burgled than a year previously.

Figure 7.1 Bar chart of respondents' gender

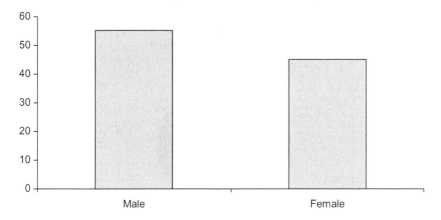

Figure 7.2 Pie chart of respondents' gender

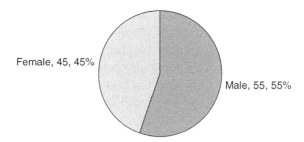

Figure 7.3 Bar chart of respondents' response to question 'I am more afraid of having my home burgled than this time last year'

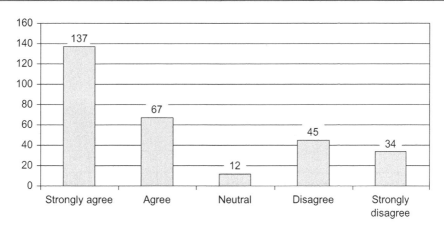

Figure 7.4 Pie chart of respondents' response to question 'I am more afraid of having my home burgled than this time last year'

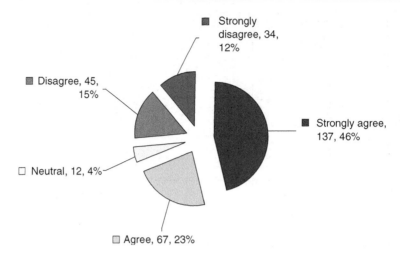

When we are dealing with interval/ratio data the range of display options open to a researcher increases quite a bit: histogram, boxplots and stem and leaf. Perhaps the most popular is the histogram. It is similar to a bar chart, with each bar representing a response category; however with a histogram there is no space between the bars as it is displaying the data in a continuous spread from the minimum to the maximum value. Figure 7.5 displays a histogram for the age of respondents in a sample. As with

Figure 7.5 Histogram for the age of respondents in a sample

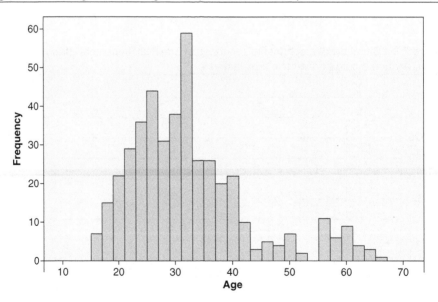

Figure 7.6 Line graph for the age of respondents in a sample

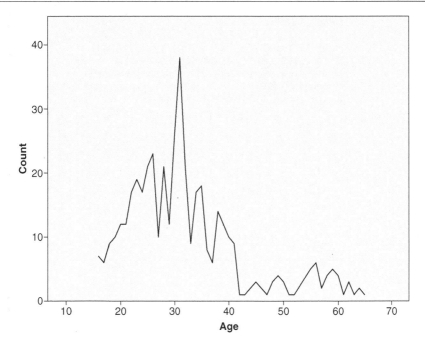

bar charts a histogram is extremely useful for visually displaying trends and patterns in the data: this one clearly shows that the majority of our sample seem to be in the 20 to 40 age range with the range being particularly dense between 25 and 35. A variation on the histogram is the line graph, which plots the responses against the numeric values in the *y*-axis instead of using bars. Figure 7.6 shows what a line graph looks like for the same data. Although like Figure 7.5 this does show that most of our respondents are in the 20 to 40 age range, it also reinforces a key problem some-times encountered with line graphs: sometimes the data produces a 'spikey' graph which can be difficult to make sense of. It is important to choose our graphs care-fully when exploring our data and communicating our findings to others.

In addition to using histograms a researcher working with interval/ratio data can plot a stem and leaf diagram. A key advantage of a stem and leaf is that they compress a great deal of information into a compact summarising form. They are also useful tools for displaying variables which are bimodal or multimodal. (If you've forgotten what this means take a quick look again at the earlier discussion of measures of central tendency and the mode.) Figure 7.7 displays a stem and leaf for respondents' age within a sample. The first column, 'frequency', refers to the number of respondents in each line of the stem and leaf: 32 in the first unit, 77 in the second and so on. The second column, 'stem', refers to the units of the variable. This usually is displayed in units of 10, which is referred to as stem width. For extremely large samples or units the stem width may be 20, 50 or even 100. So in

Figure 7.7 Stem and leaf plot for the age of respondents in a sample

Frequency	Stem and Leaf
32.00	1 . 6667777888899999
77.00	2 . 00000011111122222222233333333344444444
87.00	2 . 55555555556666666666677777888888888999999
111.00	3 . 0000000000000111111111111111111112222222222333344444444
58.00	3 . 5555555556666777888888889999999
23.00	4 . 0000011114
13.00	4 . 56899

Stem width: 10
Each leaf: 2 cases

Figure 7.8 Boxplot for the age of respondents in a sample

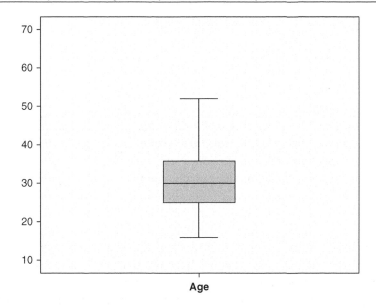

this case each unit represents 10 years: 1 is 10 years, 2 is 20 years, 3 is 30 years and 4 is 40 years. This means for the first line there are 32 respondents between the ages of 16 and 19. The third column, 'leaf', refers to each respondent's exact age when placed along the stem. In this case each leaf is said to represent two cases (two respondents). So we can see for the first line, 6667777888899999, that this means $3 \times 2 = 6$ respondents are 16, $4 \times 2 = 8$ respondents are 17, $4 \times 2 = 8$ respondents are 18, and $5 \times 2 = 10$ respondents are 19, making for 32 respondents in total. We can also see from the stem and leaf that the majority of our respondents are in the 30 to 34 age range ($n = 111$), followed by the 25 to 29 age range ($n = 87$) and then the 20 to 24 age range ($n = 77$).

Figure 7.8 displays a boxplot for the age of respondents in a sample. Boxplots visually represent the spread of the data values by placing them in rank order and displaying the median value along with the quartiles and the interquartile range. The shaded box shape represents the interquartile range: we can see from our example that the bottom of this range is 25 years old and the top 38 years old. The black line running through the box is the median, which in our example is 30 years old. The top of our interquartile range is 52 years old and the bottom is 18 years old. Boxplots are highly useful for displaying important features of the data visually. You can quickly identify the dispersion of your data around a central point and use multiple boxplots to quickly compare and contrast your variables. This can be particularly useful for looking at responses to attitudinal data.

Criticisms of Univariate Analysis

Univariate analysis involves the use of descriptive statistics. These are recommended when the objective is to explore, describe and discuss a data-set. Univariate analysis is routinely used by criminologists as it helps to summarise information and support assertions. However, a thorough understanding of descriptive bivariate statistics is essential for the subsequent appropriate and effective use of bivariate analytical techniques. Univariate analysis can be criticised for being of limited use when samples and populations are small, while it also does not help a researcher to robustly identify correlations between variables within a data-set, e.g. gender and fear of crime, in order to test a hypothesis.

Conclusion and Univariate Analysis Flow Chart

In this chapter we have looked at the univariate analysis. The chapter has outlined how the process of doing a univariate analysis involves identifying levels of measurement, measures of central tendency, measures of dispersion, as well as choosing appropriate graphs to explore data and display findings. The analysis of single variables is called descriptive statistics and the statistical tests discussed in this chapter reinforce why this is the case: doing a univariate analysis helps a researcher to examine their data and summarise its key features and themes in a rigorous and focused manner in order to draw firm conclusions about what it is telling them. The chapter has stressed how important it is to remember at the research design stage of your research the level of measurement of each of your questions. Box 7.6 contains a flow chart guide detailing the appropriate univariate statistics to use given the level of measurement. It must always be borne in mind, however, that a researcher is collecting and analysing data for a reason: to answer a research question which has been generated from current academic discourse surrounding a substantive research area within criminology.

Within quantitative criminology, survey research is done to collect data from large samples to paint a rich picture of what is happening in relation to a topic – and in doing so contribute to current academic discourse surrounding it in addition

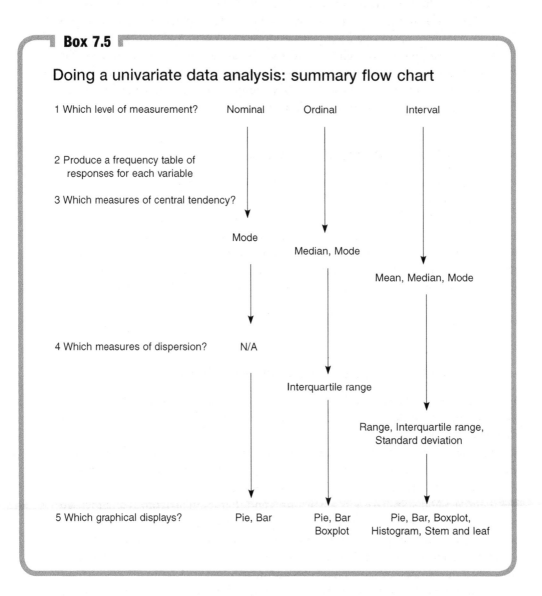

Box 7.5

Doing a univariate data analysis: summary flow chart

1 Which level of measurement?   Nominal   Ordinal   Interval

2 Produce a frequency table of
   responses for each variable

3 Which measures of central tendency?

                                    Mode
                                              Median, Mode
                                                             Mean, Median, Mode

4 Which measures of dispersion?   N/A

                                              Interquartile range

                                                             Range, Interquartile range,
                                                             Standard deviation

5 Which graphical displays?   Pie, Bar   Pie, Bar   Pie, Bar, Boxplot,
                                                    Boxplot   Histogram, Stem and leaf

to influencing the policy-making process and how criminal justice agencies conceptualise and respond to crime. However, our ability to contribute to the ongoing debates surrounding the organisation and day-to-day operation of the criminal justice system is further enhanced by being able to move past rich description and towards being able to provide a firm evidential base from which to act – as based around demonstrating relationships between variables within our data. This brings us to the importance of bivariate analysis in criminology. Criminology possesses a strong policy-orientation. It can be said to perhaps value 'armchair theorising' most when it leads to the development of a testable hypothesis concerning the possible relationship between variables. In Chapter 8 we look at how to conduct a bivariate analysis of two variables that we hypothesise are related to one another. But as we will discuss in the next chapter, a bivariate analysis can only be done against the background of a rigorously conducted univariate analysis. The information and resources provided in this chapter should enable you to achieve this goal.

CHAPTER REVIEW ACTIVITIES

1   Write a 1000-word essay which outlines the five analytical stages of hypothetico-deductive research and how your own research project will fit into this cyclical model of the research process.

2   In addition to age and gender, construct at least three and at most five questions that you could ask members of the public to identify if they have been a victim of different types of crime in the last twelve months – you may choose whichever types of crime you would like. Identify the level of measurement for all your questions and outline what measures of central tendency, measures of dispersion and types of graphs you should use to explore and summarise your findings.

3   Write a PowerPoint presentation lasting no more than 10 minutes which summarises how the different types of descriptive statistics involved in univariate analysis form an essential background to conducting a bivariate statistical analysis of two variables to test a hypothesis.

CHAPTER READING LIST

Bryman, A. and Cramer, D. (2011) *Quantitative Data Analysis with SPSS 17, 18 and 19: A Guide for Social Scientists*. London: Routledge.

Bushway, S. and Westburd, D. (2005) *Quantitative Methods in Criminology*. Aldershot: Ashgate Publishing.

Wagnar, R. (2010) *Using SPSS for Social Statistics and Research Methods*. London: Sage Publications.

8

Bivariate Analysis

CHAPTER OVERVIEW

Chapter 8 provides an introduction to bivariate quantitative data analysis. This is the analysis of two variables. Chapters 3 and 7 discussed how criminologists use quantitative research design in the form of experimental and survey research to explore a topic, answer a research question, as well as test a hypothesis concerning an assumed association between two variables, such as age and fear of crime. The chapter outlines key bivariate statistics, including phi and Cramer's V, Pearson's r, Spearman's rho and chi-square. Examples, further readings and exercises are provided to develop your understanding of bivariate analysis and help you apply this approach in your own research.

CHAPTER CONTENTS

Introduction

> ### Box 8.1
>
> ## Seven key elements of deskwork
>
> 1 Formulating an initial research area, focusing on study skills and dealing with assessment criteria.
> 2 Reviewing the literature and developing a research topic with a clear question to answer.
> 3 **Project planning and research design.**
> 4 Making contacts, gaining access and obtaining ethical approval to conduct your research.
> 5 Managing your fieldwork: timetabling.
> 6 **Conducting data analysis.**
> 7 Writing up your findings and research dissemination.

This chapter is concerned with bivariate data analysis. Chapter 7 outlined univariate data analysis and how criminologists use different statistical procedures to summarise and graphically display the answers they get to the questions they ask. This is why univariate analysis is sometimes called descriptive statistics. Some government crime data-sets – notably large-scale descriptive surveys such as the Crime Survey for England and Wales – primarily (but certainly not exclusively) use univariate data analysis to paint a large-scale national picture of respondents' self-reported experience of crime. It is certainly possible to explore in a rich and informative manner the numeric data we collect, answer our research questions, as well as even inform government policy development, using univariate data analysis alone. Yet it is useful to think of bivariate analysis as the next, somewhat deeper, stage in the analytical process, which occurs after we have completed our descriptive univariate analysis and summarised the answers we have got to our questions, not least of all because it is concerned with seeing whether there are any relationships between our responses, e.g. respondents' geographical location and whether they have had their home burgled in the last twelve months. Bivariate data analysis – also called analytical statistics – is concerned with ascertaining if there is a relationship (a correlation) between two variables. Consequently it encapsulates a key feature of quantitative research: the analysis of variables and presumed relationships between them, as stated in the form of an empirically testable hypothesis, e.g. that people living in the city will have had their home burgled more often than people living in the countryside. We previously discussed in Chapters 3 and 7 how quantitative research is typically held to follow a hypothetico–deductive model where a researcher reviews the literature on the topic in order to develop a research hypothesis to test (see Box 8.2). Exploring bivariate analysis will help you to get to grips with this approach to the analysis of criminological life.

Box 8.2

Quantitative research design: the research cycle for bivariate analysis

As was discussed in Chapters 3 and 7, quantitative research comes in two basic forms: surveys and experimental research. Criminology surveys and experimental research utilise a mixture of descriptive statistics (univariate analysis) and analytical statistics (bivariate analysis) where correlation tests are applied to two variables in order to test a hypothesis. Hence the focus of the research cycle is the acceptance or rejection of the hypothesis.

Figure 8.2.1

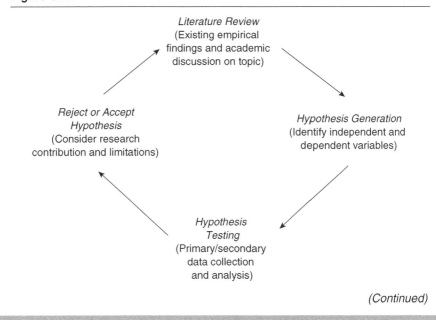

Literature Review
(Existing empirical
findings and academic
discussion on topic)

*Reject or Accept
Hypothesis*
(Consider research
contribution and limitations)

Hypothesis Generation
(Identify independent and
dependent variables)

*Hypothesis
Testing*
(Primary/secondary
data collection
and analysis)

(Continued)

(Continued)

Doing criminological research: an example exploring gender and fear of crime

In Chapter 7 (Box 7.2) we noted that in this chapter you will find an illustrative example of hypothesis testing research by looking at the difference (if any) between men and women in relation to fear of crime. Remember that being afraid of crime is not the same as actually having been the victim of crime. So you may here have a broader concern with the role played by the media portrayal of crime in 'broken Britain'. Nevertheless, your reading of the academic literature has led you to develop the hypothesis to be tested that women fear being attacked more than men. Your independent variable is therefore gender and your dependent variable is fear of being attacked. According to your hypothesis, change in your independent variable – if a respondent is a man or a woman – is associated with change in your dependent variable – fear of being attacked. We will explore gender and fear of crime at the end of chapter 8 (see Box 8.5) after we have outlined the main features of bivariate analysis (see Box 8.4) as this will help you review the contents of the chapter, as well as help guide you in how to present your own work as you complete a quantitative research project. The writing-up of findings and research dissemination is discussed in more detail in Chapter 9.

Doing a Bivariate Analysis

Imagine for a moment that you are a teacher and you have noticed that students who attend your lectures less frequently seem to do more poorly in assessment tasks than those with full attendance. You are very happy that you are clearly such a good teacher who can positively influence your students' work. Nevertheless, you are equally concerned that some of your students aren't doing so well. You have decided that you will conduct a statistical analysis of the relationship between student attendance and the grades they receive on marked work. You plan on sharing your results with your head of department who you know is equally concerned that some students drop out of their degree programme prior to graduation. But she nevertheless needs some 'hard facts' to justify resourcing a student retention and academic study skill programme. So you hope your study will help provide at least some of the data she needs. The null hypothesis for the research is that there is no relationship between student attendance and assessment grade, while the working hypothesis is that there is a relationship between student attendance and assessment grade.

Causation, in basic terms, is the process that makes an outcome happen. With regard to the variables used in this research, if student attendance is the independent variable and assessment grade the dependent variable, then attendance will influence the assessment grade achieved by a student. However, it is important to note that outcomes are rarely influenced by a single cause. Causation is too complex to reach outcomes with total certainty, therefore it can be misleading. There are sufficient conditions of causation. This means that it is not true to say that all assessment grades achieved by a student will be influenced by their level of attendance, as there may well be other factors which influence the grade achieved (these factors are called intervening variables). For example, a student may have attended all their lectures but experienced a severe personal issue, such as a family bereavement, prior to assignment submission, which led them to submit work that does not necessarily reflect their academic ability or subject topic knowledge. Correlation, on the other hand, is the pattern associated between two variables or the statistical measure used to find such patterns. This is relevant for the variables example given here, as it cannot be absolutely true that assessment grades will be influenced by attendance, as this is a causal explanation. However, it can be stated that your personal experience of teaching students has led you to conclude that there may well be a correlation, but the strength of the possible relationship needs further research, which you plan to undertake by collecting the necessary data on student attendance and assessment outcome, before conducting a statistical test entitled a measure of association.

Measures of association are sometimes called correlation statistics or correlation tests. This chapter introduces you to some of the key measures of association used by criminologists when conducting bivariate data analysis – namely Phi and Cramer's V, Spearman's rho and Pearson's r. Mastering these will enable you to conduct a basic quantitative data analysis from which you can go on to explore more complicated statistical procedures, including multivariate data analysis.

The most important thing to remember as you begin is that, as with univariate statistics, the type of statistical test which can be applied to the data values to test for a correlation is predicated by their level of measurement. So if student attendance was banded (i.e. attended 1–3 sessions, attended 4–6 sessions and so on), and grade outcome was similarly banded into possible degree outcome (i.e. second class, first class and so on), then they both would be categorised as ordinal data. This is because they can be put into a rank order, but no mathematical calculation or specific measure of relative scale can be absolutely made in relation to the distances between each category, as they could in the case of height for example (if you are unsure about this you may find it helpful to review Chapter 7). Given the level of measurement of each variable, the strength of association between the variables can be measured using the Spearman's rho statistical test. This test, and others, will be discussed in more detail shortly. First it is necessary to begin with contingency tables.

Contingency tables (cross-tabulations) _____

Regardless of the level of measurement of your data, all bivariate data analysis begins with contingency tables (these are sometimes called cross-tabulations or cross-tabs). Measures of association seek to identify the extent to which variation in one variable is linked to variation in another variable within a sample. A good way of starting the process of doing this is to produce a contingency table. A contingency table is a table setting out the cross-tabulation of two variables. It is then a visual representation of your hypothesis. When entering the two variables, your independent variable goes in the column, while the dependent variable goes in the row. A contingency table gives us visual clues as to whether there is any kind of a pattern in the relationship between two variables. Contingency tables are only the first step in measuring relationships between your variables. But like the graphical representations for univariate analysis discussed in Chapter 7 they do help in the initial process of spotting patterns in your data. Table 8.1 shows a contingency table for respondents' gender in relation to their perception of how good a job the police are doing, as recorded on a sliding scale running from 'excellent' to 'very poor'. We can see from this table that most men and women think the police are doing either a 'good' or 'fair' job. However, while the fact we have more women than men in our sample may explain some slight differences in male and female responses, it does seem that women are more likely than men to say they think the police are doing a 'good' or 'excellent' job, while men seem more likely to say they think the police are doing a 'very poor' job. Also, given there are less men than women in the sample it seems that proportionally speaking men are also more likely to say the police are doing a 'poor' job.

Table 8.1 Contingency table for male and female respondents' self-reported perception of how good a job the police do

		Respondent sex		Total
		Male	Female	
How good a job are the police doing?	Excellent	611	882	1493
	Good	4098	5776	9874
	Fair	4335	4973	9308
	Poor	1081	1086	2167
	Very poor	357	265	622
Total		10482	12982	23464

Table 8.1 reinforces how contingency tables draw attention to key patterns in the data; however, they can only tell us so much about the relationships between our variables. We can see from a well-presented table whether there is a pattern in the data so that variation in one variable corresponds with variation in the other,

i.e. as more men than women think the police are doing a 'very poor' job and more women than men think the police are doing an 'excellent' job, we may tentatively conclude that a respondent's gender is somehow related to their perception of the quality of the job done by the police. This is an interesting finding. But noticing this does not tell us whether such a link is strong enough to be more than just a chance blip. For this, we need to do a correlation test, or a measure of association as it is more commonly called. As the next section of the chapter discusses, measures of association measure the strength of a relationship within numeric data.

Measures of association

Once you have generated a contingency table the next step is to conduct an appropriate correlation test known as a measure of association. Quantitative statistical software packages, such as SPSS, enable a researcher to generate contingency tables and measure of association statistics with a few clicks of a mouse. Students nowadays do not need to know how to calculate a measure of association test; rather they must focus on understanding how to correctly interpret the result. The most important thing to remember as you begin the analytical process is that the type of measure of association you use depends on the level of measurement of your variables. Box 8.3 outlines the different statistical tests discussed in this chapter and when they should be used.

Box 8.3

Measures of association and levels of measurement

The first rule to learn when conducting a bivariate analysis is that the measure of association you use to test for a relationship between your two variables is dictated by their level of measurement. The second rule to learn is that when the level of measurement for your two variables differs (e.g. one of your variables is ordinal and one is interval) you must always use the measure of association statistical test that is appropriate for the lowest level of measurement. In this chapter we will discuss three key measures of association test – Phi and Cramer's V, Spearman's rho and Pearson's r – as well as one commonly used measure of significance – chi-square. Measures of significance are discussed in Box 8.4. For the moment it is important to make sure when doing your bivariate analysis that you apply the appropriate measure of association, as follows:

(Continued)

(Continued)

What level of measurement are your two variables?	Which measure of association test?
Nominal and nominal	Phi or Cramer's V *
Nominal and ordinal	Cramer's V
Nominal and interval	Cramer's V
Ordinal and ordinal	Spearman's rho
Ordinal and interval	Spearman's rho
Interval and interval	Pearson's r

*When both your variables are nominal and dichotomous then use the phi test, e.g. if you are testing for an association between males and females in relation to whether they own a house (which, like male/female, possesses a dichotomous response of yes/no). Use Cramer's V when either one or both variables are non-dichotomous but both are still nominal, e.g. when you are testing for an association between males and females in relation to whether they own a blue, red, yellow or green car.

Phi and Cramer's V

As Box 8.3 shows, phi and Cramer's V measures of association are used when one or more of your variables has a nominal level of measurement. These two measures of association are closely related; however, the key difference between them is that you use phi when both your nominal variables are dichotomous. These statistics, like the chi-square test we will discuss shortly, are calculated on the basis of the observed count for each cell of the contingency table compared to the expected count for each cell if there was no association between the two variables. However, the mathematics behind this calculation, as with the other measures of association discussed in this chapter, are beyond the scope of this book, and the key thing to remember is how to interpret the result. Cramer's V is measured from 0 to 1, with 0 meaning no association and 1 meaning a perfect association. The following sliding scale is useful for identifying the strength of the association between your two variables:

0 = no association
0.19 or less is a very low association
0.20 to 0.39 is low association
0.40 to 0.69 is modest association
0.70 to 0.89 is high association
0.90 and higher is very high association
1 = a perfect association

Let's examine this further by looking for a possible association between gender and fear of being attacked. Imagine the variables involved are ordinal and nominal levels of measurement, so Cramer's V as a nominal test is most appropriate. Having identified the right test to use it is now important to interpret the result. If we were to run the Cramer's V test for gender and fear of being attacked and receive a result of 0.30 then this would indicate that there is a low association between gender and fear of being attacked. We therefore need to consider the possibility that there may be an intervening variable in the relationship between gender and fear of being attacked. Is age a factor and are younger women more concerned about being attacked than older women (or vice versa)? Such considerations reinforce the need to critically evaluate the strengths and weaknesses of the data-set used, as well as to perhaps collect further data to explore such possibilities, in addition to considering new research avenues. For example, what does the fact that the data seems to show that women aren't quite as worried about being attacked as one may expect say about the role of the media, as opposed to other information sources, in influencing women's attitudes and beliefs towards violent crime?

Like Cramer's V, the association scale for phi (which is sometimes referred to as the phi coefficient) runs from 0 to 1; 0 means there is no association while 1 means there is a perfect association. However, unlike the Cramer's V, this can be a positive or negative association, while the strength of the association is also interpreted differently. So the phi result can run from -1 to $+1$. With phi the result will almost certainly vary between 0 (zero or no correlation) and 1 (a perfect correlation), which thus indicates the strength of a relationship. Hence the closer the result is to 1, the stronger the relationship; the closer it is to zero, the weaker the relationship (0 means there is no relationship). Typically a $-$ or $+$ result of 0.7 or higher is taken to mean there is a strong correlation between the two variables, while a $-$ or $+$ result of 0.5 or higher is taken to mean there is a weak to moderate correlation between the two variables. Anything less than this is seen to be a very weak correlation. This is because where the result is -1 or $+1$ the relationship between the two variables is said to be a perfect association with no other variables intervening. Anything less than -1 or $+1$, then a third (or even fourth or fifth!) variable is intervening between the two variables in question. So if we are looking at age and if a person has been a victim of crime, and our result was $+1$, then we could say that a person's age correlates perfectly with their experience of crime; however, if our result was $+0.7$ then we could say that the correlation is strong, but other variables seem to be intervening in the relationship between age and if a person has been a victim of crime, such as their geographical location or gender for instance. It is also important to note that a positive or negative value of the result indicates the direction of a relationship between the two variables. A positive result means that when one variable increases so does the other variable. So if our result for age and if a person has been a victim of crime is $+0.7$ then this means that as their age increases so does their likelihood of being a victim of crime; while a negative result means that while one variable increases the other decreases. So if our result for age and if a person has been a victim of crime is −0.7 then the older a person gets the less likely they are to be a victim of crime.

Measures of significance: the chi-square test

Clearly then, phi and Cramer's V are useful statistical tests, which can help us test for a hypothesised relationship between two variables in a relatively straightforward fashion. They are particularly important, as social scientists often find themselves working with nominal data. We will look at the correlation tests for ordinal and interval tests in a moment. But before we do so it is important for the sake of continuity to look at the next stage in the analysis of our nominal data – measures of significance. These are tests which measure whether the results from a sample can reasonably be generalised to the wider population. Measures of association seek to identify the extent to which variation in one variable is linked to variation in another variable, within a given sample. However the next question must always be whether the results from the sample can be reasonably generalised to the wider population (this is sometimes called inferential statistics). A strong Cramer's V result in a very small sample may not be strong enough to generalise from, just as a weak association in a large sample might not be enough. The statistical tests to measure such a sufficiency are referred to as measures of significance, and there are significance tests designed for variables with different levels of measurement. Chi-square is one such test commonly used with nominal data, and because it can be used with nominal data, even dichotomous nominal data, it can be used for all variables.

The chi-square test determines whether there is enough evidence from the data-set to establish that the relationship between the variables is statistically significant. The purpose of the test is to make a judgement on whether the observed differences are in fact 'real' differences and not a result of fluctuation that occur by chance. Again, we should note here that complicated mathematical equations are at play in ascertaining the chi-square result, but what is important is that we correctly apply and interpret the result. Any appropriately performed test of statistical significance lets you know the degree of confidence you can have in accepting or rejecting a hypothesis. It is also important that you conduct the chi-square test on a null hypothesis. This is the exact opposite of what you think is the relationship between your variables. So if you think a person's age influences their fear of crime, and so expect there to be a correlation between age and fear of crime, then your null hypothesis would be that there is no relationship between age and fear of crime. A chi-square of 0.05 or less is commonly interpreted by social scientists as justification for rejecting the null hypothesis (see Box 8.4). Therefore, if our chi-square test on our association between age and fear of crime gave a .001 result, then this would show there is a significant relationship between the variables, and we could reject our null hypothesis, but statistical significance does not interpret the nature or explanation of that relationship; that must be done by measures of association. So if our Cramer's V result for age and fear of crime as 0.7 – a high association – then we can say we have identified that there seems to be a strong relationship between age and fear of being attacked, while our chi-square result of 0.01 means we also seem to have a generalisable finding.

Box 8.4

Measures of significance: the chi-square test

Completing the measure of association test is the first stage in doing bivariate analysis. Having identified a correlation between two variables we next need to use a measure of significance to determine how confident we can be that our findings are not a product of chance. Criminologists, like other social scientists, use samples to collect data. This raises the possibility that our data may contain sampling error. That is, there may be a difference between the population (i.e. male and female victims of crime in the United Kingdom) and the sample you have obtained (i.e. male and female victims of crime who completed your research study questionnaire). If this happens, the sample will be unrepresentative of the wider population and any findings you have are not valid. Consequently we need to know how confident we can be that our findings can be generalised to the population. The chi-square test allows us to do this. First you must state your null hypothesis. This states that there is no relationship between the two variables in question in the population from which the sample was taken. So if we are examining the relationship between gender and cannabis drug use the null hypothesis would be that there is no relationship between gender and drug use in the population from which the sample was taken (so men in our sample will not report they consume cannabis more than women, and vice versa). The question we then have to ask ourselves is: what is the degree of risk we are prepared to accept so we can confidently reject the null hypothesis? Conventionally within the social sciences the statistical goal is to obtain a result which shows that there are up to 5 chances in 100 that we might be falsely concluding that there is a relationship when there isn't one in the population from which the sample was taken. This means that if we drew 100 samples, we are recognising that as many as 5 of them might say there is a relationship when there isn't one in the population. Our sample might be one of those 5, but the risk is fairly small. This significance level is denoted by $p < .05$ (p means probability). The smaller the chi-square value, the lower the risk of concluding that there is a relationship when there isn't one in the population from which the sample was taken. This can be expressed in the following way:

(Continued)

(Continued)

Figure 8.4.1 Interpreting the chi square result

p value	Meaning	Confidence to reject the null hypothesis
<.9	90 chances in 100	**Very low**
<.8	80 chances in 100	
<.7	70 chances in 100	
<.6	60 chances in 100	
<.5	50 chances in 100	
<.4	40 chances in 100	
<.3	30 chances in 100	
<.2	20 chances in 100	
<.1	10 chances in 100	
- - - - - - - - - - - -	- - - - - - - - - - - -	
<.05	5 chances in 100	
<.01	1 chance in 100	
<.001	1 chance in 1000	**Very high**
	of falsely rejecting the null hypothesis, i.e. of concluding that there is a relationship between 2 variables when there isn't one in the population from which the sample was taken.	

NB As the chi-square result increases, the confidence in rejecting the null hypothesis decreases. The hyphenated line (----) represents the minimum level of statistical significance accepted by criminologists (i.e. a chi-square result of 0.05 or lower). If your result is higher than this then you have to accept your null hypothesis.

Spearman's rho

Spearman's rho is the appropriate correlation test when dealing with either two ordinal variables or one ordinal and one interval variable. Like the phi measure of association, the Spearman's rho result can vary between 0 and 1 and be negative or positive. Often the Spearman's rho statistical test result is illustrated using a scatter gram. Figure 8.1 illustrates positive and negative correlations, alongside when there is no correlation, as displayed by a scatter gram. Scatter grams operate on an x- and y-axis. The independent variable is placed on the x-axis and the dependent variable on the y-axis, with each case variable being plotted along the respective axis; hence the distribution of the plots indicates the relationship (if any) between the two variables. This is why the positive correlation will run from left to right and the negative correlation from right to left. The closer the relationship is to a straight line the stronger the relationship, while the more random the plots the less likely the association.

Figure 8.1 Scatter grams illustrating correlation test results

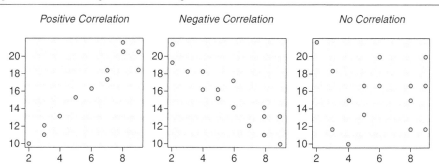

The Spearman's rho result will vary between 0 (zero or no correlation) and 1 (a perfect correlation), which thus indicates the strength of a relationship. Hence the closer the result is to 1, the stronger the relationship; the closer it is to zero, the weaker the relationship (0 means there is no relationship). Typically a − or + result of 0.7 or higher is taken to mean there is a strong correlation between the two variables, while a − or + result of 0.5 or higher is taken to mean there is a weak to moderate correlation between the two variables. Anything less than this is seen to be a very weak correlation. This is because where the result is −1 or +1 the relationship between the two variables is said to be a perfect association with no other variables intervening. Anything less than −1 or +1, then a third (or even fourth or fifth) variable is intervening between the two variables in question. Remember, the positive or negative value of the result indicates the direction of a relationship between the two variables. A positive result means that when one variable increases so does the other variable, while a negative result means that while one variable increases the other decreases. Additionally, just as with phi and Cramer's V, we also need to run a measure of significance test in addition to the measure of association test. Usually data analysis software programs such as SPSS will provide a significance result along with the correlation result in a format similar to that found in Table 8.2.

Table 8.2 Spearman's rho and measure of significance test

Income and Happiness Correlation	
Spearman's rho	.733
Significance	.001
Number (in sample)	19987

The measure of significance provided with the Spearman's rho correlation is read in the same manner as the chi-square result: a result of 0.05 or less means you can reject the null hypothesis (see Box 8.4). Consequently, the example in Table 8.2 of income and happiness shows that there is a strong positive correlation between income and happiness – the more a person earns the happier they say they are – while the significance level of .001 shows that we have one chance in 1000 of falsely rejecting the null hypothesis; so we can confidently reject the null hypothesis, as we are unlikely to be falsely reporting the relationship between our two variables when it doesn't exist within the population from which the sample was taken. Please note: what this means is that we can have strong positive or negative association between our two variables but if our significance result is too high, then we must accept our null hypothesis. Often this happens because our sample is too small; the larger the sample the better. Similarly, we can have a weak or no association between our two variables but our significance result can be strong (even if our sample is small) – a point which in itself reinforces the importance of critically reflecting on the implications of our result. After all, the hypothesised relationship between our two variables is grounded in your reading of the academic literature, so whatever result you get, make sure you interpret it within this context.

Pearson's r

The Pearson's r test is used when both your variables are interval. Like the phi and the Spearman's rho, the Pearson's r result can vary between 0 and 1 and be negative or positive. Indeed, the Pearson's r is calculated in the same way as the Spearman's rho, and you should use scatter grams to visually display your correlation (see Figure 8.1). The closer the result is to 1, the stronger the relationship; the closer it is to zero, the weaker the relationship (0 means there is no relationship). Again, typically a – or + result of 0.7 or higher is taken to mean there is a strong correlation between the two variables, while a – or + result of 0.5 or higher is taken to mean there is a weak to moderate correlation between the two variables. Anything less than this is seen to be a very weak correlation. This is because where the result is −1 or +1 the relationship between the two variables is said to be a perfect association with no other variables intervening. Anything less than −1 or +1, then a third (or even fourth or fifth) variable is intervening between the two variables in question. Remember, the positive or negative value of the result indicates the direction of a relationship between the two variables. A positive result means that when one variable increases so does the other variable, while a negative result means that while one variable increases the other decreases. Additionally, just as with phi and Cramer's V and Spearman's rho, we also need to run a measure of significance test in addition to the measure of association test. Usually data analysis software programs such as SPSS will provide a significance result along with the correlation result in a format similar to that found in Table 8.3.

Table 8.3 Pearson's r and measure of significance test

Age and Wealth Correlation	
Pearson's r	.877
Significance	.001
Number (in sample)	29987

The measure of significance provided with the Pearson's r correlation is read in the same manner as the chi-square result: a result of 0.05 or less means you can reject the null hypothesis (see Box 8.4). Consequently, the example in Table 8.3 of age and wealth shows that there is a strong positive correlation between age and wealth – the older a person the more wealth they have – while the significance level of .001 shows that we have one chance in 1000 of falsely rejecting the null hypothesis; so we can confidently reject the null hypothesis as we are unlikely to be falsely reporting the relationship between our two variables when it doesn't exist within the population from which the sample was taken.

Box 8.5

An example of how to do a bivariate analysis: exploring gender and fear of crime

Chapter 8 has outlined key procedures relating to the analysis of bivariate data, noting as it did so how this typically leads on from univariate analysis, which was discussed in Chapter 7. Often students are asked to undertake a univariate and bivariate analysis of secondary data (i.e. data which has been collected by somebody else) so they can demonstrate to their tutor their developing understanding of how to do quantitative criminological research. The following example of a report into the possible relationship between gender and fear of crime, written from the perspective of a student writing a short report for a class assignment, should help you further familiarise yourself with how to complete a quantitative data analysis involving both univariate and bivariate elements.

(Continued)

(Continued)

Important note: Although in the example the author states they are using the Crime Survey for England and Wales (CSEW) data-set, in reality this is for illustrative purposes only and should not be taken to mean that the statistical data outlined and discussed reflect the actual content of the CSEW data-set. This is because university tutors often use the CSEW in their teaching, as well as for practical assessment purposes, so it would provide the reader with an unfair advantage over their peers if they where to find the answers here to set assessment tasks without doing the analysis themselves. The following report should therefore be solely used as an illustrative self-study tool by the reader to help them get to grips with the conduct of quantitative data analysis.

Report

Introduction and rationale

This report will be based upon the secondary data analysis of the Crime Survey for England and Wales (CSEW). I have been asked to examine the relationship between two variables after looking at previous literature around the topic, and to produce a report of my findings. The two variables I have chosen to focus on are gender and fear of being attacked. Smith and Torstensson (1997) argued that women are less likely to be victims of violent crime, but in their research they found that women feared being attacked more so than men. Indeed, much of the criminological literature presents findings that imply women fear being attacked more than men (Walklate 2004). I consequently decided to investigate this matter further for my statistical class report using the CSEW as it is the largest victim survey available in the United Kingdom and as such provides a robust data-set from which to explore the relationship between gender and fear of crime.

Causation, in basic terms, is the process that makes an outcome happen. With regard to my variables, if gender is the independent variable and fear of being attacked is the dependent variable, then gender will influence the degree of fear a person feels. However, it is important to note that outcomes are rarely influenced by a single cause. Causation is too complex to reach outcomes with total certainty, therefore it can be misleading. There are sufficient conditions of causation, meaning that it is not true to say that all women fear being attacked more so than men, as there will be other factors that influence one's fear of being attacked, for example the area the individual lives in (Bryman 2008). Correlation, on the other hand, is the pattern associated between two variables. This is relevant for my variables as it cannot be absolutely true that all women will fear crime more than men, or that people who fear crime the most are all women, as this is a causal explanation. However, I can state that there will be a correlation but the strength of the relationship needs further research (Bryman 2008). The null hypothesis is that there is no relationship between gender and fear of being attacked. Based on the short literature review outlined above, I have formulated the hypothesis that women fear being attacked more than men. I will now test this hypothesis using a series of statistical tests to analyse a particular data-set.

Secondary data analysis

The data-set I will be using is the CSEW, which is a source of information that measures levels of crime and people's experiences and attitudes about crime. The survey includes crimes which may not have been reported to the police, or recorded by them, therefore providing an important alternative to crime statistics recorded by the police. Because members of the public are asked directly about their experiences the CSEW arguably provides a robust and consistent measure of crime. The results play a significant role in informing Home Office future policies. The survey is conducted annually in England and Wales by interviewing roughly 50,000-plus randomly selected people in their private households. I will be looking at data from the CSEW recorded in 2011 using a subsample of just under 20,000 people. CSEW data is available online via the Ministry of Justice website (http://www.justice.gov.uk/).

As I will be looking into the existing data of a large survey undertaken by government agencies, and analysing and presenting the findings with my own interpretations, I will be conducting a secondary data analysis. The key strength of secondary data is that I can analyse data from a large sample that would not be possible for me to collect myself. However, secondary data can be limited by the availability and quality of existing data. The CSEW data-set I will be using contains only quantitative data, which means I have no reference to in-depth qualitative data, such as semi-structured interviews (Bryman 2008). I will return to this point in my concluding discussion.

Statistical characteristics of each variable (univariate analysis)

Before I can statistically analyse the two variables, I must identify the level of measurement for each variable. The independent variable, 'Gender of respondent', is nominal data as the response cannot be categorised into any specific order as there are only two options and there is no scale or sequence. The dependent variable, 'How worried are you about being attacked?', is ordinal data because the responses are categorised and can be put into a rank order, but no mathematical calculation or specific measure of relative scale can be made in relation to the distances between each category. The rank order is characterised as *Very worried, Fairly worried, Not very worried* and *Not at all worried* (see Figure 8.5.2).

The first univariate I will investigate is gender. Table 8.5.1 shows both the percentages and frequency of each gender.

Table 8.5.1   Frequency table to show the gender of respondents

		Frequency	Percent	Valid Percent	Cumulative Percent
Valid	Male	8827	45.5	45.5	45.5
	Female	10584	54.5	54.5	100.0
	Total	19411	100.0	100.0	

(Continued)

I have constructed a pie chart to show the distribution of gender used in this sample (see Figure 8.5.1).

Figure 8.5.1   Pie chart to show the gender of respondents

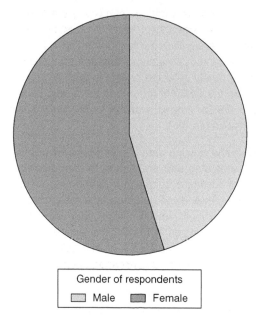

Gender of respondents

☐ Male   ▨ Female

Both Table 8.5.1 and Figure 8.5.1 show that out of a total of 19,411 respondents, the majority are female (10,584) and represent 54.5 per cent of this sample. I have constructed a bar graph that shows the frequency of respondents within each fear category (see Figure 8.5.2).

Table 8.5.2   Frequency table to show how worried the respondents are about being attacked

		Frequency	Percent	Valid Percent	Cumulative Percent
Valid	Very worried	3384	17.4	17.5	17.5
	Fairly worried	4796	24.7	24.8	42.3
	Not very worried	7589	39.1	39.2	81.5
	Not at all worried	3576	18.4	18.5	100.0
	Total	19345	99.7	100.0	
Missing	(Not applicable)	50	.3		
	9	16	.1		
	Total	66	.3		
Total		19411	100.0		

Figure 8.5.2 Bar chart to show how worried the respondents are about being attacked

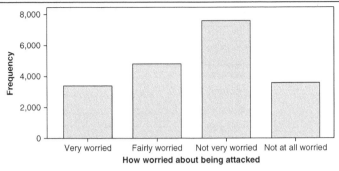

How worried about being attacked

Both Table 8.5.2 and Figure 8.5.2 show the majority of people, 7589 respondents out of a total of 19,345, chose 'Not very worried'. Of the 19,345 responses, 66 responses were missing and so have been excluded from Figure 8.5.2.

The measure of central tendency shows the typical value that summarises the distribution of values within a variable. Table 8.5.3 shows the typical value that best summarises the distribution of values in the gender variable. The mode is used in this case because gender is a nominal variable.

Table 8.5.3 Mode of the variable 'Gender of respondent'

N	Valid	19411
Mode		Female

Table 8.5.4 shows the measure of central tendency for the fear of being attacked variable. As this is an ordinal variable, I have used the median as I am dealing with attitudinal scales, and the median places the categories in rank order. The mode is the most frequently occurring value. As Table 8.5.4 shows, both the median and the mode were the 'not very worried' value.

Table 8.5.4 Mode and median of the variable 'How worried are you about being attacked?'

N	**Valid**	**19345**
Missing		66
Median		'Not very worried'
Mode		'Not very worried'

Statistical analysis of both variables (bivariate analysis)

I will now begin my bivariate analysis of the two variables. I have created a cross-tabulation and will use this to describe and explore the relationship between gender and fear of being attacked. I have placed the independent variable, gender, in the columns of Table 8.5.5 and the dependent variable, fear of being attacked, in the row. This will allow me to explore the responses of each gender with regard to their fear of crime.

(Continued)

(Continued)

Table 8.5.5   How worried about being attacked, by gender of respondent

		Gender of respondent		Total
		Male	Female	
How worried about being attacked	Very worried	682	2702	3384
	Fairly worried	1856	2940	4796
	Not very worried	3957	3632	7589
	Not at all worried	2308	1268	3576
Total		8803	10542	19345

Table 8.5.5 shows the count of the number of respondents in each fear value in the total column. It also shows the distribution of the gender of respondent within each fear category. For example, in the 'Very worried' cell, the count of the number of men is 682, and the count for women is a lot higher at 2702. From the table, I can see that the total number of men, 8803, is significantly fewer than the total number of women, 10542. Therefore, I have created a column percentage which will show the percentage of men and women for each fear cell/category. By comparing the column per cent between each of the categories in the independent variable of men and women, I have found that the differences in the column per cent in each row are large. For example, Table 8.5.6 shows that 26.2 per cent of men and 12 per cent of women felt they were 'Not at all worried' about being attacked. And from the 17.5 per cent of respondents to be 'very worried', 7.7 per cent were male and 25.6 per cent female.

Table 8.5.6   How worried about being attacked, by gender of respondent (includes %)

			Gender of respondent		Total
			Male	Female	
How worried about being attacked	Very worried	Count	682	2702	3384
		% within Gender of respondent	7.7%	25.6%	17.5%
	Fairly worried	Count	1856	2940	4796
		% within Gender of respondent	21.1%	27.9%	24.8%
	Not very worried	Count	3957	3632	7589
		% within Gender of respondent	45.0%	34.5%	39.2%
	Not at all worried	Count	2308	1268	3576
		% within Gender of respondent	26.2%	12.0%	18.5%
Total		Count	8803	10542	19345
		% within Gender of respondent	100.0%	100.0%	100.0%

I have used the data to create a clustered bar chart. Figure 8.5.3 shows each gender with a bar for each category in the dependent variable.

Looking at the bar chart, I have interpreted that more females chose the higher fear categories compared to their male counterparts, and that more males chose the lower fear categories in comparison to their female counterparts. For example, in the 'Fairly worried' category, there is a count of 2940 women and 1856 men.

Figure 8.5.3 A clustered bar chart to show the count of males and females within each 'fear of being attacked' category

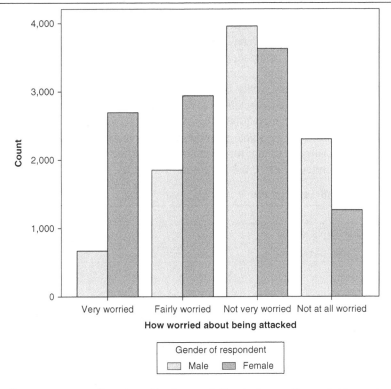

I will now measure the strength of association between the variables using the Cramer's V test. This will indicate the strength of the relationship between the two variables. Although my variables are ordinal and nominal, I will be using Cramer's V, a nominal test, because it is appropriate for the lowest value in terms of levels of measurement, which in this case is gender.

The value of Cramer's V will fall between 0 and 1, with 0 having no association and 1 indicating an absolute association. Table 8.5.7 shows the result, 0.430, which suggests a moderate strength of association between the variables. Therefore my hypothesis is correct as the measure of association shows there is a correlation, although not very strong.

(Continued)

Table 8.5.7   Cramer's V

	Value
Cramer's V	.430
N of Valid Cases	19345

The chi-square test (Table 8.5.8) determines whether there is enough evidence from the data-set to establish that the relationship between the variables is statistically significant. The purpose of the test is to make a judgement on whether the observed differences are in fact 'real' differences and not a result of fluctuation that occur by chance. Any appropriately performed test of statistical significance lets you know the degree of confidence you can have in accepting or rejecting a hypothesis. I will be testing my research hypothesis and the null hypothesis. I have read off the significant figure, which is .000 (Table 8.5.8). Chi-square probability of 0.05 or less is commonly interpreted by social scientists as justification for rejecting the null hypothesis (Bryman 2008). Therefore, .000 shows there is a significant relationship between the variables, but statistical significance does not interpret the nature or explanation of that relationship; that must be done by other measures of association (see Table 8.5.7 for Cramer's V result).

Table 8.5.8   chi-square

	Value
Pearson's chi-square	.000
N of Valid Cases	19345

Conclusion

Finally, I will relate my results to the literature I cited in the introduction. After carrying out several statistical examinations, I found that women are more afraid of being attacked than men. However, the strength of association was modest but nevertheless significant, therefore supporting my hypothesis and the published academic literature that had similar findings to mine. There may be a number of explanations for this modest association. For instance, these findings may be hindered by the socialisation of different genders, in that women may be able to openly admit fear whereas men may not (Walklate 2004). Also, women are constantly reminded by the media to be aware of their vulnerability in certain situations. In one study female respondents said they were far less confident than the male respondents in their ability to handle potentially violent situations, whereas the majority of male respondents claimed they would be willing and/or be able to manipulate violence, and protect themselves in a fight (Mehta 1999). Mehta argues that women's responses often strongly associate fear of being attacked in terms of sexual violence within public spaces such as streets and pubs, while men's responses typically do not. Thus, women's fear of attack, especially in relation to sexual violence, can perhaps be best understood as being embodied at least in part by experiences (or the experiences of women close to them) of intimidating and/or violent sexual behaviour, as well as experiences of themselves as physically vulnerable, as perhaps reinforced by popular media entertainment and crime news reporting. This is a point which in itself reinforces the need to conduct more in-depth qualitative research, perhaps using narrative life story interviews, to more fully identify the effect of media imagery, alongside the shared life story experiences of people close to them, on both women's and men's self-reported fear of crime. Indeed, as I am looking at the relationship between gender and fear of being attacked to find a correlation, I need to be aware that there may be a number of other factors which may also influence why certain people fear being attacked. Possible intervening variables mentioned in the academic literature which may influence a person's fear of crime include the neighbourhood in which the person lives, their age, their ethnicity and their sexual orientation (Walklate 2004). This may go to explain the modest strength of the association between gender and fear of crime that I found in my research study. In conclusion, the findings presented in this report showed that women fear being attacked more than men, but it is important to recognise that further research is needed, including using qualitative research methods, before any firm conclusions can be drawn.

References

Bryman, A. (2008) *Social Research Methods* (3rd edn). Oxford: Oxford University Press.

Mehta, A. (1999) Embodied discourse: gender and fear of violence, *Gender, Place and Culture*, 6(1): 67–84.

Smith, W. and Torstensson, M. (1997) Gender differences in the risk perception and neutralizing fear of crime: toward resolving the paradoxes, *British Journal of Criminology*, 37(4): 608–34.

Walklate, S. (2004) *Gender, Crime and Criminal Justice* (2nd edn). Cullompton, Devon: Willan Publishing.

Criticisms of Bivariate Analysis

Bivariate analysis involves the use of correlation statistics to investigate a possible relationship between two variables, e.g. gender and fear of crime. Bivariate analysis is routinely used by criminologists as it helps to test a hypothesis developed as a result of a review of relevant published literature, which may well include the results of qualitative research studies or the outcomes of quantitative univariate analysis. A thorough understanding of correlation statistics is essential for the appropriate and effective use of bivariate analysis. However, bivariate analysis can be criticised for offering an overly simplistic view of social reality, as often intervening variables act on relationships between two variables, e.g. there may well be a relationship between gender and fear of crime but one would also expect age and geographical location to play a role in influencing a person's fear of crime. It is important to bear this in mind when discussing the results of correlation statistical tests and the implications of one's findings.

Conclusion and Bivariate Data Analysis Flow Chart

The chapter has outlined how the process of doing a bivariate analysis involves generating contingency tables and scatter grams to display and explore data, as well as how measures of association and measures of significance enable criminologists to statistically judge the strengths of relationships they find in their data and see if they can generalise with confidence from a research sample to a larger population. Box 8.7 contains a flow chart guide detailing the appropriate bivariate statistics to use given the level of measurement. Additionally, Box 8.5 contains an illustrative example of a combined univariate and bivariate data analysis, which explores a possible relationship between gender and fear of crime, in order to illustrate not just how criminologists do quantitative data analysis, but also how the analytical process is grounded in current academic discourse surrounding a substantive criminological research area. Within criminology, like any other social science, quantitative research is undertaken to paint a rich picture of what is happening in relation to a topic, in order to contribute to current academic discourse surrounding it, in addition to seeking to influence the policy-making process and how criminal justice agencies conceptualise and respond to the problem of crime. The information and resources provided in this chapter should enable you to begin to participate in this process. However, it is important to remember that Chapters 7 and 8 together act as an introduction to 'number analysis' for the student exploring quantitative data analysis for the first time. There are a range of statistical techniques still to learn, i.e. t-tests, factor analysis and regression statistics, to name but a few. Multi-variable analysis – the analysis of three or more variables – also waits to be explored. The recommended readings in Box 8.6 will help you further develop your analytical skills.

Box 8.6

'Next steps': recommended readings

The following key readings will help you to consolidate what you have learnt in this chapter, expand your skills to include more complicated statistical techniques, and provide an introduction to how to use the software package SPSS to help you analyse quantitative data.

Bryman, A. and Cramer, D. (2011) *Quantitative Data Analysis with SPSS 17, 18 and 19: A Guide for Social Scientists*. London: Routledge.

Bushway, S. and Westburd, D. (2005) *Quantitative Methods in Criminology*. Aldershot: Ashgate Publishing.

Howitt, D. and Cramer, D (2011) *Introduction to Statistics in Psychology*. London: Pearson Education.

Box 8.7

Doing a bivariate data analysis: summary flow chart

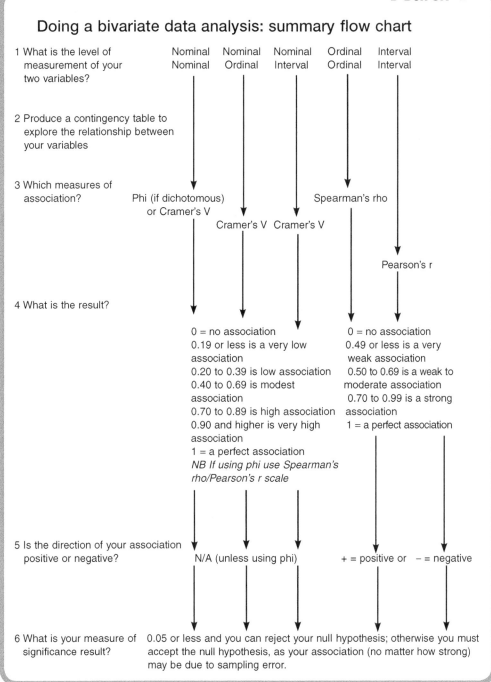

1 What is the level of measurement of your two variables?

Nominal	Nominal	Nominal	Ordinal	Interval
Nominal	Ordinal	Interval	Ordinal	Interval

2 Produce a contingency table to explore the relationship between your variables

3 Which measures of association?

Phi (if dichotomous) or Cramer's V

Spearman's rho

Cramer's V Cramer's V

Pearson's r

4 What is the result?

0 = no association
0.19 or less is a very low association
0.20 to 0.39 is low association
0.40 to 0.69 is modest association
0.70 to 0.89 is high association
0.90 and higher is very high association
1 = a perfect association
NB If using phi use Spearman's rho/Pearson's r scale

0 = no association
0.49 or less is a very weak association
0.50 to 0.69 is a weak to moderate association
0.70 to 0.99 is a strong association
1 = a perfect association

5 Is the direction of your association positive or negative?

N/A (unless using phi)

+ = positive or – = negative

6 What is your measure of significance result?

0.05 or less and you can reject your null hypothesis; otherwise you must accept the null hypothesis, as your association (no matter how strong) may be due to sampling error.

CHAPTER REVIEW ACTIVITIES

1   Write a PowerPoint presentation lasting no more than 10 minutes which summarises how bivariate statistics enable a criminologist to investigate variables with different levels of measurement in order to test a hypothesis and check that their sample is representative of a larger population.

2   Download a copy of the Crime Survey for England and Wales from the Ministry of Justice (http://www.justice.gov.uk/) and identify two variables to investigate to see whether there is a relationship between them. Conduct an appropriate univariate and bivariate analysis and provide a report of your findings using the example report provided in Box 8.5 to guide you.

CHAPTER READING LIST

Bryman, A. (2008) *Social Research Methods* (3rd edn). Oxford: Oxford University Press.

Bryman, A. and Cramer, D. (2011) *Quantitative Data Analysis with SPSS 17, 18 and 19: A Guide for Social Scientists*. London: Routledge.

Bushway, S. and Westburd, D. (2005) *Quantitative Methods in Criminology*. Aldershot: Ashgate Publishing.

Howitt, D. and Cramer, D. (2011) *Introduction to Statistics in Psychology*. London: Pearson Education.

Mehta, A. (1999) Embodied discourse: gender and fear of violence, *Gender, Place and Culture*, 6(1): 67–84.

Smith, W. and Torstensson, M. (1997) Gender differences in the risk perception and neutralizing fear of crime: toward resolving the paradoxes, *British Journal of Criminology*, 37(4): 608–34.

Walklate, S. (2004) *Gender, Crime and Criminal Justice* (2nd edn). Cullompton, Devon: Willan Publishing.

9

Deskwork Revisited: Writing a Project Report

CHAPTER OVERVIEW

Chapter 9 returns to the topic of deskwork and outlines how to write up your research findings for dissemination. The chapter discusses a generic research report format which can be adapted for several different purposes, e.g. journal articles, government reports and for a dissertation project. Further readings and a chapter review activity are provided to help you apply what you have learned in your own research.

CHAPTER CONTENTS

Introduction

> ### Box 9.1
>
> ## Seven key elements of deskwork
>
> 1 Formulating an initial research area, focusing on study skills and dealing with assessment criteria.
> 2 Reviewing the literature and developing a research topic with a clear question to answer.
> 3 Project planning and research design.
> 4 Making contacts, gaining access and obtaining ethical approval to conduct your research.
> 5 Managing your fieldwork: timetabling.
> 6 Conducting data analysis.
> 7 **Writing up your findings and research dissemination.**

After outlining different forms of data analysis used by criminologists in previous chapters, in Chapter 9 we return to the theme of deskwork and discuss the writing-up and dissemination of research findings. Criminologists often present their research findings in different formats to different audiences, e.g. as an oral presentation for delivery at an academic conference, as a formal governmental report for a criminal justice agency such as the police service, as an article for a criminology journal, or as a PhD dissertation for submission to a university examiner. Also, as we have touched on when discussing qualitative forms of data analysis, notably narrative and discourse analysis, the emergence of anti-realist social constructivism has led some researchers to experiment with a range of alternative forms of research dissemination, including poetry, dramatic plays and collage work. As this book is aimed at the first-time researcher it is presumed you will be presenting your findings in a written report format for an assessed piece of coursework. Bearing this context in mind, Chapters 2 and 3 together reinforced the importance of deskwork and the need to carefully organise your research project, both during the topic identification and research design stage as well as subsequently as you collect your data. Furthermore, subsequent chapters, as they have discussed the process of doing data analysis, have reinforced that criminological research, whether it is qualitative or quantitative, or indeed a mixture of the two, is typically conducted while bearing firmly in mind academic and policy-making communities as well as the published literature which surrounds the topic under investigation.

What this means in practical terms is that the commonly held idea that a researcher first collects and then analyses their data before they begin to write their report, is somewhat false. Indeed, if you have followed the guidance offered in earlier chapters, then you will have already produced an account of what you know about your chosen topic in the form of a literature review. This, together with your proposed research methodology, will have formed an important part of your original research proposal. When producing your research proposal, the books, policy documents, research reports and journal articles you have discussed, as you initially outlined your research topic and the associated research question you are seeking to answer, will have been fashioned into an initial form that you can and should use to help you write your final research report. Of course, this does not necessarily make the act of writing up your research findings easier. The 'blank page' syndrome, where you stare at the empty computer screen, cursor flashing, but feel unable to put what you know into words, happens to everybody from time to time. Furthermore, the idea of communicating your research findings to an audience, who you know may well not agree with all of what you have to say, can be intimidating. Hence, a certain amount of nervous procrastination is common, particularly amongst first-time researchers. The sense of achievement a researcher often feels when they successfully collect and analyse their data can quickly give way to a sense of dread when they are faced with the task of communicating their findings to other people, often with the result that household chores like cleaning the windows, reorganising a book collection, or finding out how to make a green Thai curry, can seem much more attractive alternatives to sitting down at a computer screen to write. This is where the structure of the project report becomes important: it provides scaffolding you can use to help organise and plan your writing.

It is not possible to state exactly the form in which you will be expected to write up and present your research as this can vary depending on a range of factors, such as the academic qualification you are pursuing, or the type of academic journal or policy-making body you are submitting your work to. But you should expect to present your research in something along the lines of the generic format outlined in Box 9.2, which was first discussed in Chapter 2. This format is sufficiently structured to provide a guiding narrative form while at the same time is broad enough for it to be used for writing up your research findings for a range of purposes.

Box 9.2

Generic report format for presenting written research findings

All criminological research must be written up into a report for presentation to another person if it is to make a contribution to existing knowledge. Criminologists embed their research within current thinking surrounding their topic under study, as expressed in the form of the literature review where gaps in current knowledge

(Continued)

(Continued)

are highlighted and a project to fill them proposed; as well as later on when findings are reported, their implications discussed and further research plans outlined. Academic research is an accumulative exercise which never ends – all knowledge, no matter how persuasive and well evidenced, is temporary and open to ongoing debate and subsequent revision. Your goal is to become part of that ongoing conversation surrounding your topic through making some small but nevertheless important contribution to your chosen field of study, and perhaps just as importantly, outlining what to do next, now you have found out what you have. The generic report format discussed in this chapter will enable you to achieve this goal while also helping you to structure your writing as you try to organise your thoughts and present your findings for public consumption.

1 *Title page* (research title and author name).
2 *Abstract* (brief summary of research aims and key findings).
3 *Introduction* (overview of topic; statement of research aims and objectives; justification of why it is important; summary of subsequent chapter content).
4 *Literature review* (discussion of literature leading to the identification of key themes, issues, concepts and theories relevant to topic; identification of gaps in reviewed literature; statement of research aims and objectives in relation to these omissions).
5 *Methodology* (discussion of strengths and weaknesses of research strategy designed to meet stated research aims and objectives; consideration of access and research ethics alongside the process of data collection and analysis, e.g. questionnaire development and proposed statistical analysis procedures, given the type of data collected).
6 *Findings* (clear thematically organised discussion of findings obtained using a mixture of text and graphs to illustrate key findings as appropriate).
7 *Discussion* (analysis of findings obtained and their contribution to existing literature based on a critical appraisal of whether and how they fill previously identified 'literature gaps'; consideration of possible next steps for future research on topic).
8 *Conclusion* (evaluation of implications and consequences of research findings).

Writing your research report should not be a frantic exercise in brinkmanship. If you are writing up your research at the last minute you are approaching the task of managing your project incorrectly; it is strongly recommended that you take a step back and critically reflect on how you approach your studies. As we discussed in Chapter 2, you cannot achieve your full academic potential if you don't self-regulate your study skills and how you approach learning tasks. The structure outlined in Box 9.2 reinforces that the process of writing a research report has various stages which are completed at different points in time. First drafts may well need to be revised and rewritten over the duration of a project, but nevertheless the foundations for your project report should have been laid early on. The goal is to revise and redraft your work into an acceptable narrative form as you proceed from the initial research proposal stage through to obtaining ethical approval to conduct your study, collecting your data and analysing it, and finally, considering the implications of your findings. You are telling your reader a story about your topic: what its key features are, why it is important, how you went about finding out what you did, what the implications of your findings are, and so on. To achieve this goal you must approach your writing with discipline and carefully plan your work. Although there are no hard and fast rules about writing, the recommended readings in Box 9.3 will help you to better manage the writing process, while in the rest of this chapter we will discuss each of the report headings outlined in Box 9.2 to further help you.

Box 9.3

Recommended readings for writing up a research project

The following recommended readings will help you to manage the writing process and develop how you approach communicating research findings to different audiences:

Becker, H.S. (1986) *Writing for Social Scientists: How to Start and Finish Your Thesis, Book or Article*. Chicago: University of Chicago Press.

Harrison, J., Simpson, M., Harrison, O. and Martin, E. (2005) *Study Skills for Criminology* (*Sage Study Skills Series*). London: Sage Publications.

Thody, A. (2011) *Writing and Presenting Research*. London: Sage Publications.

Generic Research Report Structure

Title page

The title page should contain the title of your study, your name and the date. You may also need to include the title of the qualification you are studying or the name of the organisation you are submitting your report to. Chapter 2 reinforced the importance of knowing your assessment criteria at the proposal writing stage; you may need to include a statement on your title page stating your report is all your own work. Your title should be succinct but at the same time priority must be given to ensuring it accurately reflects the purpose of your study. Include a subtitle if it helps to clarify what your study is about. Don't panic if a clear title does not immediately come to mind. It can take some time to finalise your title. I often find myself hastily rewriting a title after I have finished a report and put it to one side for a few days so I can give it a final run through with a fresh pair of eyes (I usually also find I catch spelling mistakes this way too!). So remember, it is OK to revise your initial working title as a result of your research findings.

The example in Box 9.4 states the aim of the proposed research as 'undergraduate criminology student retention'; it is concerned with the issue of undergraduate students who drop out of their studies, while the subtitle raises the question of how important student grades and attendance are to this issue. Sometimes, asking a question as part of your title can help you keep your work focused as well as capture the reader's interest when it comes to communicating your findings. However, the most important thing is to make sure your title is clear and to the point. Asking a friend who does not study on the same course what they think about your title – Is it clear? Does it make sense? Does it tell them what to expect if they were to read your work? – can prove invaluable in helping you to finalise your title. Do not fall into the trap of thinking there is only one right way to present your work but make sure you talk to your supervisor to double-check that your title is acceptable before you submit your work.

Note: After your title page you may need to include an acknowledgements page, where you thank any individuals or organisations that helped you undertake your research, followed by a contents page, which outlines the main sections of your report and their page numbers. Again, remember to double-check the format you are expected to adhere to when you submit your research report.

Box 9.4

Report example: title page

Undergraduate criminology student retention: are grades and attendance really that important?

By Dr John M. Chamberlain

June 2012

Abstract

An abstract provides a brief summary of your work; usually it is between 150 and 250 words in length. The goal is to provide a succinct introduction to the problem under study, the key findings obtained, as well as the main conclusions made. The example abstract in Box 9.5 outlines in short and clear sentences the aims of the research – Is there a relationship between student attendance and the grades they achieve? – and how this is related to a broader concern with helping individual students academically to minimise the drop-out rate from a programme of study. It notes that although a relationship was found, other factors also seem to be at play in influencing students' academic achievements, so it concludes that student retention requires a broader focus on a range of possible factors. This concluding point ensures the reader's interest is maintained, because although the study's main findings are outlined, not everything is revealed: sometimes it can be useful to try to 'hook' your reader in this way.

Writing a clear abstract is a skill which can take time to develop. Reading the abstracts at the beginning of journal articles can help you to become familiar with the expected style: does reading it provide you with a good idea of the content of the paper, how the data presented was collected and from whom, as well as what key conclusions were reached? Be prepared to take your time and draft and redraft your abstract as you write up your findings – talk to a friend and ask their opinion, and ask your supervisor what they think about your abstract. Talking to your supervisor is particularly important as sometimes you will not need to include an abstract with your work. Nevertheless, under these circumstances, it can still be highly useful to produce an abstract as it can help you develop a focused and clear answer for when your tutors (and friends and family!) ask you about your research and what you are *actually* doing, while it can also be helpful when it comes to finalising the content of your project report.

Box 9.5

Report example: abstract

This report discusses the findings of research concerned with analysing the relationship between first-year student attendance and the grades they receive in their first summative assessed coursework task. The research took place against the background of a concern with improving student retention and minimising academic failure. The research found evidence of an association between student attendance and grade outcomes. However, it was also noted that other factors, such as entry qualifications, age, gender and personal circumstance, can play an important role in influencing the grades students achieve. It concludes that the findings presented reinforce the need to introduce innovative multi-dimensional retention programmes if academic departments are to improve student retention.

Introduction

The introduction section of your report should provide an overview of your topic: just what is your research problem and why is it important? If you have a research hypothesis to test, state it here. This section should end with a brief summary of subsequent report content. The example of an introduction in Box 9.6 provides a clear introductory background to the study that will be subsequently discussed: the aims and objectives of the research are stated, its importance justified, as well as the structure and content of the report briefly outlined. Note here that the outline of the third section actually covers the last three sections of the report format found in Box 9.2. This is because we are here providing a brief summary of our report – this final section will be broken down into a series of interrelated subsections: 'findings', 'discussion' and 'conclusion'. Remember, it is important to make sure you are flexible in your approach to structuring your report while also adhering to expected presentational requirements. Again, seek guidance from your supervisor if you are unsure what to do.

Box 9.6

Report example: introduction

This report outlines the results of research concerned with examining the relationship between first-year criminology student attendance and their assessment outcomes for core programme modules. The stated research aims and objectives were to examine the commonly held assumption that students who attend class achieve better grades while students who do not attend class achieve lower grades. The research was undertaken against the background of a concern with, as far as possible, minimising student academic failure and promoting student retention. In the face of the current economic climate – which increasingly sees higher education institutions worldwide vying for a piece of the competitive fee-paying educational marketplace while operating within the context of a global recession – it is arguably more important than ever before that criminology programmes focus on the issue of student retention. The report is divided into three sections. In the first section it discusses relevant literature pertaining to its topic; it then moves on in the second section to outline the research methodology; and finally, the third section outlines the report findings and discusses their implications before highlighting areas for further possible research.

Literature review

The literature review section of your report should cover the literature researched around your topic as a background against which your own research takes place. Remember, Chapter 2 and Chapter 3 discussed how your review of the literature must cover key relevant material in a critically aware fashion to set the scene for your own research. The key is not to include everything you have read for the sake of it, but rather to tell a story using key information to evidence your points as needed. You will have originally written your literature review when you fashioned your original research proposal, yet you are likely to have discovered new material as you collected your data and analysed it; hence at the report-writing stage it should be a matter of redrafting what you have already written and adding any additional material as needed, so your final review provides a framework in which your own research is clearly positioned. Remember to include any sources you cite in a reference list at the end of your report. The example provided in Box 9.7 begins by focusing on literature relevant to student retention before moving on to discuss student attendance and why it is important to investigate this issue when seeking to minimise the number of first-year students dropping out of their university studies. In doing so it provides a clear, well-evidenced context against which subsequent research findings can be outlined and discussed.

Box 9.7

Report example: literature review

Student retention: a multi-dimensional issue

The research described in this report was conducted as part of a broader concern with improving undergraduate criminology student retention. This section of the report will outline relevant academic literature to highlight the importance of analysing student attendance and grade outcomes in relation to the issue of student retention. Over the last three decades research studies have highlighted a number of commonly occurring personal and academic factors surrounding why students leave a degree programme (e.g. Tinto 1975, 1987; Rickinson and Rutherford 1995; Yorke 1997; Johnson 2002; Wilcox et al. 2005; Zepke et al. 2006). Davies and Elias (2003) found the main reasons for student withdrawal were 'a mistaken choice of course', 'financial problems' and 'personal problems'. Unpacking 'personal problems', Rickinson and Rutherford (1995), Gann (2003) and Collins and Lin (2003) found that financial and job worries, poor accommodation, as well as feelings of homesickness, loneliness and isolation, were commonly self-reported by students withdrawing from their studies or transferring to another university (often so they could be nearer to the parental home). Poor study skills, a lack of self-confidence and a general sense of dissatisfaction with their higher education experience all also play a role in student withdrawal (Assiter and Gibbs 2007). Finally it has also been noted that socio-economic background and race and ethnicity can play a role in influencing the decision to withdraw (Parry 2002).

Clearly, there are a number of factors which can to varying degrees influence an individual student's decision to withdraw from their studies. Student withdrawal is a multi-dimensional issue, not easily solvable by a single 'one-size fits all' intervention (Zepke et al. 2006). Furthermore it is arguable that 'in house' transfers between academic programmes, or academic transfers between universities, are

(Continued)

(Continued)

a consequence of the contemporary emphasis placed upon promoting opportunity and student choice within a consumer-led higher education marketplace (Johnson 2002). Similarly it can be said that students postponing or withdrawing from their studies for health, financial or family reasons will to some extent always be a reoccurring feature of the higher education system (Johnes and McNabb 2004). However, it is equally arguable that a concern with equity and widening participation means universities need to do all they can to help students with the complex interplay of academic and personal issues which can cause them to withdraw from their studies (Cavico and Mujtaba 2010), particularly in today's competitive global educational marketplace (Yorke and Longdon 2004).

Richardson and Skinner (1991) suggest academic and other university departments (e.g. student welfare and study skill support services) can address the issue of student retention through working in tandem with students and associated student-led organisations, as well as local and national voluntary and statutory agencies, in relation to the following three key areas: 1) student recruitment, financial aid and admissions; 2) outreach work, peer mentoring, accommodation and the student experience of university life outside of the educational process; and 3) the learning environment, teaching and assessment strategies, as well as learning and study skill support. Critically reflecting upon the third key area highlighted by Richardson and Skinner (1991), and in particular looking at learning and study skill support for students, Syndow and Sandel (1996: 10) argue that individual academic teaching departments within universities should develop 'a process for monitoring student behaviours associated with failure (e.g. excessive absenteeism, failing grades, failure to turn in assignments etc.) … and intervention strategies should be employed to help these at-risk students succeed.'

It is important that teaching staff identify, follow up and meet with students who fail an assessment, provide what support they can to help each student, as well as where necessary refer them to specialist services for further guidance and support. The assumption that all students who fail an assessment are under-prepared or intellectually deficient must be challenged (Tinto 1975). Students are not solely responsible for academic failure and therefore should not be solely responsible for seeking support to address it (Yorke 1999). Indeed academics concerned with student retention (e.g. Johnson 2002; Yorke and Longdon 2004; Wilcox et al. 2005; Zepke et al. 2006) argue that it is important – particularly during a student's first year of university – to focus on course design and teaching and assessment methods, in addition to providing targeted learning support, to address study skill issues as well as learners' self-awareness of how they approach educational tasks. Research shows that integrating study skills sessions within interactive and collaborative teaching and learning methods, on discipline-specific topics for first-year students, seems to be beneficial in fostering

ing peer-group and staff–student relationships – which in turn can help student retention and address academic failure (Lowe and Cook 2003; Yorke and Thomas 2003; Wilcox et al. 2005).

Focusing on student attendance

One possible way of addressing student retention is to assign a core first-year teaching module as an 'induction module' which contains within it a targeted referral process as part of a broader focus upon helping students manage the transition into the higher educational system (Lowe and Cook 2003; Wilcox et al. 2005). Integrating a referral process within a subject-specific module, which utilises an interactive (as opposed to didactic) teaching approach during targeted sessions through the use of small-group work and formative assessment, could arguably support students to develop their understanding of the approaches to learning and study skills necessary to succeed in higher education, while also developing discipline-specific content knowledge (Ward et al. 2000).

Any referral process designed to address the issue of student retention in general, and the risk of academic failure in particular, must first identify those students who need further targeted pastoral and academic support. Syndow and Sandel (1996) and Gibbs (2003) note that poor attendance can be a useful indicator when seeking to first identify students at risk of academic failure as well as those who are struggling more generally to adjust to the requirements of the higher education system. It certainly is a commonly held belief amongst academic teaching staff that student attendance and grade outcomes are linked (Yorke 2000; Taylor and Bedford 2004). Furthermore, there is supportive published research evidence for the viewpoint that student attendance can be a useful indicator of assessment outcome, although other factors such as student age and degree entry qualifications have been shown to also play a role (Woodfield et al. 2006). This said, analysing student attendance in relation to the outcomes of an assessment task could arguably be a useful starting point for developing a protocol for identifying and supporting students at risk of academic failure, particularly in their first semester at university (Syndow and Sandel 1996; Gibbs 2003; Halpenn 2007). It was therefore decided to test the assumption that student attendance and assessment outcomes are linked, to provide an evidential basis for the implementation of a referral process identifying undergraduate criminology students at risk of academic failure as part of a broader departmental and university-wide concern with addressing student retention. In order to do this the following null research hypothesis was defined: there is no relationship between student attendance and assessment outcome. The next section of this report outlines the research methodology used to analyse the relationship, if any, between student attendance and assessment outcome.

Methodology

The methodology section (which is sometimes called 'research methods') is where you outline how you sought to address your research aims and objectives and so answer your research question/test your research hypothesis. Here you will also consider issues such as access to research participants and sampling and research ethics, as well as outline the process of data collection and analysis, e.g. questionnaire development and proposed statistical analysis procedures give the type of data to be collected. The example outlined in Box 9.8 discusses the research sample, the type of data collected, as well as how research participants (in this case first-year undergraduate criminology students) were reassured that they did not have to participate in the research unless they wanted to. When you have to apply for formal ethical approval to conduct your study you should briefly discuss this process here. Remember to include blank copies of your project consent forms and the associated information provided to research participants in an appendix at the end of your report, after your reference list. Of course, as with your literature review, you should already have a working draft of your research methodology ready for when it comes to writing your research report. A useful tip I often give my students to further help them is to remember that a key thing you are trying to achieve when you outline your research methodology is to give enough information to the reader so they could repeat the study themselves, if they wanted to. Remembering this can help you to finalise what you need to put into the methodology section of your report: as you read through what you have written ask yourself if you now have all the information you need to replicate this study, or is some piece of important information missing? If so, make sure you revise what you have written so you include it!

Box 9.8

Report example: research methodology

Research sample and ethics

Given the research aim of identifying whether there is a relationship between attendance and assessment outcome, it was necessary to, first, obtain a record of student attendance, and second, statistically compare this record of attendance with the grade obtained by a student on an assessed learning task. As of September 2011, 123 students were registered on the first year of the undergraduate-degree criminology programme. Ten students withdrew from their studies between September and December 2011. Three of these students withdrew in the first three weeks of the academic year; seven had withdrawn by December 2011.

The reasons for withdrawal included homesickness, transfer to another programme within the university and transfer to a programme at another university. These students were excluded from the data analysis process on the grounds of incomplete data owing to their not submitting coursework for assessment. This left a research sample of 113 undergraduate criminology students. Students were informed that the research was taking place, that research findings would be subsequently shared with them, and that they could refuse to participate if they so wished. All students agreed to participate, with each signing a consent form, and a student-nominated representative was fully consulted throughout the lifetime of the research project and regularly kept informed as to progress being made.

Data collection

Research data was obtained from the university record system which all academic teaching staff have electronic access to. All first-year students must complete two core criminology programme modules, respectively entitled Introduction to criminology and Introduction to criminal justice. Departmental policy requires student attendance be formally recorded each week, with the resulting data being forwarded to the departmental office. The attendance records for the introduction to criminology and introduction to criminal justice modules were obtained for the September 2011 to December 2011 teaching period and entered into a research database alongside students' marks for their first assessments for these two modules. Both these assessments were written academic essays due at the end of the first semester. The final student grade results were made available electronically by mid-February 2012 after their work had been marked and subjected to moderation to ensure consistency. Student assessment outcomes and their attendance data were retrieved from the central university database pre-coded as ordinal levels of measurement. Attendance at lectures was banded into four categories: 1) attended none, 2) attended between 1 and 3 sessions, 3) attended between 4 and 6 sessions, and 4) attended 7 or more sessions (maximum of 10). Grade was banded into the five categories associated with final degree result grading: 1) First Class degree (70%-plus mark), 2) Second Class First Division (60–69% mark), 3) Second Class Lower Division (50–59%), 4) Third Class (40–49%), and 5) Fail (0–39%).

Data analysis

The null hypothesis for the research was that there is no relationship between student attendance and assessment grade, while the working hypothesis was that there is a relationship between student attendance and assessment grade. Causation – in basic terms – is the process that makes an outcome happen (Bryman and Cramer 2011). With regard to the variables used in this research, if student attendance is the independent variable and assessment grade the

(Continued)

(Continued)

dependent variable, then attendance will influence the assessment grade achieved by a student. However, it is important to note that outcomes are rarely influenced by a single cause. Causation is too complex to reach outcomes with total certainty, therefore it can be misleading. There are sufficient conditions of causation. This means that it is not true to say that all assessment grades achieved by a student will be influenced by their level of attendance, as there may well be other factors which influence the grade achieved. For example a student may have attended all their lectures but experienced a severe personal issue prior to assignment submission which led them to submit work that does not necessarily reflect their academic ability or subject topic knowledge. Correlation, on the other hand, is the pattern associated between two variables or the statistical measure used to find such patterns (Treiman 2009). This is relevant for the variables examined here as it cannot be absolutely true that assessment grades will be influenced by attendance, as this is a causal explanation. However, it can be stated that there will be a correlation, but the strength of the relationship needs further research.

The type of statistical test which can be applied to the data values to test for a correlation is predicated by their level of measurement (Treiman 2009). Both attendance and grade awarded are classified as ordinal-level data because they can be categorised and put into a rank order, but no mathematical calculation or specific measure of relative scale can be absolutely made in relation to the distances between each category, as they could in the case of height or age for example. Given the level of measurement of each variable, the strength of association between the variables can be measured using the Spearman's rho statistical test (Bryman and Cramer 2011). The next section of the report outlines research findings.

Findings

This section of your report should contain a clearly organised discussion of the findings obtained using a mixture of text and graphs to illustrate key points, as appropriate. Of course, although frequently the longest section of a research report, as the example in Box 9.9 illustrates, this isn't always the case. What matters most in this section of your report is providing a clear summary of your research findings in a well-organised manner. This part of your report may well need to be drafted a few times as, unlike previous sections, you probably will not already have draft versions at hand when you begin to write it. Again, I always advise my students to get a friend to read through what they have written to make sure they are presenting their findings in as accessible a manner as possible.

Box 9.9

Report example: findings

This section of the report outlines the research findings. Table 9.9.1 shows the results for the Spearman's rho test and their significance. The results show a positive association between student attendance and grade outcomes for both modules: the greater the student attendance the higher the grade achieved. However, the results are classed as being in the weak to moderate association range (Bryman and Cramer 2011). It appears the association is slightly stronger for the Introduction to criminology module than Introduction to criminal justice, although the difference is small. The significance value determines whether there is enough evidence from the data-set to establish that the relationship between the variables is statistically significant. The purpose of the test is to make a judgement on whether the observed differences are in fact 'real' differences and not a result of fluctuations that occur by chance. Any appropriately performed test of statistical significance lets you know the degree of confidence you can have in accepting or rejecting a hypothesis. I have read off the significant figure, which is 0.001 (Table 9.9.1). A probability of .05 or less is commonly interpreted by social scientists as justification for rejecting the null hypothesis. Therefore, .001 shows there is a significant relationship between the variables, but statistical significance does not interpret the nature or explanation of that relationship; that must be done by the measure of association result, that is, the Spearman's rho test. Consequently the research project's null hypothesis must be tentatively rejected as it appears attendance and assessment outcomes do share an association and this is statistically significant. But it nevertheless should be added that the relatively low strength of the measure of association result reinforces the need for further research to be conducted into the topic. This is a point the report will discuss in the next section.

Table 9.9.1 Spearman's rho measure of association result for attendance by grade

Session	Spearman's rho
Introduction to criminal justice lecture and exam grade	−0.591 Sig 0.001
Introduction to criminology lecture and exam grade	−0.610 Sig 0.001

Discussion

The discussion section of your report is where you analyse the findings obtained and their contribution to existing literature based on a critical appraisal of whether and how they fill previously identified 'literature gaps'. Any deficiencies in the research should be critically discussed at this point. But it is equally important to make sure you highlight the contribution of your research to the existing literature as well as outline what next steps should be undertaken in light of your research findings. Again, ask a friend to read through what you have written if you are unsure about your work. Along with the findings section this element of your report will perhaps need the most work, although you should be referring to literature you have already read when you interpret the impact of your research. The example in Box 9.10 outlines the limitations of the research conducted into student attendance and assessment outcome, but it balances this with a discussion of its contribution to existing literature surrounding the topic under investigation, while also considering what further research could now be undertaken in light of the findings outlined.

Box 9.10

Report example: discussion

The research found evidence of a positive correlation between student attendance and assessment outcome; however, although significant the strength of the association is relatively weak, and consequently it arguably reinforces that other factors also play a role in determining student assessment outcomes. Before this is discussed further the limitations of the research need to be acknowledged. This was a relatively small-scale research project concerned with the outcomes of first-year criminology students' first submission as they enter the higher education system. How students approach assessment tasks may well change as their studies progress and their learning styles develop, and possibly even change to suit particular learning contexts as they become more acquainted with the range of different learning environments they will encounter during their university studies. It therefore would be useful to undertake longitudinal research with a larger research sample to find out more about how criminology students' approaches to learning tasks change as they progress through their undergraduate degree and they become more familiar with the academic criminological corpus.

Although the study's limitations are readily acknowledged, the findings presented in this paper are nevertheless supported by the published research literature. This by and large finds a stronger association between student attendance and assessment outcomes than the one found by the research reported here, but most importantly, it equally shows that entry qualifications, age, gender and personal issues (e.g. part-time employment, health problems or family situation) all play vitally important roles in influencing the grades students obtain (Martins and Walker 2006; Halpenn 2007). This lends further weight to the argument that further research is needed to expand on the findings presented here. Such research could collect qualitative data from students alongside relevant statistical data, to more fully explore the intervening variables which seem to mediate the relationship between student attendance and assessment outcomes, such as entry qualifications, age, gender and part-time employment and so on.

It should also be noted that it is arguable that evidence of a weaker correlation between student attendance and assessment outcome than commonly found in the published literature fits with a constructivist view of learning and teaching (Gibbs 2003). This is the view that knowledge cannot exist outside of the mind, nor can it be transferred from one mind to another; rather, new knowledge is personally constructed by an individual in and through direct personal experience. If one accepts this position then what matters is not students' attendance to lectures per se, but rather the nature of their total engagement with their disciplinary subject as well as the general higher education environment they find themselves in (Gibbs 2003). Consequently the research discussed in this paper can be said to arguably reinforce the view that it is vital that academic departments and teaching staff focus upon study skill support and developing students' self-awareness of how they learn, instead of focusing upon transferring core disciplinary subject knowledge, particularly in the first year of a student's degree programme (Duffy and Cunningham 1996; Gibbs 2003). In relation to the development of support for students to tackle academic failure and help them manage the transition into higher education, this means teachers must play close attention to how they structure teaching episodes and provide students with learning resources so they can take more personal responsibility for their learning outcomes (Johnson 2002). For example, tutors may wish to make greater use of online resources and module discussion boards to stimulate student-led engagement with course materials outside of designated teaching sessions, as well as to facilitate informal student-led group discussion and self-appraisal of progress with module learning and assessment tasks (Cavico and Mujtaba 2010).

Conclusion

In the conclusion to your project report you should discuss the implications and consequences of your research findings in a succinct and research-informed manner: your conclusion is drawn from the evidence you have presented so do not include new information here. Where your research is focused on policy issues you may wish to provide recommendations for policy development in your conclusion. It can be helpful to carefully review what you have written in previous sections and make a note of the key points you have made to help you focus your writing. After your conclusion you should provide a full reference list of the published literature you have used in your report. The example in Box 9.11 provides a concluding summary for the research into student retention and the issue of the relationship between student attendance and assessment outcomes. Typically you will include a reference list immediately after your conclusion, with any further information such as example respondent consent forms being placed in appendices after your reference list.

Box 9.11

Report example: conclusion

The research presented in this report was undertaken to aid the development of a student retention referral process to help identify first-year criminology students in need of further study skill and pastoral support as they make the transition into the higher education system. The research found that student attendance and assessment outcomes do share a relationship, but this is not as strong as is often presumed, which reinforces the validity of the viewpoint that it is important to focus holistically on the multi-dimensional factors at play in generating student assessment outcomes when seeking to address instances of academic failure, not least of all because if these are not identified early enough and consequently are left unchecked, then they may well lead to a student withdrawing from their studies. After all, although it is undoubtedly the case that for various academic or personal reasons not all students who enter university will be able to successfully complete their programme of study, the fact remains that in today's competitive economic marketplace it is vitally important that individual teachers and their academic departments do all they can to help their students succeed.

References

Assiter, A. and Gibbs, G.R. (2007) Student retention and motivation, *European Political Science*, 6: 79–93.

Bryman, A. and Cramer, D. (2011) *Quantitative Data Analysis with SPSS 17, 18 and 19: A Guide for Social Scientists*. London: Routledge.

Cavico, F.J. and Mujtaba, B.G. (2010) An assessment of business schools' student retention, accreditation and faculty scholarship challenges, *Contemporary Issues in Education Research*, 3(1): 107–18.

Collins, R. and Lin, H. (2003) *The Challenge of Transition*. York: Higher Education Academy.

Davies, P. and Elias, P. (2003) *Dropping Out: A Problem of Quality or Student Finance?* Paper presented to the British Educational Research Association Annual Conference, University of Sussex, 2–5 September.

Duffy, T.M. and Cunningham, D.J. (1996) Constructivism: implications for the design and delivery of instruction. In D.H. Jonassen (ed.) *Handbook of Research for Educational Communications and Technology*. New York: Macmillan.

Gann, R. (2003) *An investigation into recruitment, retention and programme preferences of first year social science students at UCLAN: report of findings*. C-SAP Project 10/SP/02. Available at: www.c-sap.bham.ac.uk

Gibbs, G. (2003) *Implementing Learning and Teaching Strategies*. London: Open University Press.

Halpenn, N. (2007) The impact of attendance and student characteristics on academic achievement: findings from undergraduate business management, *Journal of Further and Higher Education*, 30(4): 335–49.

Johnson, V. (2002) Improving student retention – by accident or by design, *Exchange,* 1: 9–11.

Lowe, H. and Cook, A. (2003) Mind the gap: are students prepared for higher education? *Journal of Further and Higher Education*, 27(1): 53–76.

Martins, P. and Walker, I. (2006) *Student achievement and university classes: effects of attendance, size, peers and teachers.* IZA Discussion Paper, December 2006.

Parry, G. (2002) A short history of failure. In M. Peelo and T. Wareham (eds) *Failing Students in Higher Education.* London: Open University Press.

Richardson, R.C. and Skinner, E.F. (1991) *Achieving Quality and Diversity: Universities in a Multicultural Society.* New York: Macmillan.

Rickinson, B. and Rutherford, D. (1995) Increasing undergraduate retention rates, *British Journal of Guidance and Counselling*, 23(2): 161–72.

Syndow, D.L. and Sandel, R.H. (1996) *Making Student Retention an Institutional Priority.* Paper presented at the National Institute for Staff and Organizational Development Conference on Teaching and Leadership Excellence (Newcastle University, 26th–29th May).

Taylor, J.A. and Bedford, T. (2004) Staff perceptions of factors related to non-completion in higher education, *Studies in Higher Education*, 29(3): 375–94.

Tinto, V. (1975) Dropout from higher education: a theoretical synthesis of recent research, *Review of Educational Research*, 45(1): 89–125.

Tinto, V. (1987) *Leaving College: Rethinking the Causes and Cares of Student Attrition.* Chicago: University of Chicago Press.

Treiman, D.L. (2009) *Quantitative Data Analysis: Doing Social Research to Test Ideas (Research Methods for the Social Sciences).* New York: Jossey Bass.

Yorke, M. (1997) *How Significant is the Problem? Select Committee on Education and Employment Sixth Report.* London: Department for Education and Employment.

Yorke, M. (1999) *Leaving Early: Undergraduate Non-completion in Higher Education.* London: Fulmer Press.

Yorke, M. (2000) The quality of the student experience: what can institutions learn from data relating to non-completion? *Quality in Higher Education*, 6(1): 61–75.

Yorke, M. and Longdon, B. (2004) *Retention and Student Success in Higher Education.* London: Open University Press.

Yorke, M. and Thomas, L. (2003) Improving the retention of students from lower socio-economic groups, *Journal of Higher Education Policy and Management*, 25(1): 63–74.

(Continued)

(Continued)

Ward, I., Crosling, G. and Marangos, J. (2000) Encouraging positive perceptions of economics: the effectiveness of the orientation tutorial, *Economic Papers*, 18(3): 273–82.

Wilcox, P., Winn, S. and Fyvie-Gauld, M. (2005) 'It was nothing to do with the university, it was just the people': the role of social support in the first-year experience of higher education, *Studies in Higher Education*, 30(6): 707–22.

Woodfield, R., Jessop, D. and McMillan, L. (2006) Gender differences in undergraduate attendance rates, *Studies in Higher Education*, 31(1): 1–22.

Zepke, N., Leach, L. and Prebble, T. (2006) Being learner centred: one way to improve student retention? *Studies in Higher Education*, 31(5): 587–600.

Chapter Conclusion

Chapter 9 has outlined an example report structure which criminologists commonly use to write up their research findings for dissemination and public consumption. This discussion has reinforced the importance of placing your research within the context of the published literature surrounding your topic so you can assess its contribution to current academic discourse while also acknowledging its limitations and detailing future possible research avenues. An illustrative example of a research project examining the relationship between criminology student lecture attendance and assessment outcomes has been outlined which you can use to help you write up your own research (see Chapter Review Activity). One of the key themes running through previous chapters has been the need to engage with the academic and policy-making communities when undertaking criminological research. The most common method for doing this being in the form of the literature review.

The writing process reinforces this truism and how the study of criminological life not only needs to use both numbers and words in equal measure; it also needs an audience – that is, if we are to make a difference with our research. Of course, we must acknowledge the limitations of our ability to reach our audience and influence policy development. For better or worse, policy-makers do not make their decisions solely on the basis of what academic research tells them is the most appropriate course of action. Yet it is important to remember that rigorously conducted criminological research possesses its own intrinsic value. Furthermore, the primary purpose of your first research project as an undergraduate criminology student is educational and to pass an assessment task, rather than to influence policy development. In part, this is why this book has been written with the novice first-time researcher in mind. Although you are at the beginning of your undergraduate career and so more focused on exploring a topic of interest for an assessed piece of coursework, rather than to influence the formation of social policy, it is nevertheless still important to use this opportunity to begin to develop your ability to communicate research findings in an appropriate format. After all, you never know who might end up reading your work aside from your research supervisor.

CHAPTER REVIEW ACTIVITY

Write up your research using the structure outlined in this chapter. You can adapt the format if you need to so your report meets the assessment submission requirements of your educational institution. Give a copy of your report to a fellow student to review who is also conducting a research project, but on a topic different from yours, so you can look at each other's work. Ask them to check your spelling in addition to the clarity and impact of what you write. Do they understand what your study is about? Is your literature review well-argued and appropriately evidenced? Are you highlighting the strengths and limitations of your research as well as its contribution to existing literature surrounding your topic? Is there anything that you have missed which they think may be important? Agree that you can be critical of each other's work, but set the rule that you must highlight *at least* three good points and two areas for improvement (this is in addition to any referencing, spelling and grammatical errors you may notice). Set a deadline to meet – at the latest – a week before your final project report is due for submission to your tutor, to allow yourselves plenty of time to make any final changes you feel may be needed as a result of completing this exercise.

CHAPTER READING LIST

Becker, H.S. (1986) *Writing for Social Scientists: How to Start and Finish Your Thesis, Book or Article*. Chicago: University of Chicago Press.

Biggs, J.B. (2003) *Teaching for Quality Learning at University: What the Student Does* (2nd edn). Buckingham SRHE and Open University Press.

Harrison, J., Simpson, M., Harrison, O. and Martin, E. (2005) *Study Skills for Criminology* (*Sage Study Skills Series*). London: Sage Publications.

Hendry, G.D., Frommer, M. and Walker, R.A. (1999) Constructivism and problem-based learning, *Journal of Further and Higher Education*, 23 (3): 359–371.

Thody, A. (2011) *Writing and Presenting Research*. London: Sage Publications.

Glossary

ANALYTICAL GENERALISATION   A form of generalisation based on the development of a conceptual framework thematically developed from textual data. It is most associated with qualitative research, but more so grounded theory analysis than narrative or discourse analysis, as these approaches tend to be less concerned with the generalisation of research findings and more with ensuring both narrative authenticity and that previously silenced and oppressed voices are heard.

AXIAL CODING   A form of coding used in grounded theory analysis which is focused on the exploration of the attributes and dimensions of an emergent thematic category as a result of completing the process of open coding. Axial coding is sometimes subsumed within the selective coding process.

BIVARIATE ANALYSIS   The analysis of two variables to identify if there is a relationship between them, e.g. gender and fear of crime.

CONTINGENCY TABLE   A contingency table (also referred to as cross-tabulation or cross-tab) is a table or matrix which displays the frequency distribution of variables.

CONVENIENCE/SNOWBALL SAMPLING   A form of sampling where respondents are selected on the basis of immediate availability, e.g. passers-by in the street. A popular variation of convenience sampling is snowball sampling where a research participant guides the researcher to their next respondent. Convenience sampling is popular in survey research concerned with public perceptions of topical issues, and snowball sampling is popular in qualitative research studies concerned with hard-to-reach groups.

DISCOURSE ANALYSIS   A qualitative data analysis technique – heavily influenced by social constructivism – that takes as its starting point the position that language is constitutive of reality and which seeks to deconstruct the socio-cultural norms and power relations present within different forms of talk. The analytical tools of interpretive repertoire and subject position are used to assist this deconstructive process.

GROUNDED THEORY A form of qualitative data research and approach to data analysis which advocates the inductive generation of theory from respondents' accounts rather than the deductive testing of a pre-stated hypothesis. Grounded theory adopts a theoretical sampling strategy and follows an analytical process which moves from open coding to axial and selective forms of coding, in order to achieve theoretical saturation and analytical generalisation.

INTERPRETIVE REPERTOIRES Interpretive repertoires are more or less coherent ways of describing ourselves and the world around us. Discourse analysts hold that interpretive repertoires provide ready-made explanations and subject positions which individuals creatively use within a social situation to achieve certain ends.

INTERVAL VARIABLE Interval variables are determined by categories which can be ordered, and furthermore possess discrete value differences between each other which are consistent and can be expressed in numeric terms, e.g. height is expressed intervally as follows: somebody who is 180 cm tall is exactly 1 cm taller than somebody who is 179 cm, and exactly 1 cm shorter than somebody who is 181 cm.

LEVELS OF MEASUREMENT The term used to express the difference between nominal, ordinal and interval forms of data in terms of their relative value, with nominal being lowest, ordinal middle and interval highest. Levels of measurement dictate which measure of association test can be used.

MEASURE OF ASSOCIATION Measures of association are statistical tests used to test for a relationship between two variables. Commonly used measures of association include Phi, Cramer's V, Spearman's rho and Pearson's r. Which measure of association test is used is decided by the lowest level of measurement of the two variables under analysis.

MEASURE OF CENTRAL TENDENCY The numeric expression of the middle values of data-set variables using the mean (the average value), the median (the central value in the distribution) or the mode (the most frequent value). Which measures of central tendency are used is decided by a variable's level of measurement.

MEASURE OF DISPERSION The range of distribution within the variables of a data-set between the lowest and highest values. Key measures of dispersion used in univariate analysis include the range, the interquartile range and the standard deviation. Which measures of dispersion are used is decided by a variable's level of measurement.

MEASURE OF SIGNIFICANCE A statistical test which measures whether the results from a sample can reasonably be generalised to the wider population, e.g. chi-square. When the measure of significance result is not held to be robust (i.e. it is higher than 0.05) then this indicates the possible presence of sampling error.

MIXED METHODS An approach to empirical research that uses more than one research method to collect empirical data. Mixed-methods research often involves using both quantitative and qualitative methods.

NARRATIVE ANALYSIS A qualitative data analysis technique which possesses a social constructivist orientation and focuses on exploring the storied nature of social life. Narrative researchers are concerned with how people creatively use narrative structure, rhetoric and plotting to construct a sense of personal identity, negotiate social situations, as well as locate their lived experience within broader social processes and events.

NOMINAL VARIABLE Nominal variables are determined by categories which cannot be ordered, e.g. gender is expressed nominally in terms of male and female categories but these categories cannot be ordered in terms of value.

NULL HYPOTHESIS A statement concerning the relationship between two (or more) variables. The null hypothesis is the opposite of the working hypothesis developed by a researcher as a result of their literature review. It is the null hypothesis that is tested by a researcher using measures of association to check for a correlation between variables and measures of significance to check for the possibility of sampling error.

OPEN CODING A form of coding used in grounded theory analysis which is focused on the initial identification of pertinent themes within textual data. Open coding must be completed before moving onto axial and/or selective coding.

ORDINAL VARIABLE Ordinal variables are determined by categories which can be ordered but to which an exact numeric value between the categories cannot be determined, e.g. attitudes can be expressed ordinally in terms of a ranked scale running from 'Strongly disagree' to 'Strongly agree'.

POSITIVISM Until recently this was the dominant model of the criminological research process. Positivism first emerged during the mid-nineteenth century but was increasingly challenged by various social constructivist forms of criminological research from the mid-twentieth century onwards, i.e. narrative and discourse analysis. Positivism assumes there is an objective reality which exists independently to human beings and can be readily accessed by them. It emphasises the need for a researcher to engage in systematic observation and experiment in a value-neutral and dispassionate manner in order to discover underlying causal laws of behaviour. Positivism is most associated with quantitative forms of research but qualitative grounded theory analysis has been criticised for seeming to possess positivistic assumptions.

QUALITATIVE RESEARCH Empirical research in which the researcher explores a topic using textual data. Key research methods used to collect textual data include interviews and observations (although experimental research can be used to collect qualitative textual data as well). Policy documents and organisational files, e.g. police reports or legal documents, can also be used for qualitative research purposes, as can visual and media materials, e.g. films, photographs and TV adverts. Key data analysis techniques include grounded theory analysis, narrative analysis and discourse analysis. In qualitative research, emphasis is generally placed on analytical as opposed to statistical generalisation.

QUANTITATIVE RESEARCH Empirical research in which the researcher explores a topic using numeric data. Key research methods used to collect numeric data include surveys and experimental research (although experimental research can be used to collect qualitative textual data as well). Key data analysis techniques include univariate and bivariate analysis (which are sometimes called descriptive and inferential statistics, respectively). Emphasis is placed on statistical as opposed to analytical generalisation. It is important to account for sampling error when conducting quantitative research.

RANDOM SAMPLING A form of sampling where respondents are selected at random from a possible sampling frame. Typically the sampling frame is numbered and then a sample is selected using a random number generator. Random sampling is popular with researchers seeking to reduce sampling bias by reducing their own role in the selection of research participants, and is frequently used in both survey and experimental research studies.

RELIABILITY The extent to which a research method yields the same result on repeated trials.

SAMPLE A sample is a group selected from a sampling frame which a researcher will collect empirical data from using qualitative and/or quantitative research methods. All researchers take steps to ensure they select a sample that can be considered representative of the people to whom their results will be generalised. There are several different sampling approaches adopted by researchers: convenience sampling, stratified sampling, random sampling and theoretical sampling are amongst the most popular. Sample size is important as generally the larger the number in the sample, the higher the likelihood of obtaining a representative distribution of the targeted sampling frame, which in turn reduces the threat of sampling error.

SAMPLING ERROR The degree to which the results from the sample deviate from those that would be obtained from the entire population.

SAMPLING FRAME The population which is a focus of a particular study is known as the sampling frame, e.g. victims of crime in the United Kingdom in the last year. Typically a researcher will seek to select a sample of research participants so they can generalise their findings to the sampling frame using statistical generalisation if they are using quantitative research, or analytical generalisation if they are using qualitative research. This process is complicated by the fact that it is not always feasible to define a sampling frame, e.g. it is impossible to know exactly how many people have been victims of crime in the United Kingdom in the last year, as not all crimes are reported.

SELECTIVE CODING   A form of coding used in grounded theory analysis which is focused on the exploration of dominant thematic categories within textual data to identify a central theme around which all others can be placed.

SOCIAL CONSTRUCTIVISM   A model of the criminological research process which first emerged in the social sciences during the mid-twentieth century. Social constructivism argues, in contrast to positivism, that reality cannot be accessed in an objective and value-neutral manner by a researcher. It emphasises the presence of multiple possible interpretations of reality while at the same time noting the role of language in creating shared meanings and narrative stories about the nature of the world and the place of human beings in it. A distinction can be drawn between strong and weak constructivism, with the former arguing that it is completely impossible to access reality outside of the language and cultural norms used to describe it, and the latter holding that a limited form of access is possible while still rejecting positivistic assumptions regarding the ability of a researcher to be objective and value-neutral in their research.

STATISTICAL GENERALISATION   A form of generalisation based on numeric data concerned with the extent to which research findings from a study conducted on a sample can be applied to the population at large – also known as the sampling frame. Survey and experimental forms of research utilise statistical generalisation.

STRATIFIED SAMPLING   A form of sampling where respondents are selected on the basis of fit to a particular aspect of the sampling frame which is often expressed in terms of 'quota filling', e.g. if out of 50,000 known victims of knife crime 35 per cent were Asian, 45 per cent were black and 20 per cent were white, then a stratified sample would be selected that reflected the distribution of this split. Stratified sampling is often used in large-scale survey research, for example the British Household Survey, to help ensure validity, reliability and statistical generalisation.

SUBJECT POSITION   Subject positions are socially defined identities made relevant by specific ways of talking about a person, thing, event or social situation. Discourse analysis is concerned with the examination of how different subject positions are offered, accepted or resisted within discursive exchanges between two or more people in order to identify underpinning socio-cultural norms and power relations.

THEORETICAL SAMPLING   A form of sampling used in qualitative research, particularly in grounded theory, which emphasises respondent selection based on their ability to contribute to the development of a thematic framework that is analytically generalisable.

THEORETICAL SATURATION In grounded theory analysis, theoretical saturation is held to occur when collected data contains within it reoccurring thematic categories, which revolve around a core explanatory thematic category, in spite of a researcher deliberately and systematically attempting to disprove their emergent understanding of their data through repeatedly collecting further data. There is no set guide to when theoretical saturation occurs, hence every grounded theory researcher must articulate a convincing reason why they have stopped collecting further data.

TRIANGULATION Triangulation is used by a researcher to bolster the validity and reliability of their study. It comes in different forms: 'data triangulation' involves using different types of data concerned with the same topic; 'investigator triangulation' involves using different researchers in the same project to collect and analyse data; 'theoretical triangulation' involves using different theories in the same study; finally 'methodological triangulation' involves using different methods to study a topic.

UNIVARIATE ANALYSIS The analysis of single variables.

VALIDITY The degree to which a method accurately reflects or assesses the specific concept that the researcher is attempting to measure, e.g. a respondent's attitude towards a person, thing or event.

VARIABLE (NOMINAL, ORDINAL AND INTERVAL) The characteristics that vary among individuals. These are typically expressed in nominal, ordinal and interval forms.

WORKING HYPOTHESIS A statement concerning the presumed relationship between two (or more) variables; e.g. in the working hypothesis 'women have a higher fear of crime than men' the two variables held to possess a relationship are gender and fear of crime. A working hypothesis is developed by a researcher as a result of conducting a literature review of their research topic. The working hypothesis must be turned into a null hypothesis – e.g. 'there is no relationship between gender and fear of crime' – and subjected to a correlation test using an appropriate measure of association, as well as an appropriate data-set robustness test using a measure of significance to check for the possible presence of sampling error.

Index

Page references to Figures or Tables will be in *italics*

radical criminology, 9
Randall, W., 113
random sampling, 243
randomised control trials (RCTs), 46–7
  and experimental criminology, 44–5
range, 182, 183, 241
realism, 77
reflexivity concept, 52
relativist philosophy, 77
reliability, 57–8, 144, 243
replacement discourses, 141–2
report, research *see* research report,
    writing
research methods, research report, 24, 222,
   230–2
research report, writing, 219–38
  abstract, 24, 222, 224–5
  'blank page' syndrome, 221
  conclusion section, 24, 222, 235–8
  data analysis, 231–2
  data collection, 231
  discussion section, 24, 222, 233–5
  findings, 24, 222, 232–3
  first drafts, revising, 222–3
  generic report structure, 221–2, 223–35
  introduction section, 24, 225–6
  literature review, 24, 222, 226–9
  methodology, 24, 222, 230–2
  sample and ethics, 230–1
  subtitles, 223–4
  title page, 24, 222, 223–4
research topic development, 25–37
  doability, 26–9
  explaining areas of criminal life, 32–3
  literature review *see* literature review
  square of crime, 26–9
responsiveness, 93
Richardson, R.C., 228
Riessman, C.K., 110, 116, 125, 146
Roberts, B., 111
Rosenweld, D.L., 110

safety, 94, 95
sampling
  convenience, 80, 240
  defined, 243
  ethical considerations, 230–1
  random, 243
  snowball, 80, 240
  stratified, 244
  surveys, 48–9
  theoretical, 76, 79–82, 85, 244–5
sampling errors, 241, 243
sampling frame, 243–4
Sandel, R.H., 228, 229

saturation
  data, 96
  theoretical, 81–2, 92–3, 245
scatter grams, 204–5
scientific forms of criminology, 8
search engines, 35
Searle, A., 145
secondary data, 16, 27, 29
  analysis, 49, 209
Secret Policeman, The, 68
selective coding, 86, 91, 92, 96, 244
self-evaluation, 94, 95
self-identity, 124
sex trafficking, 29, 34, 36, 61
sexual abuse, 61, 64, 94, 95, 125
Shaw, C., 109, 112
Shipman, Harold, 4
Siegel, Larry, 18, 25
significance measures, 199, 202–4, 241
Silverman, D., 65
Simmons, J., 48
Skinner, E.F., 228
Smith, Adam, 159
Smith, W., 208
snowball sampling, 80, 240
social classes, 43
social constructivism, 136, 140, 145, 242, 244
  see also discourse analysis
social control theory (SCT), 9, 63
social disorganisation, 9
social interaction, 160
social networking, 112
social sciences
  analytical approaches, 4
  criminology as, 10
  and narrative analysis, 111
  numbers and words, 3
Society for the Study of Social Problems in
    America, 68–9
sociological criminology, 6, 9, 50–6
  mixed methods, 55–6, 242
  qualitative research methods, 51–4
Spearman's rho, 197, 199, 204–6, 207, 232, 241
specialist guidance and support, 19
speech acts, 136
Spencer, Herbert, 159
SPSS (Statistical Package for the Social Sciences),
    171, 172, 199, 205
square of crime, 26–9
  exercise, 28–9, 30, 67
standard deviation, 183, 241
statistical generalisation, 59–60, 79, 244
statistical information, crime patterns, 47, 50
statistical skills, 5
status frustration, 9

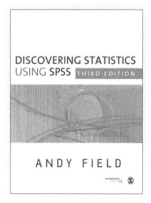
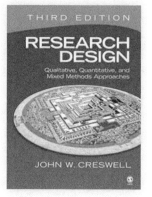
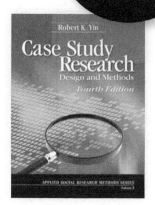

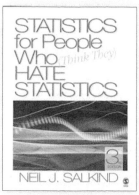

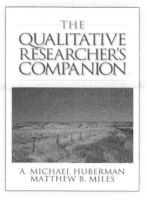
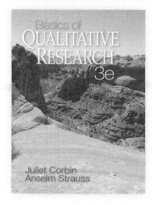

Research Methods
Books from SAGE

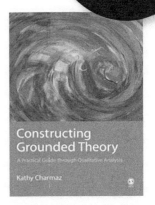

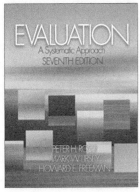

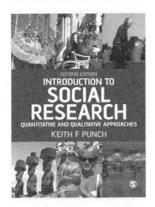

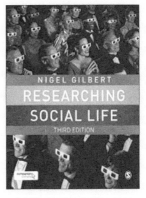

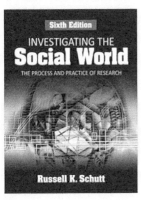

www.sagepub.co.uk